D1429120

The
Action Learning
Handbook

To our family and the late Roger Grant

The
Action Learning
Handbook

Powerful techniques for education,
professional development and training

Ian McGill and Anne Brockbank

Routledge
Taylor & Francis Group

LONDON AND NEW YORK

First published 2004 by Routledge
2 Park Square, Milton Park, Abingdon, Oxfordshire OX14 4RN

Simultaneously published in the USA and Canada
by Routledge
711 Third Avenue, New York, NY 10017

Routledge is an imprint of the Taylor and Francis Group, an informa business

First issued in hardback 2015

Transferred to Digital Printing 2010

© 2004 Ian McGill and Anne Brockbank

Typeset by Saxon Graphics Ltd, Derby

British Library Cataloguing in Publication Data
A catalogue record for this book is available from the British Library

Library of Congress Cataloging in Publication Data
A catalog record for this book has been requested

ISBN 978-0-415-33511-9 (pbk)
ISBN 978-1-138-12658-9 (hbk)

Contents

Acknowledgements

In the last months before completing the handbook, Reg Revans died. Whilst not having had the privilege of working with him, we would like to commend his longstanding contribution to the development and growth of action learning and our debt to his innovative work.

We approached a number of experienced facilitators to offer stories about critical and significant moments in their work. We have recorded them in the text at points where they highlight what is being written. All the names in the stories have been disguised to protect confidentiality. We would like to thank Belinda Dewar, Development and Research Manager, Scottish Centre for the Promotion of the Older Person's Agenda, Queen Margaret University College, Edinburgh; Judith Hunt, Chair of the London Health Observatory, consultant and executive coach; Dr Barbara Johnson, Senior Research Fellow, City University, St. Bartholomew School of Nursing and Midwifery; Professor Brendan McCormack, Professor/Director of Nursing Research, University of Ulster/Royal Hospitals Trust; Jane Neubauer, The Creative Leadership Retreat, Washington, USA; Linda Smith, consultant and Chair, South East London, NHS Strategic Health Authority.

A thank you to Lennie Egboma, Abyd Aziz and Stella Binns who led and supported the developments in action learning at Ealing; and to Sandra Taylor, Charles Obazuaye and Lorna Wallace at Birmingham City Council, Social Services for championing action learning in the Department with guidance from Judith Hunt. Both organisations also supported the accreditation of facilitators at City University with the encouragement and critical support of Dr Yvonne Hillier in ensuring validation of the relevant part of the MSc programme.

To colleagues at the NHS Leadership Centre a debt for initiating the programme and evaluation of action learning for chief executives of health authorities and trusts, and chief executives and directors of social services of local authorities, in particular Tessa Brooks, Gillian Black and Manjit Smith.

To Tom Bourner for our continuing association over the years to mull over ideas about the application of action learning in organisations and, particularly, universities. His reflections for the handbook have been invaluable.

We are grateful to Gerard O'Connor for some of the diagrams in chapters 10 and 11.

Appreciation to Brendan McCormack, at the University of Ulster/Royal Hospitals Trust for being a reader along with Brendan Harpur, Head of

Human Resources at FAS, the Training and Employment Authority for Ireland. They provided valuable feedback when the handbook was completed which we were able to heed and incorporate in the final text. Nevertheless, we take full responsibility for the resulting outcome.

Finally, we are indebted to all the willing participants in our action learning sets who have provided us with so much in the way of ideas and reflection for the handbook

Ian McGill and Anne Brockbank
London 2003

I.McGill@mailbox.ulcc.ac.uk
A.Brockbank@mailbox.ulcc.ac.uk

Introduction

This handbook is written for users of action learning. We include amongst users: experienced users as well as those embarking upon action learning for the first time; those with some experience who wish to deepen their understanding; and those who are becoming, or are, facilitators of action learning. The handbook may also be useful for those responsible for staff and management development in organizations considering using action learning as part of the repertoire of development.

The handbook endeavours to reflect the life of an action learning set (the term used for a group engaged in action learning). Thus Part I is mainly about the activities necessary to create, initiate and start sets. Part II is designed to enable a deeper understanding of action learning with recourse to theory. Part III underpins the earlier part of the handbook by conveying the skills for effective set work. Part IV investigates the value of action learning and aims to provide users with the means for reviewing the journey undertaken by set members, sets as a whole and the organizational benefits. The handbook structure endeavours to reflect the beginning of the process, the journey itself, and the end of the life of action learning sets.

Part I, Starting action learning, is particularly for those new to action learning as well as those who wish to revisit the range of approaches to the fundamentals and familiarize themselves with the types of action learning that can be created and in what contexts. Practitioners who are introducing action learning to colleagues can make use of Chapter 3, which offers a range of workshops depending upon the depth of introduction required. Chapter 4, Starting a set, is a key chapter designed to ensure a high degree of commitment to action learning from the initial set meeting. We include the second meeting in this chapter to ensure integration of set members who may have been unable to attend the crucial first meeting.

Part II, Understanding action learning, is the theoretical part of the handbook and may, for users less familiar with learning theory, be omitted until a point is reached when access to theory is felt appropriate. Significant is the idea of reflection, and reflective dialogue as an introduction to reflective learning. Our aim is make the theory accessible, and to enable the use of theory relating to reflective learning to be integrated into the work in action learning sets. While engaging in action learning, practice locks into theory, and theory locks back into practice. Practical understanding becomes underlined with theory.

There are three key roles in an action learning set, set member, presenter and facilitator. In Part III, Facilitating action learning, we explain the roles of each in depth. These roles are related to the skills desirable for each role. Part III is designed to enable users to acquire and deepen the skills necessary for effective set working as well as fully attending to the skills and qualities needed for being a facilitator. Although Chapter 8, Group dynamics in action learning, is a theoretical chapter, we have included it in Part III as it underlies the way in which groups, and in particular, action learning sets work; thus, it may be appropriate here. Readers wishing to immerse themselves in the roles of presenter, set member and facilitator may wish to return to Chapter 8 at a later stage.

Part IV, Evaluating action learning, is about reviews, endings and evaluation of action learning programmes. In Part IV we offer review methods through the language of process, by which sets can reflect on their work. Reflection on the process is crucial to the learning of set members and to the effective use of action learning – hence our concentration on process review. Evaluation of action learning may be part of the ending of a set as well as being conducted after the set has concluded. We wished to end the book with the chapter on the endings of sets and have therefore included evaluation as the penultimate chapter. The appendix offers a variation on the traditional action learning set format, for issues common to set members.

We begin by describing our own journeys to action learning.

How we came to action learning

Below each of us conveys in our story how we came to use action learning in our work. Ian shows how he first experienced action learning in a self-facilitated set and Anne will convey how she first facilitated a set.

Ian's story

I worked in a business school in a polytechnic in England in what became the University of Brighton. Having just returned from a three-year secondment in the public sector I was excited about making some transitions in the business school. I had returned to take lead responsibility for a postgraduate management development programme. The programme, a two-year part-time course, had been mainly subject/lecture based with examinations at the end of each year. The programme was due for revalidation and I was to lead the review and relaunch of the programme. The course had been successful but we considered that it was becoming less relevant to participant needs.

The original programme had been subject/tutor and examination led. Tutors in the silos of their subject lectured students for preparation for an examination at the end of each year's study without collaboration across the subject field. There was little application to the participants' experience and their world of work in which they were being prepared to apply the fruits of their learning. Case study analysis was the only area of application and these case studies bore no direct relationship to student experience. We had been increasingly concerned at the lack of relevance of the programme to current and potential areas of professional and work development. We were not utilizing the enormous potential of participants' experience.

Some of the staff had been engaged in learning that centred on the learner and in experiential learning (Weil and McGill, 1989). In order to ensure that the programme became more relevant to the participants' experience, we decided to revise it by making it student centred and making student-based projects, both individual and group, the driving force for the programme. The projects were live in that each student had to develop a theme that was implementable in his or her work. The project might 'fail'. However, the key was the learning derived from the experience entailed in undertaking the project. The assessment of the students' progress and attaining the qualification would be by an examination of their reflective learning derived from the projects. Each work-related project was to be agreed by the organization in which the student worked, the student and the teaching staff, with the latter having a veto until the project satisfied the requirements of the programme.

A pedagogical concern was to ensure that the project was relevant to the participants' learning and management development. We thus faced the issue of how to integrate progress on the project firmly into the participants' learning as the course proceeded. All students on the programme faced similar issues of process in undertaking the project even though their content may differ widely. How could we utilize that experience to enhance learning?

We chose action learning as our main vehicle for student learning. Some of us in our journeys into experiential learning had heard of action learning but we had not directly experienced the process. However, we rapidly agreed that if we were to ask students to engage in action learning, we would have to be familiar with the process ourselves, be confident in using the approach, as well as being positive about the potential benefits for participants.

Hence my interest in action learning (originally in an academic setting) derived from my work in experiential learning and enabling student learners to have much greater autonomy in their learning. Action learning provided a promising vehicle for postgraduate courses in management development for part-time students.

As a first step, a few of us invited other staff in the business school to an introductory discussion about action learning. Eight staff came to the meeting. It was a rather one-dimensional affair as we did not actually engage in action learning but simply talked about it, drawing upon the work of Revans (1980, 1983). Nevertheless, following the meeting some of us decided we would try it ourselves. At its formation the set comprised five persons: four with academic and one with administrative responsibilities; two women, three men; ages ranged from 32 to 47. Three of the five, including myself, were likely to be facilitating action learning sets on the new programme or on a similar postgraduate management development programme. We thus had a vested interest in endeavouring to make our own experience a success as a precursor to using action learning as a vehicle for learning on the programmes.

For a fuller version of this story please refer to McGill *et al* (Weil and McGill, 1989: 116).

Rapidly it became clear that action learning could be used much more widely than this. Action learning offered staff as well as students a means of addressing and learning from their own concerns and problems. We each took many issues to this first set. These included:

- enabling the successful progress of two postgraduate management development programmes through validation to implementation;
- reviewing work priorities to clarify direction;
- progressing a (static) dissertation through to completion of a PhD;
- working with a recalcitrant colleague in a course development team.

What became clear was the extent of our own learning, not only about the progress we made on the issues like the above, but also a growing awareness and deepening appreciation of the way in which we were working. We could not have had a better initiation into how action learning worked for us as well as for those we were subsequently to facilitate.

From the outset there were three important ways in which this set differed from the traditional notion of an action learning set. First, action learning sets within organizations tended to have a 'client' outside the set to whom the set members were responsible for the progress of the task or problem. Although each of us was working on real problems directly pertinent to our job responsibilities, we did not have a client. We were our own clients using the set for our own purposes, although there would be a benefit to our organization (the business school) for those of us concerned with pursuing tasks based in the organization. An example of this was taking a postgraduate management development programme from an interesting and rather novel idea through to successful validation and implementation. The novel idea was the use of action learning as the major vehicle for learning! Hence the desire for some of us to do action learning if we were going to prescribe it for those embarking on our courses.

Second, and in our view most important, we decided to work without a facilitator. We would do that task ourselves. We will look at the implications of this in Chapter 2 on types of sets.

Thirdly, we set up our particular group voluntarily. While we all worked in the same organization, the set was created by ourselves and was not formally recognized by the organization. We met in our own time. We were a self-facilitated and an independent set simultaneously.

The first meeting of the set established our procedures and ground rules, in particular for length of meetings, frequency and duration, confidentiality and time-keeping. Because we were self-facilitating we had to take more responsibility early on for the maintenance of the group. We very quickly developed a sense of commitment to the group and priority that once a meeting was in the diary, we would endeavour to ensure that it was not set aside for anything else that might subsequently emerge. Within the meeting we would agree time allocation and set aside some meetings for a longer amount of time for the set.

This first set continued in existence for six months and at that point we reviewed our progress as well as what we had learnt. We decided to continue with a second cycle of meetings. At the same time as starting a second cycle we each agreed to initiate a new action learning set ourselves. From these early beginnings the business school started to use action learning on undergraduate courses as our approach and methods became better known and successful across the school.

From this start I began to use action learning more widely in organizations concerned directly with the management development of their staff.

Anne's story

I found out about action learning by accident. I came across Casey and Pearce (1977) and found that the principles of action learning I was reading about were the ones I was using in my work as a facilitator in the Faculty of Management and Business at Manchester Metropolitan University (MMU). I realized subsequently that my development as a facilitator supported my entry into action learning.

The term facilitator was rather unusual in higher education and I found that I had to justify what I was doing to many colleagues who challenged the whole idea of facilitation. The term was seen as floppy and ill-defined and unsuitable for higher education. I was a founder member of the team at MMU which developed the first-ever UK degree in retail marketing. My role as a lecturer in the department was to develop a programme of Interpersonal Skills Training for retail marketing students. The programme included an assessed final year module, using the laboratory group model (Luft, 1984), described in more detail below, where participants operate in a small experiential group, with clear guidelines but no defined task other than their own behaviour. The experiential task was identifying interpersonal behaviours in self and others, with the aim of developing the interpersonal skills which had been identified in my research as necessary for potential managers in the retail sector. These included listening, responding to others, empathy, questioning, and clarity. As far as I know, this was the first and only time that interpersonal behaviour was included in a final year assessment at undergraduate level.

The process was like action learning in that active listening was a key factor in empowering members of the group. Also, the group established a culture of responding-to-others, questioning and empathy which is a characteristic of action learning. The ground rules were almost identical to action learning ground rules, including confidentiality, use of 'I' statements, respect for difference, rights to express feelings etc. Where the laboratory group departed from action learning was that there was no allocated time for each individual. As facilitator, I made it my business to ensure that members got roughly equal 'air time'. However, because the experiential group was unstructured, the members experienced some of the group dynamic effects discussed in Chapter 8. For instance, some members struggled with the freedom they had to speak, wanting me to act as their leader and tell them what to do.

The Interpersonal Skills (IPS) module was a new departure even for a 'new' university like MMU. Staff were unsure of the value of such so-called 'soft' material, and had agreed to its inclusion under protest. My colleagues were doubtful and at the start were unwilling to be involved. I found myself running the first IPS module three times in the year, as I was the only person delivering it, in the far-from-desirable slot of Fridays from 2 to 5 pm.

To the surprise of almost everyone in the faculty, the Friday slot became the best attended in the programme. Participants were unwilling to miss the experiential group, as they were excited by it, valued what they were doing, and made sure they attended, even if it meant leaving for the weekend later. The success of the Interpersonal Skills module is now history and very soon my colleagues asked to be trained as facilitators.

How did I approach the work? I drew from my experience of the work and practice of Gerard Egan (1976, 1977) who had developed clear behavioural indicators of interpersonal skill, in relationships and at work. In addition to the technical input, which was delivered in the usual lecture/seminar style, I ran the group of 12 as a laboratory group, an experiential group, without an externally imposed task, where group members were able to interact freely (Luft, 1984). This offered them the opportunity to identify effective interpersonal behaviours in themselves and others, to assess their own behaviour, and practise alternative patterns if desired. An important part of the process was the group contract or ground rules, which included confidentiality so that group members felt able to explore issues which were not in the public domain, ie not known to their other tutors or fellow students. We discuss ground rules in action learning in Chapters 4 and 8.

I facilitated this experiential group in what would be termed a humanistic way, using the principles laid down by Carl Rogers for effective learning (Rogers, 1983, 1992). I had learnt the technique in my training as a counsellor where I had facilitated a variety of groups of mostly young people. I had discovered that a 'hands off' approach, where I said little and responded a lot, produced a much richer quality of exchange in the groups. I had learnt to listen before speaking and to respond first in a simple restating-the-facts kind of way, and then, where appropriate, to respond with empathy. I was particularly excited about how powerful a simple statement of empathic understanding by me, the facilitator, was for group members, who would then move out of their 'comfort zone' and work with difficult and sometimes uncomfortable personal material. This method transferred well to my group of young undergraduates who, I found, were hungry for self-knowledge and development.

When I read Casey and Pearce's book, I became interested in action learning, and when I obtained the resources to facilitate staff development groups, I used the action learning method. I continued to use the facilitator style described above, and added an action learning element to the process by structuring the sessions, giving each set member equal time. When the presenter in a set declared an intended action, I recommended that this be recorded by the set, not by me, and revisited at a future set meeting.

My career moved on, I moved south, learnt more about action learning, and contributed to the first edition of Action Learning (McGill and Beaty, 1992). I began to use action learning as a vehicle for groups of postgraduate students doing projects or dissertations, and the method worked really well, because set members heard about each other's difficulties, and learnt about solutions from each other. This contrasted with one-to-one supervision where the only source of expertise was the tutor. Action learning enabled set members to take responsibility for themselves and to support each other in the way described in this book.

This did not always suit some members of the set, who had been led to believe that learning was a passive process, where lecturers 'force fed' their students. One of the set members challenged me, at the ground rules stage, saying that it was my job to teach them, and this method meant that 'they had to work instead of me'. I was rather nonplussed by this challenge and felt paralysed by it. Fortunately, this left space for set members to express their opinion about what their colleague had said. Without knowing anything about learning theory, the group embarked on a dialogue about how adults should learn, and several set members described their unhappy learning experiences in the past, when they were passive learners, and compared them with productive learning where they had been active. Eventually, the principle of 'each member is responsible for their own learning' emerged and was included in the ground rules.

I have since facilitated action learning sets for managers in local government, and for staff and students in higher education. The method is far more efficient than supporting learning and development on a one-to-one basis. The facilitator needs to be skilled and we discuss these skills in later chapters, but can soon transfer those skills to set members, who thereafter share the task of facilitating the set. The method is relevant in the workplace, as it accommodates the need for action in many organizational contexts, as well as giving members the space for reflection which is so desperately needed in organizational life.

Facilitator contributions

We write as experienced users and facilitators of action learning. We have benefited from participating in sets and enabling others to become practitioners and facilitators. Significant for us is the learning from our collaboration with others in the field, whether as colleague set members or facilitators. A continual surprise is the ever-open opportunities of being faced with challenges that ensure we are never complacent in undertaking action learning. We have included across the handbook appropriate examples of where we and our facilitator colleagues have been faced with situations that have not been experienced before or in a different way from those previously experienced. The incidents have frequently been critical in the sense that the life of the set was apparently on the line. We include them not to put readers off but to show that we can live through them and move with them. Action learning does require courage. The work and the process is enormously rewarding from whatever standpoint – presenter, set member or facilitator. Our greatest satisfaction has been acquired as facilitators in enabling set members to work with often hugely significant issues in their lives, their work and their relationships. Many have worked in sets with the intention of becoming facilitators themselves – this too has been some of the most rewarding work. Finally, having the time to reflect is a necessary attribute of a civil life, one for which we make no excuse. It is essential as well as desirable.

PART I

Starting
Action Learning

Chapter 1

Introducing action learning

Action learning is a continuous process of learning and reflection that happens with the support of a group or 'set' of colleagues, working on real issues, with the intention of getting things done. The voluntary participants in the group or 'set' learn with and from each other and take forward an important issue with the support of the other members of the set.

The collaborative process, which recognizes set members' social context, helps people to take an active stance towards life, overcome the tendency to be passive towards the pressures of life and work, and aims to benefit both the organization and the individual.

As definitions don't always give a clear picture, we explore here the answer to the question *What is action learning?*, a regular question in introductory workshops and sessions.

Personal and management development

Action learning was initially developed by Reg Revans in post-Second World War Britain and he worked intrepidly, ploughing a very innovative path compared to the prevailing norms of training and development. He was very much at the frontier. Advances made in the USA, emanating from the west coast and found in such excellent works as Pfeiffer and Jones (1977), enabled people engaging in personal and management development to work in ways that involved them – that is, their whole person – in activities that at least they could relate to their own direct experience. In the UK, learner-centred development was slower to develop. In higher education lecturing to students was the norm, and case studies of past events used as material for qualifications like the MBA, modelled on the Harvard one, where the expertise lay mainly with the lecturer leading the case, represented the mainstream. The main alternative in the development field lay with the emphasis on 'up front' training.

In both the above examples, authority and expertise lay firmly with the lecturer or trainer. This simply reflected the tendency to authoritarian ways of inculcating learning, even though it ignored much of the research, which suggested that in adult learning the significance of personal experience is crucial. Relatively advanced programmes in the development field at least used simulations that emphasized key issues such as the need for planning, strategy and task/process. In these programmes the participant was actually involved in undertaking a task, albeit using Lego or film. It is perhaps unfair from this vantage point to be critical of the latter methods – for they are still useful as part of the overall development of individuals both within and outside organizations. Outdoor activities that promote personal and group understanding and team development, for example, come to mind. However, all the above come under the critical gaze when attention is paid to the life experience of the individual and the utilization of that experience by the individual. That experience was usually overtly left at the door to the training or development event.

It is here that action learning becomes increasingly relevant for it does just the opposite – bringing life experience to the fore as the single most important resource in enabling the individual to move and learn and develop with the support of others. Moreover, action learning is increasingly in line with the resistance to what are in effect authoritarian methods to induce learning. By its nature there is, in action learning, a fundamental respect for where people are coming from, their values and their right to learn at their own pace in a democratic environment.

Action learning also reflects the growing recognition that learning and development can be, and is, supported by a social context in which learning is shared as a social activity. This again is in contrast to the notion that learning is best conducted in isolation and in competition with others. There is a tension here in that much of the contemporary life of work is competitive. Again that is part of the appeal of action learning. It creates the conditions for collaboration amid that competitive environment that are also needed for a sane life.

Further, while capitalism is the current order, it nevertheless has enormous downsides, and developing alternative collaborative ways of working and living may be pointers to the future.

In the 1980s, one of us, for our research leading to a PhD, investigated the organization of work and the advocacy of industrial democracy by those primarily on the left of politics – including the British Labour Party. A key feature was the advocacy of collaborative ways of working, a facet of industrial democracy. The espousal of that appeal to democratic ways of working was almost always defeated in the lack of realization of that appeal. While there were often '*real politik*' reasons why it was not feasible, even where the conditions were possible, it did not work for the simple reason that the actors did not know *how* to work collaboratively.

What is the connection here with action learning? It is this: to work effectively, action learning requires in the participants a value criterion that promotes collaborative approaches to the task in hand. This includes sets where there is a facilitator. The facilitator is, in the early stages, creating the conditions within the voluntary framework for collaborative work and learning. While the facilitator may lead the process, once set members become aware of and familiar with it, the set can move to more collaborative modes, sharing responsibility and gradually moving into autonomous mode without the facilitator.

Moreover, members of sets collectively share their concerns, issues and proposed actions, which itself may be novel. Just as important is the process by which the learning set works through a set member's issues. The process is a shared, collective one where the learning about how to work on issues collectively is made explicit. Thus set members gain practice in a way of working that is designed to be collective as well as reflecting upon that practice. This reflection on practice ensures that the learning is made explicit – the practice is sensed, articulated, and incorporated into the set member's repertoire of behaviour. This enhanced and 'different' repertoire is then applicable in other contexts outside the action learning set, in work as well as in other social contexts. The repertoire of behaviour is different in that the aim is to learn, develop, and engage in tasks in a collaborative way, typified by the term 'win–win' rather than 'win–lose' strategies. The approach is not adversarial.

Another facet of our experience in working with a wide range of people employed in organizations is the tremendous pressure, often oppressive, from which it is very difficult to disentangle oneself without total withdrawal through voluntary or involuntary retirement or burn-out. It is quite clear that some enthusiastic participants are attracted to action learning because the set is a haven of sanity and reflection. Working conditions commonly provide little time for shared reflection. Asked if time is feasible in the day, week, month or year for reflection (and the necessary conditions for learning and development), the answer is usually raised eyebrows and laughter. Yet we are asking organizations to make that leap to engage in organizational learning without providing the means for it, often for their most senior staff, let alone the seedbed staff of the future.

What is action learning?

Action learning builds on the relationship between reflection and action. Learning by experience involves reflection, ie reconsidering past events, making sense of our actions, and possibly finding new ways of behaving at future events. We believe that reflection is a necessary precursor to effective action and that learning from experience can be enhanced by deliberate attention to this relationship. The theoretical basis for reflection is discussed at length in Chapter 6.

Taking part in an action learning set provides the time and space to attend to the relationship, ie the link between reflection and learning. Set members enable their colleagues to understand, explore and judge their situation as well as helping them to realize underlying feelings which influence behaviour. The action learning process is supportive *and* challenging, while recognizing the subjective world of set members and the social context of their work and lives.

Action learning is often assumed to be an everyday activity – 'Oh yes, that's learning by doing' or 'I use action learning all the time but I've never been in a set' (Pedler, 1997: 263).

Why is a set necessary for action learning?

Casual conversations in groups or one-to-one or even just talking through ideas with colleagues may be seen as reflective – why use a special name for it?

The answer lies in the deliberate and intentional provision of time and space for set members to engage in reflective learning. Action learning multiplies the kind of support which a trusted friend or colleague would offer, listening without judgement and, without giving advice, helping the individual concerned to discover his or her own solution. Not one but several people focus on supporting one person, with the knowledge that this will be reciprocated later in the session or at a later session.

Action learning sets formalize reflective learning and legitimize the allocation of time and space to it, with consistent voluntary group membership over an extended period of time.

How is action learning different from ordinary groups?

Action learning is unlike other kinds of group such as:

- formal meetings;
- seminars;
- teams;
- support or self-development groups;
- counselling or therapy groups.

Formal meetings have a chairperson, an agenda, open discussion, minutes and sometimes a vote. An action learning set focuses on the presenter's issue and set minutes are simply action points, not a record of the meeting.

A seminar is a presentation of prepared material for discussion by the group. The material is based on factual knowledge in the public domain. The rules are rarely helpful to the presenter, being adversarial in style, and no consequent action is expected. Action learning sets are wholly focused on assisting the presenter to reflect on action and move towards action.

A team is a group with a well-defined group task. Members may support each other but the objective is primarily completion of the task. Action learning sets work for the benefit of individual set members, not an externally imposed task. If set members share a task or project, they become a team, and the action learning process would have to be created in addition to team/task-focused meetings.

Support or self-development groups are often focused more on support than challenge. See Chapter 11 for challenge vs. support in action learning sets. The aim in action learning is to enable the individual to take responsibility, decide on action, and move on.

Action learning is not a counselling or therapy group. The presenter will be listened to and will be offered empathic support – aimed at helping. Counselling will not be offered in an action learning set. When personal problems arise, set members should seek counselling or therapy elsewhere.

So if it's not a team, support group or seminar, what issues can set members bring to a set? For action learning to be effective, the presenter's issue should be:

- important to her;
- something where she has authority to act (or is concerned about her lack of it);
- not trivial;
- owned – not about someone else.

The 'authority to act' issue may well look different after the set discussion and the presenter may use the set to work with feelings related to her perceived lack of power. We look now at what the provision of time and space means in action learning.

Time and space

How long should the action learning set meet for? How often should the set meet? How much time should the set and each person have?

How long?

A typical set cycle is likely to be over one calendar year, but set cycles vary from six months to two years depending on the nature of the set. Sets may re-contract at the end of cycle review stage and start a second or even third cycle. What is important is the need for a clear commitment to an agreed number of meetings, which include a review, an ending and an evaluation. We discuss endings in Chapter 15 and evaluation in Chapter 14.

How often?

The frequency of set meetings is negotiated and agreed at the start of the cycle, and set meeting dates are decided and diaried in advance. This is particularly important with independent sets (described in Chapter 2) where set members are coming from different organizations and different geographical locations. An interval of one month or six weeks between set meetings is usual; any longer affects the momentum and work of the set.

How much time?

The total time for each set meeting will also be agreed at the start. The set members may not be totally free to determine how much time they can commit to each meeting. There may be personal and organizational constraints or, for independent sets, logistical limits to their commitment. Two models are currently in use:

- *Half-day*: This is rather short for a set of five or six members but a typical choice for many. We recommend an absolute minimum of 30 minutes per member, plus 30 minutes each for opening and closing the set meeting, as the minimum below which the action learning work of the set would be compromised. One approach is to accept that only two set members can present at each set meeting, ensuring that every set member has the opportunity to present over the whole set cycle.
- *Full day*: Here it is possible for five or six members to take their time at every set meeting, as well as providing time for a process review. When set members become familiar with the action learning format, they can confidently adapt the process to suit their own situation. A set may choose to have fewer presentations to enable greater depth and consideration.

How much time each?

Time within the set meeting can be allocated evenly to each set member. If the set chooses to alter this arrangement by consensus, timing can be flexible. This may occur when a presenter's issue has stimulated deep issues or strong emotion.

When not presenting, set members are actively working to support the presenter – there is no let-up in activity! Set meetings can be exhausting; they are not cosy chats, so the environment, the setting and venue are important.

Space

We recommend that set meetings take place in a comfortable and quiet environment. The set needs privacy as sensitive issues may be discussed and strong emotions may be expressed. The meeting room must be appropriate for the session, without interruptions. Fixed phones should be disabled, while mobile phones or pagers should be switched off as part of the ground rules. When it is necessary for people to be available for urgent calls, these can be taken at the breaks. Refreshments are an important ingredient for keeping the set's energy levels up and a sandwich or buffet lunch, well presented, ensures that the set keeps active in the afternoon.

Beginning and ending set meetings

Set meetings are likely to be productive if they begin with attention to 'nurture' issues such as greetings, tea/coffee, seating, welcoming, toilets etc. The need for nurturing and relaxation should be met by suitable short breaks, between presentations if possible. Opening exercises are essential to enable set members to share any recent experiences that there are to surface (Chapter 4). Time-keeping will have to take account of these. This ensures that set members can re-enter their creative cycle with high energy levels. The creative cycle is shown in Figure 1.1.

Process review

Somewhere in the set's time there should be time for a process review. This is where set members talk about 'how' the set worked, without re-entering the content of presentations. The facilitator's role is to ensure that the set remains in process mode and records their reflections in some way. We discuss levels of reflection in Chapter 6 and give details of a process review in Chapter 13.

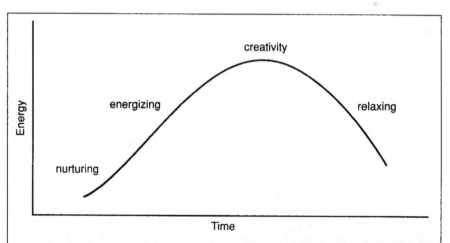

This cycle shows that energy-flows over time require periods of nurturing and relaxation. As well as the set meeting as a whole becoming more effective with the use of an approach to the event taking into account different stages within it, throughout the meeting energy will come and go. Keeping energy high for each individual may be greatly aided by periods of nurturing and relaxation. These periods do not have to be long to be effective but ignoring the need for them by rushing on to next business will make the meeting as a whole less successful. This cycle applies to the whole set meeting but also to the presenter during her time.

Figure 1.1   *The creative cycle, adapted from Randall and Southgate (1980)*

Ending a set meeting

The tangible outcome of a set meeting is the intention to act by set members. Action points emerge from each presenter's time, decided by the presenters themselves, after the set dialogue. We discuss action points, recording, and closure in Chapter 4.

Evaluation

Much of the writing on action learning has been advocatory. This book still has that – put it down to our enthusiasm. Indeed McGill and Beaty (1992, 1995, 2001) were rightly accused of that. However, we seek in this text to underpin that enthusiasm with evidence of the value of action learning to participant set members and organizations.

Why is evaluation of action learning important? For individuals coming to set work it is necessary to justify, given the importance of the time devoted to such personal and management development. A set can amount to 8–10 days over a year, to take just one time approach. Given a working year of 220 days, that amounts to under 5 per cent of the person's time. Taken as the figure of 8–10 days it looks a lot. As a percentage it is very modest against the investment simply to maintain an organization's capital! Yet such time for the individual is often baulked at.

By evaluation we mean the aim to measure the outcomes of action learning and an examination of the effect of process outcomes. We consider evaluation in detail in Chapter 14.

The values in action learning

Working with action learning presumes a core of values, ideas and assumptions that are worth making explicit at this stage in the handbook. Action learning is very different from traditional methods of education, learning and most forms of training and development. We review below some of the core values that are essential to action learning. These values will be developed in later chapters. The section below is not intended to be conclusive – some other values will emerge later in the handbook.

Voluntary nature of action learning

Participants in action learning engage in the process voluntarily. That is, they make a positive conscious decision to join an action learning set. Action learning does not work where it is imposed on the person. Voluntary implies a willingness to engage with the process. Resistance to the process may result in negative outcomes, leading to behaviour that militates against constructive learning. The effect is likely to lead to departure from the set and potentially the breakdown of the set as a whole.

Because the action learning process is unusual in the context of traditional forms of learning, potential set members may come to the early meetings of a set with a degree of scepticism or doubt about its potentiality. This is understandable given the past that most of us have experienced in education and subsequent development where we have had to accept the burden of endurance before the benefits. Provided the facilitator accepts this healthy scepticism and set members are asked to suspend judgement until some experience of the process occurs, new set members are likely to pass beyond their scepticism into a positive approval of the novel form the process takes.

Voluntarily embarking on action learning is more likely to yield a positive approach to the whole experience and substantially underpins the trust that emerges.

Confidentiality and trust

Confidentiality is an essential precondition for action learning to work effectively. We will say more about this subject later (Chapter 4). Essentially it means that set members do not disclose the content of other set members' contributions outside the set. Each set member may take their own issues elsewhere. This forms the basis of any trust that develops in the set and is a core need to enable significant learning and development. Without trust, set members are not going to disclose what may be, to them, a vulnerability, a perceived weakness or helplessness. Yet these qualities in each of us can also be a strength, when revealed, that enables us, with the support of others, to move on.

Emerging trust is also the basis of the story and history that will inevitably be created by the set about its life, which in turn has the effect of endorsing and building that trust.

Recognition of all the domains of learning

Traditional learning lays emphasis upon knowledge or cognition and its transmission and acquisition. We do not underestimate its importance in our development. The approach, however, understates the other two aspects. The three 'domains' of learning have long been identified by educationalists (Bloom, 1964), and they cover the three aspects as follows: cognitive (knowing); conative (doing); affective (feeling) (Brockbank and McGill, 1998).

These terms are abstractions which overlap in practice. However, they may be presented in terms which describe the outcome of learning in each domain, eg cognitive learning results in knowledge; conative learning results in action/changes in the world; affective learning alters appreciation of the self in relation to self and others.

If learning is limited to one of these domains, the others are affected and learning is limited. The emphasis on cognition in adult (including higher education) learning has neglected the development of conative and affective intelligence. While practical applications have become an integral part of much adult development, the denial of emotion in learning remains in place for many parts of adult development.

In action learning the affective and conative aspects of learning are given their significance in the learning and development process – a recognition of the emotional and action dimensions in learning. In the facilitator's role is embodied knowledge, self and world, the three domains of expression, whereas in traditional teaching and training the practice emphasizes primarily one domain, that of knowledge.

Autonomy and *mutuality*

Action learning is noted for its development of the individual with greater autonomy and independence. Action learning works primarily by individual set members bringing their issues to the set and working towards some form of resolution and potential action. This journey to autonomy and independence needs to be qualified. We are not suggesting an individualistic journey, for we are asserting that while the learner may be experiencing a journey towards that autonomy and independence of learning, it is one undertaken with others. Learning is a social process. Here we are using that term to convey the interdependence between facilitator and learners and between learners. The interaction between these 'actors' represents a *relationship* between them. By relationship we are implying a mutuality. In the words of Buber 'I-Thou establishes the world of relation' (1994 p.18), in contrast to an object relation where thou is an it or object. We explore this notion more extensively in Chapter 8.

Such a different way of relating with the learner can be achieved through facilitation, where the focus is on the learner, as learner (not as object). Therefore, we are putting forward the idea that facilitators of learning, both facilitators and other set members, will move into a different way of seeing their role, a different way of being and relating with the set member as presenter, and will do things that are different from traditional teaching or 'up front' training.

Learning as a social *and* collaborative *process*

Reinforcing the idea of mutuality is the idea of learning as a social process. The idea of learning as a social and collaborative process sits strangely on our traditionally competitive Western education system, with its emphasis on detachment and distance. When the social context of learning is recognized, and collaboration is valued rather than penalized, the significance of relationship in learning makes sense, prioritizing involvement and connection, nurturing joint endeavours and stimulating the creativity of constructed knowledge.

Relationship in traditional adult education and learning has emphasized separateness and isolation, causing learners to be 'estranged' from each other, their teacher, and the material ideas they seek to learn about (Radley, 1980: 34). As non-participants in the process, learners have been presented with their subject as the teacher's 'product', often an alien 'buffet of ideas' (Radley, 1980: 40) and quite foreign to the student learner.

When relationship replaces estrangement, and learning is recognized as having implications in the realm of ideas, values, social interests and assumptions, then learning becomes 'the expression of a social system... which is grounded in the ways in which student and teacher together work with their material' (Radley, 1980: 36), suggesting connection between facilitator and learner and, we would add, learner and learner.

Belenky *et al* (1986) differentiate connected learning from separated knowing with reference to the deep relationships that characterize the former (1986: 115) in contrast to the detachment of the latter. Connected learning recognizes the significance of relationship as learners jointly construct knowledge for themselves and each other. Chapter 5 gives a detailed account of the terms 'separated knowing' and 'connected learning'.

The learner as a model of 'abundance' rather than 'deficiency'

Implied from what has been stated so far is the idea of individuals being resources of abundance that can be drawn upon to further learning. This is in contrast to the deficiency model of the individual being an 'empty bucket to be filled'. The former model begins with an openness to abundance, an assumption that the learner already possesses in abundance what is needed for learning. In this model, given the opportunity, space and encouragement, learning will happen. Thus in action learning set members bring their whole experience to the set as a resource to be applied to the issue presented by the presenting set member.

Belenky *et al* (1986: 190ff) contrast stances taken by two college professors and their impact via stories told by two women who had each experienced one of the professors. The first professor, introducing a science class, asked the students to guess how many beans a jar contained. After a host of inaccurate answers he gave the 'right' answer and added: 'You have just learned an important lesson about science. Never trust the evidence of your own senses.' The effect destroyed the confidence of the student who left and did not return to science for years, having had her notion of first-hand experience trashed. In the second example a philosophy professor put a cube on the table and asked what it was. In response to its being called a cube, she asked what a cube was. The response brought forth that a cube contained six equal square sides. 'But how do you know? We can't exactly see six sides, can we, when we look, yet you know it's a cube. You invent the sides you cannot see. You use your intelligence to create the "truth" about cubes.'

The contrast between the approaches of the two professors is interesting. The science professor, in a benign way, wanted to teach students that experience is a source of error. In isolation this had the effect of rendering the student dumb and dependent. The philosophy student's lesson was that although raw experience is insufficient, by reflecting upon it the student arrived at a truth. It did not diminish but enhanced her self-esteem and built upon her lived experience. The latter is the basis of action learning from the outset, that a set member is resourceful rather than resource empty; abundant rather than deficient. An action learning set unlocks (and sometimes unblocks) the experience that people bring with them. In addition, a set will also surface prior tacit learning.

Making a difference

Working in an action learning set yields another value, having a positive outlook on life, with the idea that in situations fraught with difficulty and apparently intractable it is possible to find some 'room for manoeuvre', however small, that will create some resolution or action. Believing that something can be done is not the same as saying that everything is under our control and still less that all problems are our fault. There is clear recognition that we are deeply influenced by our environment. It does mean that we take responsibility to review the situation, context and identify our position and ability to manoeuvre within the situation. The presenter can become clearer about his or her own contribution to the situation as currently presented. Identifying what action it is possible to take may also mean deciding to take no action. Reflecting on past action as well as reviewing the present may reveal that the best thing to do is *nothing*. The set may enable the presenter to *see* the situation differently, from a new perspective not previously considered or experienced. Such a recognition may not require any action – the recognition may be sufficient in itself, involving a different way of seeing reality.

Personal responsibility for learning

A basic principle in action learning is that each set member is and remains responsible for their issue, problem or concern that they bring to the set. Set members are not there to tell a presenter what or how to progress an issue. They are not there to give the presenter advice, but rather to enable each individual to understand his or her situation by exploration through reflection and to challenge assumptions underlying these reflections in order to move to some resolution and potential action.

Thus in action learning each set member is recognized as the expert on their situation in terms of their context, feelings, and knowledge. A corollary of this is that other set members may have insights that the set member has not realized by virtue of that proximity.

Underlying this responsibility by each set member is personal responsibility for the learning that may derive from attending to their issue. This is fundamental to action learning and the *raison d'être* for this is developed throughout the handbook.

Support and challenge

Set members new to action learning are often in work situations where support is absent and isolation is the prevailing feeling, sometimes unrecognized until the advent of the set.

A set can provide the support that is necessary to development and learning, which are the critical aspirations and measures of whether an action learning set is successful.

Support is necessary but not sufficient. Support can be beneficial but alone may produce a cosy, collusive atmosphere that will not enable a set member to move on. Challenge is the counterpoint to support. Set members and facilitator will, in an effective set, challenge the assumptions and perspective that a presenter may hold and have taken for granted. An example for one of us was a senior manager presenting who assumed that a seemingly recalcitrant member of his staff was exhibiting that behaviour because she disliked the senior manager. The set did not know whether this was valid or not but just questioned the basis of the recalcitrance. The set member, on reflection, recognized that there may have been an assumption determining his behaviour. The action which later flowed included the task of checking out how she felt about her work. The feelings behind the recalcitrance had nothing to do with the manager, but rested with a personal tragedy she had experienced. The manager moved and changed his working relationship with her, as did her work.

Empathy

Central to the action learning process is empathy. By empathy is meant the understanding of the position, context and emotional state of the other set members, usually when they are presenting. The deeper and fuller my understanding of a set member, the more easily I can find the right words to enable progress. Learning how to use empathy within a set is important for set members' development as well as the success of the set, yet it is not something that comes easily to most, even though it is useful beyond action learning. We describe and discuss empathy in much greater detail in Chapters 10 and 11.

Quality of attention

A significant feature of action learning, emphasized by set members, is the degree and quality of attention each set member receives, particularly when presenting. Indeed, it is common at the end of an action learning session for set members to say that they are exhausted, yet energized, from the sheer concentration levels that are maintained.

Most work meetings require more selective attention depending on agenda requirements. In action learning presenters are the 'agenda' and the whole set gives their attention to the presenter even though it is about their world. Set members really attend to the person and their issue. The reason for this is that their issue is usually presented as a 'story' even though a more formal picture may also emerge. The story is about the presenter told from their perspective and includes what they know about it, how they feel about it and what they may have done about it up to now and imminently. It is not 'out there' as some arid description distant from the actor. It is the actor. This spirit of attending, once experienced, is engendered for others, with concomitant commitment to the set.

Development takes time

A surface or instrumental understanding of the process might suggest that it is about reflecting upon a person's current circumstance relating to one or more issues and then taking action to change or improve the situation. Action learning is about development and the associated learning that is linked with development. Set members may bring issues that evolve over the life of the set and/or projects that require progress and implementation. Reflection on issues may well evolve over time. Those issues or projects will be explored between set meetings following some commitment to action from a set meeting. Let us look at an example. A set member changes her career. She commences a new form of training in the community development field for fifty per cent of her time and starts a new job working for a charity that uses her senior administrative skills from her previous post. This happens during the life of the set. Six months in, she experiences tensions in the administrative post while greatly valuing the community development training. She reviews the tensions and potential actions she can take in the job. Slowly, with questions, she realizes that the job is not really important for her any longer and that she had taken the post, without realizing it, for status reasons. The satisfaction from the study and training helped her surface the status issues with the support and challenge of the set. The process in the set enabled her to recognize and make explicit the development that had taken place. Such a summary does not do justice to the tentative evolution that occurred over a number of set meetings and was expressed after an hour by her at one of the meetings. This example reveals how development and learning about ourselves is slow but can be very radical in the change it yields.

Finally, we distinguish between development and learning that results in improvement and that which yields transformation. The former is gained by making a change within the confines of current ways of doing things, eg clarifying priorities within a current work role. Transformative development results in working with a different way of seeing the world or reality. Action learning is able to work at both levels, though whether either occurs depends upon the context and issue for the set member. We explore this further in Chapter 7.

A spirit of enquiry

Action learning can be a powerful and potent form of learning and development. But it is not an automatic fix. It can go awry. We consider in the book some of the difficulties that can be experienced by practitioners of the process.

As we proceed through the handbook, we will reflect these values and expand on them where appropriate.

Chapter 2

Types of action learning

In this chapter we emphasize the flexibility of action learning and how it may be adapted to the needs of organizations and individuals. We distinguish two main types of action learning: sets created by organizations and sets independent of organizations. Sets can also be facilitated or self-facilitated, the latter sometimes referred to as self-managed. In addition, we identify the nature of the issues that individuals may bring to sets, continuing professional development where action learning may be a support, and applications to organizations. We conclude with a reference to the various 'schools' of action learning and where we consider this handbook fits across the schools.

First, there are sets initiated and supported by organizations. Organization-initiated action learning includes sets usually formed for management development purposes. Secondly, independent action learning sets can be found within or across organizations or may be organizationally free. In addition, independent sets may be formed without organizational support with their own development aims. Independent sets can be organized by the participants themselves or by facilitators inviting participants to join a set.

Action learning sets can be facilitated by a facilitator or be self-facilitated. With the latter, responsibility for facilitating the set is shared by the set members themselves.

The variety of action learning types is shown in Figure 2.1.

The diagram shows that sets can be organization initiated or independent; and sets can be facilitated or self-facilitated. We will consider the purposes for which sets may be used by organizations and the use of independent sets by individuals. We consider a recent innovation in action learning – the use of pair sets. This is followed by the particular requirements of self-facilitated action learning sets.

Facilitated sets sponsored by organizations

Taking initiative and gaining commitment for action learning

Two groups of people may initiate action learning within an organization. The first are those who have responsibility for development and wish to use

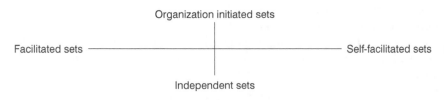

Figure 2.1   *Types of sets*
Source: McGill and Beaty, 2001

action learning as an important means of enabling staff and management development to happen. The second are the people who wish to be participants in sets for their personal and management development. Both groups have responsibilities for ensuring that the sets are created and maintained.

The key here is the source of influence for initiating the creation of sets. For organizational support, there is a need for a champion in the organization to make action learning happen. This is particularly important where resources of time, finance and project initiatives are required. The champion may be a managing director, head of staff/management development, trainer or someone who is an enthusiast to make action learning happen. Ideally the champion will be familiar with the use and effectiveness of action learning, what it is like to do action learning and the personal/managerial and organizational benefits.

Determining issues brought to the set

Here we consider the basic approaches organizations may take to how they expect participant managers and staff to use sets.

The continuum in Figure 2.2 can be used to describe the range of ways in which sets can be used by set members. With organizationally initiated sets it is important to clarify for the sponsors, set members and facilitators (in facilitated sets) at which ends of the continuum sets are expected to work.

The person responsible for initiating action learning can take a stance along the continuum. Let us call him the development manager. At the right-hand end of the continuum, the development manager negotiates the parameters of a project with three other people, the set member, a 'champion' and the facilitator. There is shared 'ownership' of the project and accountability by the set member is maintained mainly through project management. At the personal end of the continuum, the set

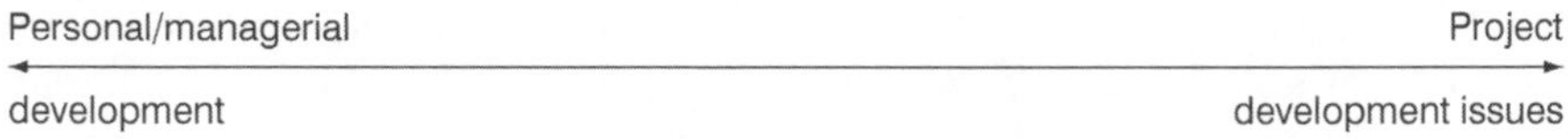

Personal/managerial   Project

development   development issues

Figure 2.2   *Organizationally initiated set continuum*
Source: McGill and Beaty, 2001

member is left to decide the issues she brings to the set. Responsibility rests here more with the set member to use the set for her development. The set member may be accountable for her development in supervision or reflection with her line manager and the management developer responsible for creating the sets.

The organizational project

At the project end of this continuum, the development manager will require staff joining sets to undertake a project that is directly geared to the needs of the organization. The member of staff joins a set to enable her to gain support while undertaking the project which has direct pay-offs for the organization. The project may be directly geared to the organization's strategic purposes or be a one-off problem-centred issue for resolution. A project could be based on an operational or a developmental problem. An operational problem would be one that concerned the way in which a product is currently produced or a service delivered. The problem becomes a project to resolve or at least reduce its incidence. Examples may include:

- low morale and low customer satisfaction in a frontline service department of an organization;
- a chief executive endeavouring to embark on a modernization programme and dealing with resistance to change;
- reducing the number of return visits by clients in order to deal with their needs more effectively first time.

A developmental issue or problem would be one that takes the organization and its members beyond the operational into new pathways of potential action:

- implementing a management development system;
- planning and implementing a monitoring strategy to reflect equalities policy;
- developing and implementing a new marketing strategy;
- introducing performance measurement into customer care programmes;
- identification, design and implementation of a staff development policy.

Enabling management development through project work via action learning sets has two crucial aspects. First, the problem tackled must be one for which there is not a prescribed solution. If we know how the problem can be resolved it is not a problem. We just need to get on with it. However, 'I' may have a problem doing it. This is a different matter. 'I' may have a problem in undertaking the task I am addressing. An example would be where 'I' lack the confidence to do a particular task. We will address this below at the personal development end of the continuum. An organization, in agreeing an organizational problem for resolution through a project, will want the project to be one that is at least intractable initially. Otherwise, resources are being wasted. If we know how a problem can be resolved, go ahead and do it!

Secondly, there is the 'ownership' of the project. The project has to be owned by its initiators to ensure the planning, implementation, and outcomes of the project. The 'ownership' of the project is shared three ways, the first two of which are essential:

1. The person in the set, the set member, will have ownership in wanting to undertake the project to completion over a period of time. If the set member pursues a project without really wanting to do it, then a lack of commitment to the project may mar its successful progress. The inherent danger here is the project 'imposed' on the set member. The culture prevailing in the organization will partly determine whether the imposed project is successfully implemented. The desire to undertake the project will be negotiated with:
2. A 'client' elsewhere in the organization for whom resolution of the problem is also important. This person will negotiate with the set member the purposes of the project, its implementation and a review of its outcomes.
3. The third interested person will have some ownership in the project. This person may be responsible for management development, the set member's line manager and/or our management developer in the organization who will wish to be assured of the development of the individual beyond completion of the project.

The facilitator and set may have an additional and useful contribution. They provide a focus for the set member to decide the feasibility of the project within the set framework. The set member takes any problems to the set so that she can think them through with the support of the set and the facilitator.

Personal development issues

At the other end of the continuum, the 'personal development issues' end, the set becomes the forum for staff to bring their issues to the set with the simple rule that the issue is one of significance to the set member. Sets are formed with staff who:

*   will potentially benefit from action learning;
*   voluntarily wish to become members of a set with other colleagues in the organization;
*   and who (usually)[1] do not have direct line relationships to each other.

The sets commence, leaving the participants in the sets to address their own issues, problems and opportunities.[2] In this way participants start from where they are 'coming from' with their issues, problems and concerns. Examples could include:

- reviewing management team relationships;
- line relationship as a manager with colleagues for whom the manager is responsible;
- completion of a research degree with field work in the manager's employing organization;
- prioritization of work for self and staff;
- forthcoming redundancy and 'moving on';
- future work/career direction.

As at the organizational end of the continuum, the set member could design some of the above issues and problems as a project with specific targets in respect of planning, implementation and review. Other problems may require more short-term attention and, once resolved, the set member can go on to other issues. For example, a set member may bring her desire to improve her working relationship with an 'awkward' colleague to the set, attention to which may enable the problem to be resolved fairly quickly. However, to the set member this relationship may be *the* intractable problem facing her at the time.

The choices along the continuum

Both ends of the continuum are justified but they do start from different perspectives. At the organization end is the view that any initiated project should have direct organizational benefits. The manager, as set member, gains her personal and management development en route. At the personal development end is the view that the manager has her 'baggage' of skills, qualities, attributes and 'ways of seeing the world'. This is the starting point. The set enables that person to work on her issues. In this way her management development will derive from those issues most significant to her, from which the organization may also benefit.

Between the ends of the continuum are combinations of the above. For example, once the personal development issues have reached a degree of resolution, wider organizational issues and projects can be negotiated with clients elsewhere in the organization.

Both ends of the continuum have their disadvantages. At the personal development end, the manager and other set members may stay in a 'crisis'-centred mode, always returning to operational issues of concern. In the example above, we gave the instance of a set member addressing the operational issue about working with an 'awkward' colleague. The set member could stay in the mode of always addressing issues like this one so that they recur in one form or another. The set may, even with a facilitator, collude with this mode and the set member may not rise above the parapet to look at developmental issues. At the organizational project end, the manager may address the issues of the project, 'safely' ignoring her personal developmental issues by immersing herself in the content of the project. Facilitators need to be aware of these potentialities.

In an organizational context, participants will face a pay-off with the organization regarding benefits to both. An organization may, at the personal development end of the continuum, be content to enable the participant to choose his or her personal development needs without any explicit organizational demands. At the project development end of the continuum, the organization may require the participant to meet the demands of the project as well as having developmental requirements that satisfy the participant. If there are no perceived benefits for the participant, the latter may engage negatively in the process, with similar implications for the organization.

Independent action learning sets

'Independent' means that an organization is not involved in the creation of an action learning set, in determining the parameters of the set, or providing direct resources for the set. Members form sets for their personal needs without support or constraints by an organization.

An independent set has advantages of being released from the constraints, demands and expectations of an organization. This freedom can be positive. There is usually a sense of commitment and responsibility to make the set function, to meet, to continue and to ensure that the set works for each member. The negative side may be that maintenance of the set imposes a responsibility of time and resources that the set member cannot provide but that an organization can.

In an independent set, members can bring issues to the set that they may not bring to one supported organizationally, particularly where the organization requires a client-based project. This leads us to another continuum, shown in Figure 2.3.

In contrast with the organizationally sponsored set, the set member has complete choice and total responsibility for what she brings to the set. In Figure 2.3, by project/task we mean:

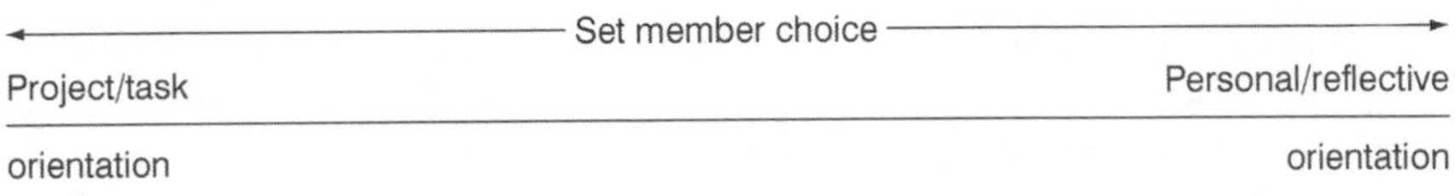

←————————————— Set member choice —————————————→

Project/task   Personal/reflective

orientation   orientation

Figure 2.3   *Independent sets continuum*
Source: McGill and Beaty, 2001

- producing a report or project to a deadline;
- how to work with a 'difficult' colleague;
- how to overcome being reactive in work.

A reflective issue or problem brought to the set could include those examples given above in an organizationally sponsored set at the personal development end. We could add more here:

- What am I doing this work for anyway?
- What makes me do what I ought to do as opposed to what I want to do?
- How do I balance my work with the rest of my life?
- Where am I going in my life?

A set member may start at the task end but gradually (and even deriving from the task end) move to the more reflective/personal development end of the continuum.

Another advantage of independent action learning sets is that they enable those not attached to an organization to join a set. Here we include people who are home based, not in paid work or self-employed who would like support plus action from a set.

With an independent set, each member can decide what to bring to the set without any accountability to external providers. The only accountability is to themselves supported by the other set members!

Sets created and supported by an organization benefit by having a champion. The champion can initiate or obtain agreement for this form of development, the resources of time allocation, funding of facilitators and possible cover for set members' work. Independent sets require being their own champions in creating and maintaining the sets. This can appear a more daunting task.

Consideration of the need for a facilitator to facilitate an independent set may be an impediment on grounds of cost for the facilitator's time. However, as we show below, depending on the skills that set members bring to the set, a facilitator may not be necessary. Alternatively, a facilitator could facilitate the set for a short period to enable take-off to self-facilitation.

Pair sets

Pair sets are a recent innovation. Normally, set members join sets as individuals from across organizations or within organizations but not usually in direct working relationships. Pair sets consist of a number of paired individuals who have a working relationship in their organization, who come together in a set with others in the same working relationship to work on issues common to the pairs in the set.

An example of pair sets is a programme recently organized by the NHS Leadership Centre in association with the British Association of Medical Managers for chief executives and medical directors of NHS Trusts to work in development sets together, using the action learning model. Chief executives and medical directors are expected to work closely together in British health organizations such as hospitals and in primary care. The innovative element of this form of action learning was that they would work together on issues which were common to both, with a view to applying the results of their work together in the action learning set back at their organization. Four sets were created with eight members each, with a facilitator appointed by the NHS Leadership Centre, for six day meetings over one year.

Two of the sets had a mix of chief executives and medical directors from a range of Trusts but no set members came from the same Trust. In these sets there was simply a commonality of the two roles in the set. These sets became known as the 'singles' sets.

Two sets were created specifically for a chief executive and medical director from the same Trust to be part of the same set. Thus in a set of eight members there would be pairs of chief executives and medical directors from four Trusts. These became known as the 'pairs' sets. Because of the experimental nature of these sets they were preceded by day workshops, particularly where there was to be joint working.

The aims of the sets were to facilitate cross-professional working, improving mutual insight into carrying out responsibilities at a senior level in the NHS, and to provide personal development in a challenging and supportive environment. The members of these sets were asked what their expectations of the programme were. These included:

- to have a safe environment in which to share and explore issues;
- to problem solve, learn and reflect from the experiences of others;
- to develop a better understanding about the way in which chief executives and medical directors think and work;
- to try to understand with greater effect the wider 'political' environment;
- managing difficult issues in the Trust and rapid change in the NHS.

This was added to in the pair sets by:

- to develop the relationship between the chief executive and medical director.

This last expectation goes to the core of the experiment of the pairs work. The 'singles' sets shared overlapping roles but were not in each other's patches. The 'pairs' sets were exceptional in each pair being from the same patch. This was the point of these latter sets. It was intentional. The purpose of these latter sets was to enable the pair to work on issues with which they were both concerned and had a common interest in moving forward and getting resolution. What is the reservation in such an arrangement? Coming together in a set with replicated relationships across the set would require significant trust between each pair, let alone the whole set. The reservation of such an arrangement is that the pair would 'freeze' any tendency to openness and simply work in a purely surface manner, ensuring that no risks were taken. The initial workshop for pairs explicitly addressed this issue alongside an introduction to action learning. Their Trusts were in the vanguard of major reform and change. The themes addressed by the pairs included:

- management team dynamics;
- clinical governance – dealing with difficult colleagues and service failures;
- developing new healthcare communities and managing changing organizations;
- personal management, career and life dilemmas;
- interventions to manage the political context.

In addition, there was particular mutual support for facing questions such as:

- Is what I am doing/we have done right?

Outcomes included specific changes in behaviour; doing things differently and more effectively; gaining clear support from the set through: recognition; commonality of problems; access to wider sources of experience and information; understanding their work by comparison with other Trusts.

Singles set responses were more tentative about effects upon their work and their organization than the pairs. For the pairs there were very positive statements of improvement in the relationship between each of the pairs as well as gaining insights from other pairs. The set process was considered effective because it engendered trust between pairs and within the sets. There was a willingness to take time to consider issues in depth.

The sets were occasionally marred by lack of attendance. Where a pair was working together and one was absent, the person attending was often unwilling to pursue the common issue without the presence of the other person in the pair.

Facilitating pair sets is considered more complex than sets where individuals are simply representing themselves.

The pairs programme was regarded very positively overall. However, much more experimentation is necessary before more evaluative conclusions can be made about this use of action learning.

Self-facilitated sets

We define a self-facilitated action learning set as one that operates without using a facilitator. In self-facilitated (sometimes referred to as self-managed) sets the set members take responsibility for the facilitation role and action learning process.

Developmental activities for staff can be resource-hungry and can be wasteful if the activity does not lead to pay-offs for the organization and the individuals experiencing the development. We now examine the use of self-facilitated sets to promote staff and management development. An external facilitator may initiate the process.

Organizations may use self-facilitated groups more frequently as they move from hierarchic and rigid forms of working to flatter, more flexible structures with people across and between organizations. We recommend that readers refer to particular chapters that support the running of self-facilitated sets. In Chapter 1 we outline the start of the set process, the basic insights, procedures and processes by which a set works; Chapter 4 is concerned with commencing a set; Chapters 9 and 10 convey the essential roles of set members as presenters and enablers of the presenter; Chapter 11 considers the role of the facilitator, and gives the self-facilitated set member an insight into the skills and attributes of facilitation; Chapters 9 and 10 explore the skills required for effective set interaction by addressing skills development. We recommend that potential self-facilitated set members, who have limited facilitation experience, should use the chapters mentioned above.

We use the term self-facilitated action learning sets. Some writers and practitioners have referred to self-development groups (Pedler *et al*, 1990). We would distinguish a self-facilitated set from a self-development group by the former using explicit action learning processes.

We also make a distinction between self-facilitation and unfacilitated sets. It is a small but crucial point. Self-facilitation means that all set members consciously take on the role of facilitator to progress the set meeting. Each set member takes and shares responsibility for facilitation as part of their set membership. Only when being presenter will they relinquish that responsibility. The term 'unfacilitated' connotes a meaning that suggests the set does not require facilitation. Given the structured nature of action learning, we prefer not to use such a term.

The story of how one of us started using action learning in a self-facilitated set is to be found in Ian's story in the Introduction.

Benefits of self-facilitated sets

Self-facilitated sets using the action learning approach give a coherent structure and way of working that combines individual action and reflection and is an effective means of maintaining the group. Often, when people get together in groups that are unstructured the result can be failure or group-destruct. The action learning process is a sensitive format that meets the needs of its members and the group as a whole. The action learning way of working in groups does not guarantee success, but it does reduce the chances of failure. Action learning methods are also very explicit and clear. This makes it easier for participants new to group working to practise, reflect and add to their repertoire of skills.

Traditional ways of progressing tasks in organizations can be isolating, that is, 'do it on your own'. Presenting that work to a meeting where there are varying degrees of commitment is a discouraging environment in which to work. Sabotaging a project is a typical tactic of the cynical. Alternatively, working in sets can create rapport, commitment, and collaboration beyond the set.

What does a self-facilitated set need to be effective?

Potential set members

Personal commitment is important for a set member in a traditional set. That commitment is even more important in the early stages of a self-facilitated set. Drawing upon Heron's (1999) modes of facilitation, this form of action learning is at the autonomous end of the spectrum. Set members share responsibility for the maintenance of the set, its procedures and processes (Chapter 4). There is no facilitator to take responsibility when the set is detracting from its purpose. Each set member in a self-facilitated set shares the responsibility otherwise vested in a facilitator.

When creating a self-facilitated set, set members need to gain commitment that is voluntary. We do this by ensuring that the first meeting is a 'taster'. At the first meeting it is open to anyone to say that it is not what they anticipated and that they may choose not to come to subsequent meetings. This is similar to facilitated sets. A potential set member should not feel obliged to join a set just because it has met, or feel any group pressure to continue. It may mean that the set is stillborn. However, as long as there are sufficient numbers who wish to continue, the basis for real commitment has been identified.

Drawing upon our experience of self-facilitation (McGill *et al* in Weil and McGill, 1990), we saw that: 'For each person, personal commitment to the set and the way it worked was a priority. Being at the set was very important compared to other activities associated with our work. This generated a feeling of protectiveness towards the time of the set. Something that required so much effort to protect and sustain could not fail to attain significance.'

Procedures

At the first meeting of a set, basic procedures and ground rules are agreed. These can be modified at subsequent meetings to suit the set. These include:

- Life expectancy of the set. The set agrees the length of time for which it will hold a cycle of meetings. It may meet for six months, nine months or a year. The set reviews its progress during and at the end of the designated period. (See Chapter 13 for review processes.)
- Frequency of meetings. This is dependent on the needs of members. However, meetings once every four to five weeks enable set members to maintain momentum and to fulfil actions between set meetings.
- Set numbers and duration of set meetings. There is a relationship between the number of members in a set and the duration of each set meeting. These are usually two to three hours, dependent upon the number of set members. A small set of three or four may get through business in three to four hours. Five to six members will need at least four hours. We do not recommend sets below four unless there is a degree of action learning experience among members. The set may agree to have a day meeting to give set members more time, to review the set process and to celebrate the set!
- Time allocation at meetings. This may be divided equally after allowing sufficient time for informalities (how we are feeling today), common business (diaries for subsequent meetings) and a process review. The set may agree that a set member has more time if there is a felt need.
- Time-keeping and note taking. Without a facilitator, these key functions are allocated between set members. Time-keeping is necessary to prevent time drifting, with the effect of reducing another set member's time. One person also needs to maintain a note of set member actions for circulation among the group so that recall is prompted by the note before and at the next set meeting.
- Review of the set. The set may wish to review its effectiveness for each member by allocating time either at the end of a presenter's session or near the end of the meeting
- 'End' of set review meeting. The set may determine to end after the review meeting, continue for a further period and/or add to or alter the membership. This final review stage is an important learning process. The finite period of meeting also provides a limit, enabling all set members to make a judgement about whether they continue or not.

Continuing professional development

Professional development presupposes that qualifications have been acquired with additional experience gained. Continuing to enhance that experience in a structured way throughout the professional's career is considered essential. However, development can be isolated and lonely. Structured development can be expensive and lonely! Action learning can provide structured development that is collaborative. The use of self-facilitated sets or, with experience, a gradual move from facilitated to self-facilitated sets can keep the cost down, as the need for a facilitator is reduced and eliminated.

Development should be continuous for the professional. That continuity can be maintained with the support of colleague professionals over time in an action learning set. In the early years following acquisition of professional status, the support of a set is particularly useful in order to attain an ease with the notion of reflection and learning how to learn (Chapters 5 and 6).

The working assumption from which sets start is to begin from the learner's current learning state. Linked to this principle is clear recognition that the effective learner knows best what he/she needs to learn. The set member is encouraged to clarify what her learning needs are. An example of this approach in making continuing professional development (CPD) work for an individual is that drawn from self-managed learning (Cunningham, 1994). The professional asks herself five key questions and potential subsidiary questions:

1. Where have I been? This is biographical in nature, drawing upon her background, previous experience, significant events in her learning about herself and the person she is.
2. Where am I now? This question invites her to articulate her skills and qualities that she possesses and what kind of person she is.
3. Where do I want to go to? This elicits important subsidiary questions. What do I want to do? What kind of person do I want to be? What skills and qualities do I need to gain to get/be there?
4. How do I get there? What learning programmes, opportunities and processes do I need?
5. How will I know that I have arrived? The questions that will provide evidence here include: How do I evaluate my learning? How will I assess myself so that I have the means to know that my learning goals have been met? What measures do I need in order to assess myself?

Questions 1 and 2 enable our professional to clarify her learning needs. Question 3 is the basis for defining and setting her goals. Question 4, the *how* question, provides the means of attaining her goals. Question 5 provides the basis for her assessment of her learning achievements in the form of tangible evidence. This approach, or variants of it, can help to ensure that a professional can treat her development like a project with learning objectives that can be clear, though they may be complex.

Action learning does reflect the last principle of CPD that investment of time in learning should be regarded as being as important as investment in any other activity. With, say, an annual cycle of CPD, the questions above could be spread over that period. Membership of an action learning set can provide the base for creating a personal contract that sets out what 'I' want to achieve with the agreement of significant others (such as colleagues in the set; line managers for project planning, implementation and review; joining a post-qualification programme). A contract and an agreement with others to go for it (even though it may be modified) helps to maintain momentum and tenacity. A planned intention to undertake something can remain at the planning stage for ever. With a challenging set the professional is encouraged to move from planning to implementation.

Having the continuing support and encouragement of an action learning set can provide the bridge over dips in motivation surrounding development. Development can be painful and isolating as well as pleasurable and exhilarating.

Continuing professional development often requires evidence for the person engaged in the process, as well as for the profession's institute. The action learning set process creates the conditions and a framework for that evidence to be adduced. An action record of the set is itself evidence of the developmental process.

The use of action learning sets enhances the set member's understanding of task and process. Facilitation skills develop in each set member that are valuable as the professional moves forward in his or her career.

Applications in organizations

The self-facilitated Brighton set described in Ian's story (Introduction) provides a useful example of how sets can be extended in organizations. As it happens, it started as an independent self-facilitated set. Over a period of about three years it led to more independent sets being created, then the organization officially started creating sets for course delivery purposes. There are an infinite variety of ways in which sets can be created in organizations with or without the organization's support. Below we explore some which we have experienced across organizations.

From that first set in Brighton we each went on to invite other colleagues in the organization to join a new set. Diagrammatically it looked as shown in Figure 2.4.

The new sets were created by each of us inviting potential members to an initial meeting preceded by informal conversations. People had heard about the first set and wanted to join. Starting new sets seemed the logical next step. Not all new members remained, but the effect overall was to put action learning on the map in the organization. It was recognized as an effective form of self-development among colleagues. The experience outlined above took place in a university business school, an organization interested in the learning process and in developing effective methods of student learning. The independent sets helped create a culture by which staff with personal experience of sets began to use them on their courses as a key learning method for postgraduate courses. These staff now acted as set facilitators

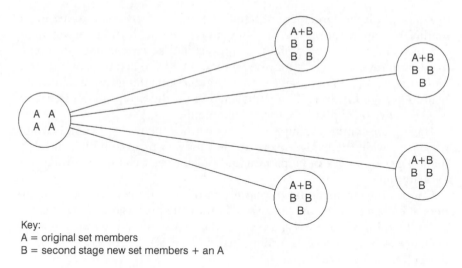

Key:
A = original set members
B = second stage new set members + an A

Figure 2.4   *Extending independent self-facilitated sets*
Source: McGill and Beaty, 2001

guiding managers on management development programmes. So the model in Figure 2.4 became as shown in Figure 2.5.

Example 2.5 shows how an organization can make effective use of limited resources and achieve development of its staff. We are not advocating that those responsible for staff/management development in organizations leave their staff to start sets themselves as a cheap way of encouraging development of staff. However, the model is adaptable, as in Figure 2.6, to organizations that take responsibility for using action learning as a part of their developmental repertoire.

In Figure 2.6 the organization appoints an external facilitator (if the resource is not available internally), who facilitates a set consisting of members with little experience of group facilitation. The members gain, over time, an understanding of the set process. Over a period of, say, one year, with the initial set focusing increasingly on facilitator skills, those set members who are confident of initiating a set move on to new sets consisting of staff who are invited to join and wish to become set members for their own development.

This second stage has two possible pathways. Pathway one is where the original set members become facilitators for the new sets. Pathway two is where original set members merely act as initiators and all members of the set move into self-facilitation mode. We recommend the latter when new set members have some experience of group work.

Both pathways require the initial resource of time from the set members plus the costs of employing the external facilitator. The advantage of this form of development is that it is modest on external costs.

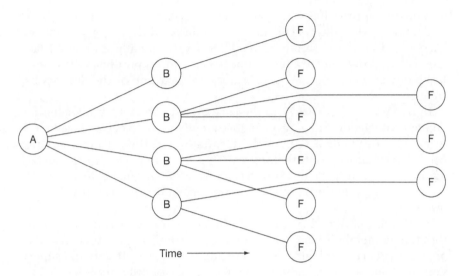

Key:
A = the original set and its members as in Figure 2.4
B = self-facilitated sets initiated by set members from A
F = sets facilitated by set members from B sets

Figure 2.5   *Organizationally supported facilitated sets*
Source: McGill and Beaty, 2001

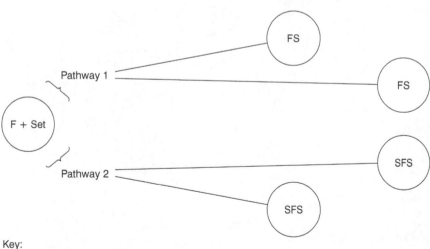

Key:
F = facilitator of the first set
FS = facilitated set
SFS = self-facilitated set

Figure 2.6   *Development with action learning: pathways*
Source: McGill and Beaty, 2001

A further approach is where an external facilitator is asked to organise a facilitator set with the specific task of training and developing facilitators. They will either concurrently as in fig 2.8 or subsequently as in fig 2.7 facilitate sets with continued training, supervision and support from the external facilitator in a support set. This is a model that one of the authors uses frequently.

In pathway 1 (Figure 2.7), in the facilitator set, the set members become familiar with action learning and subsequently learn to become facilitators. After six months or a year in the facilitator set, the set members then become facilitators of sets themselves. They continue in their original facilitator set, with support and supervision from the original external facilitator for a defined period, until as internal facilitators they can provide their own support.

Finally, in pathway 2 (Figure 2.8) the facilitator set is run concurrently with the set members being facilitators of sets consisting of other staff of the organization. The facilitator development set provides support and supervision alongside the set members being facilitators for other sets.

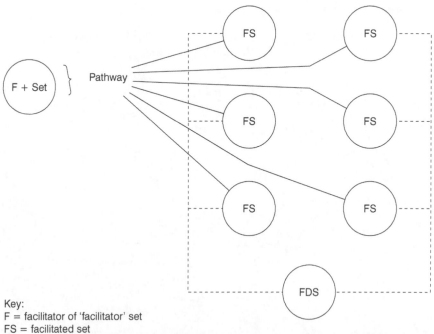

Key:
F = facilitator of 'facilitator' set
FS = facilitated set
FDS = facilitators' continuing development and supervision set for the facilitators of new sets with 'supervising' facilitator for facilitators of the other sets

Figure 2.7   *Support for internal facilitators: pathway 1*
Source: McGill and Beaty, 2001

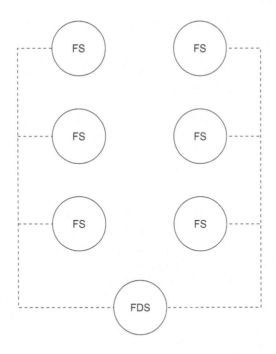

Key:
FS = facilitated set
FDS = facilitators' development and supervision set run concurrently for the facilitators
of new sets with facilitator for facilitators of the other sets

Figure 2.8   *Support for internal facilitators: pathway 2*
Source: McGill and Beaty, 2001

An example of in-house action learning

We would like to cite an example of successful self-facilitated sets used in the public sector. The directors of a large British public health care organization wanted to make a strategic development intervention that would allow managers at all levels to be innovative and cross traditional boundaries within the organization. The programme was designed to combine management development and organizational development in partnership with external developers that would be taken over and run by the organization itself. Bourner, O'Hara and Webber (2002) convey the full nature of the programme. The programme was created by the University of Brighton Management Development Research Unit for the organization's managers who signed up and committed themselves to carrying out a change project that would fulfil some element of their service plan and bring about an improvement in the workplace and also to engaging in personal and professional development. The programme comprised a combination of projects, personal development plans, workshops and self-managed action learning set meetings over a period of one year.

The key to the success of the programme was the initial and continuing support the managers had while facilitating their own sets. The programme organizers referred to the sets as self-managed rather than self-facilitated. This was intentional as they wished to endorse the skills that managers already had from their work for running set meetings and simultaneously empower the managers. The programme organizers were following a salutary concern that self-facilitated sets can go off the rails if the sets are inadequately facilitated. They were recognizing that sets supported by a skilled facilitator tend to be more successful in operation and achievements. To ensure that the 'self-managed' sets would be effective, an initial five-day foundation residential course enabled participants to develop the skills required to manage their own sets, and to identify potential change projects and elements of a personal development plan. The action learning sets then met monthly for a full day throughout the year. Over the year, one-day workshops were additionally provided on change management, project management, performance management and basic research skills to support the participants in their change projects and the implementation of their personal development plans. A process review workshop enabled managers to reflect on how the sets were working and to develop action plans to address any problems. The final element was an end-of-year review and evaluation workshop.

The programme organizers developed a close relationship with the organization and the participating managers. However, they were able to avoid the more extensive costs that would have been incurred by directly facilitating the sets themselves as external facilitators. Nevertheless, the programme organizers built in supports that were designed to ensure that the self-managed sets did not fail:

1. The opening workshop contained an intensive training in the skills of effective set participation and of managing a set effectively.
2. Each set would be provided with support materials to help them to self-manage.
3. Each set meeting would have a half-hour process review with a set process adviser (set PA).
4. A set could request a session of intervention by an external set adviser if they encountered problems that they couldn't (yet) manage.
5. The programme contained a full-day workshop to review the action learning set process approximately four months after the start of the programme.
6. The first two set meetings would be externally facilitated.
7. The values and beliefs underpinning action learning were to be made explicit. This would provide a set of 'operating values' to work from when managing the action learning sets. It also would make it easier, at

the outset, for people either to commit to action learning as participants or to decide not to get involved.

8. The set meetings would be managed by individual members of the action learning set on a rotating basis.
9. The set PAs would be mentored by University of Brighton staff.
10. A structured process for set meetings (with a 'round' for reflection followed by a second 'round' for planning next actions) would be provided.
11. Adoption of the name 'self-managed action learning' (SMAL) rather than 'self-facilitated' action learning would help to empower managers, because 1) it would enable them to bring their management skills to managing the process of the set meetings, and 2) it would help to demystify the process by avoiding the use of the less familiar term, 'facilitation'.

(Bourner, O'Hara and Webber, 2002: 65)

The programme was deemed a success as well as affordable. The first author, Tom Bourner, considered that the programme was transformational for many of the participants and that it did lead to organizational improvement.

In addition, one of the important features the organizers learnt from the programme was that the skills of managing an action learning set are very similar to the skills of facilitative management and similar again to the soft skills of managing change needed by internal change agents. This was a very important lesson in the context of the client's organization as: 'one senior member of the management team expressed concern that if some managers were prevented from using a "command and control" style of management they would be left with no method of managing at all. By acquiring the skills of facilitative management such managers acquired a real choice about how to manage' (Bourner, O'Hara and Webber, 2002: 66). This quotation reflects one of the key incidental benefits of participating in action learning – the impact on approaches to management that enables managers to support their staff in taking responsibility rather than relying on the manager to 'solve' their problems.

Action learning in higher education

Throughout the UK and in the industrialized nations mass higher education is a reality. Often this is happening without a commensurate matching of staffing. Teaching staff face higher numbers of students from a greater diversity of backgrounds. The one-to-one or one-to-few tutorial or seminar is less common. Learners have to rely much more on their own resources of time and application than in the past.

Tom Bourner, in an unpublished paper (2003) on the broadening of the higher education curriculum in the past 30 years, posits the view that:

> any summary description of the purpose of higher education will need to reflect the increased emphasis on developing student's *powers of learning*. In the 19th century the main espoused aim of higher education was to expand the *powers of the mind* of the student... For most of the 20th century the emphasis has been on a higher education to support the advancement of knowledge. In the 21st century higher education will be increasingly aimed at developing the powers of learning of the student. [original italics]

Learning how to learn is the premium challenge for learners and their teachers. For learners to become flexible and more self-managed requires methods that enable that to happen. Self-facilitated action learning is one path through higher education expansion, ensuring that the experience of learning in higher education is a positive one where real learning is enhanced rather than diluted by numbers. Teachers can use action learning methods to enable that positive experience to happen. Facilitated action learning sets can be used as a vehicle for enhancing student powers of learning with a possible transition to self-facilitated sets. However, the transition from facilitated to self-facilitated sets must be treated with caution. The latter should not be used as a cynical way of avoiding tutor responsibility for developing the skills for working in action learning sets (Brockbank and McGill, 1998).

A typology of action learning

Another way of considering the uses of action learning is to view them in terms of different approaches or 'schools' of action learning.

Action learning has developed according to different philosophies of learning and change that in turn have influenced its design and practice. For more detail on philosophies of learning, readers may refer to Part II and Brockbank and McGill (1998).

Marsick and O'Neil (1999) have provided a very useful typology of action learning, which classifies three 'schools' of action learning. The schools have commonalities and differences. Marsick and O'Neil importantly point out that 'these "schools" do not exist in practice' (1999: 161). We would endorse this. One of the healthy characteristics of action learning is that its advocates and practitioners have sought to build on each other's work without corralling a particular approach.

The first 'school' is characterized by its originator – Reg Revans – as being the 'scientific' method of action learning (1980, 1982, 1983). Given Revans' physicist background, he validated action learning with recourse to the scientific method. For Revans this involves three stages: 1) understanding the system in which the problem being addressed resides; 2) negotiating and implementing a solution against a background of the scientific method – survey, hypothesis, experiment, audit and review; 3) finally the action learner brings his or her ways of seeing the world to check reality.

The second 'school' is characterized as the 'experiential' school based on Kolb's ideas on the learning cycle of: action, reflection, theory and practice. Here set members have a starting point of a current, proposed or emerging action which they are undertaking and reflect upon it with the support and challenge of others in order to yield changes in actions and behaviour rather than simply repeat previous actions and habits. Marsick and O'Neil cite the first edition of action learning by McGill and Beaty (1992) as exemplifying this school. Further characteristics of this school include making the learning of set members explicit by attention to the importance of process of the set and enabling the set members to learn how to learn. In addition, crucially, is the recognition and significance of emotion and the social context in contributing to learning.

The third 'school' is characterized by 'critical reflection'. In addition to the experiential school, proponents of critical reflection highlight the need to reflect on the assumptions and beliefs that shape practice. This approach draws upon Mezirow's (1990) notion that critical reflection can transform perspectives. Perspectives drawn from life experience may be 'flawed' for being filtered through unexamined views, which may distort the person's understanding of their situation. We have drawn attention to this above in relation to the work of Schön as developed in Part II and in Brockbank and McGill (1998). This is where action learning can have a transformational effect for the set member and for organizational change. An explicit recognition of this radical potential is appropriate for set members who wish to embark on this route. Marsick and O'Neil conclude their article with a cautionary note for those who embark upon action learning and that:

> it is often a first step for participants in a journey toward greater self-insight, greater capacity to learn from experience, and greater awareness of the political and cultural dimensions of organizational change. For organizations, it is often a first step toward linking individual learning with systemic learning and change. (1999)

Our experience is that transformational change is possible at the individual level. Transformational as opposed to instrumental change (for improvement) at organizational levels is more an aspirational than a practical reality. Where individuals have senior roles in an organization they may be able to effect significant change, particularly in association with others who have experienced action learning. The example of the public sector organization preceding this section is a good example of action learning leading to organizational improvement.

NOTES

1. Where sets are formed, they are usually recommended not to have set members in line relationships with each other. Where this does occur it is essential that the facilitator negotiates the arrangement with the set and the set members concerned so that line issues are considered outside the set.

2. We are sometimes asked why we use the terms 'issue, problem, opportunity' when inviting set members to bring what is pertinent and relevant to them to the set. We do this partly because we used to ask set members to bring a 'problem' to the set. The danger of using this term is that it might convey they may have a problem and they may not, that they may feel that they should have one and/or that they are a problem! There may indeed be a genuine problem, eg a sticky relationship with a 'difficult' colleague. However, by using a wider range of terms we avoid centring on problems *per se*. Further, an opportunity might be, say, an advertisement in the press for a post to which the set member is considering applying but is uncertain because it is not in their immediate purview. This is not a problem – at least not at the outset. Similarly, a person may have a project they are pursuing which they bring to the set.

Chapter 3

Introductory workshops

Our purpose in this chapter is to describe a workshop method that conveys to potential users of the method a real sense of what action learning is, before they fully commit themselves to working in action learning sets. Potential users can be informed about action learning by listening to someone talking about what action learning is, how it works and what it may achieve. However, given the experiential nature of the approach, it is best understood and appreciated by doing it. Below we set out a number of activities that enable participants to do or get very close to appreciating the approach. Exactly which activities we use depends upon the nature and context of the group, its purpose for being together and the amount of time available for the workshop.

We offer three options:

- a full-day workshop;
- half-day workshop;
- one hour/one and a half-hour session.

If a group has been brought together with the explicit intention of forming an action learning set then we recommend the approach conveyed in Chapter 4. If the anticipated audience is more tentative about using action learning then we suggest one of the formats given below, or a combination depending upon the potential commitment of the group and where necessary their sponsors.

The workshop designs are based on four phases or kinds of activity:

Phase 1: Introduction to action learning and triads
Phase 2: Action learning in concentric circles
Phase 3: Simulating action learning
Phase 4: Process review.

Before examining workshop options, we consider below the likely uses and benefits of such a workshop.

We are addressing two potentially overlapping identifiable groups. The first are managers, trainers, staff developers etc who may be considering using action learning as a potential for personal, professional managerial development of their staff. This group could also include educationalists and teachers who may wish to use action learning as a vehicle for learning in courses. The second potential group are those staff, managers, students etc who may be the participants in a set for their developmental and learning needs. The latter would also include those considering an independent set.

The most effective way to convey the potential value of action learning is to *do* it. Those who wish to use action learning may have read about action learning, may have had action learning described to them but they may still remain sceptical because of an unfamiliarity with this way of working together. There are severe limitations to the verbal description of the process because the description lacks the key ingredient of people actually engaging together. *Doing* action learning overcomes these problems and gives them a real feel for the process – how it works for them.

Uses of the workshop

This workshop method and approach can be used for the following purposes:

1. To introduce participants, who are unaware of the process of action learning, to action learning as a vehicle for their personal and/or management development. Participants may then follow through with planned programmes of action learning sessions.
2. As above, but with the intention to follow the session with a programme of action learning that is self-facilitated, ie without a facilitator (McGill *et al*, 1990). Here the facilitator models practice that is later emulated by all members (Chapters 9 and 10).
3. With participants who are familiar with action learning but who wish to become facilitators, the workshop gives them the opportunity to observe the process of action learning.
4. As a basis for 'cascading' in organizations. Once action learning becomes an organic part of the development of staff of an organization, the workshop can be used to introduce staff new to the method.

Workshop benefits

The workshop conveys the nature of action learning. The method has the following advantages:

1. Experimentation before commitment. The method acknowledges that participants at an introductory workshop may not yet have fully committed themselves to joining or starting a set. The participants can

therefore obtain a close understanding of the process before fully committing themselves.

2. Working with a large group of potential action learners who may form more than one set. The workshop method enables us to reach a wide number of interested people. We have had as many as 40 engaged in this initial workshop, but the more usual number is between 12 and 20 participants.

3. Convey more accurately the *how* of action learning. The workshop enables potential action learners to get an idea and a feel of what it is like to be in a set. The key to action learning is in the process as well as what is dealt with in the set – the content. The process is about *how* a set works. An analogy might be learning about a new activity, say cycling or swimming. You can read about it, have it described to you but it is not the same as doing it. Similarly with action learning – doing it makes all the difference to understanding and feeling what it is like to be a member of a set.

4. The workshop method works. The method serves its purpose and engenders enthusiasm beyond that associated with merely reading or having action learning described.

5. Self-screening. The workshop has a benefit for it means that, once action learning sets are created, there is a greater likelihood of the set(s) continuing and maintaining themselves. 'Self-screening' occurs at the workshop stage. This is useful as it reduces the number of those who may join a set but subsequently decide that it is not really what they expected and then leave. When such early withdrawal from a set happens, the numbers in the set may be reduced so that the set is no longer viable. This in turn can be dispiriting to the active and committed set members. A new set that has experienced the introductory method is thus more likely to take off successfully, maintain its numbers and be effective for each individual and as a set.

6. Cost-effectiveness. The workshop is cost-effective in reaching a wide number of potential users and ensures that sets which are created are more likely to maintain numbers and use the process of action learning more effectively and at an earlier stage. We have used the approach in universities, local authorities, companies, and at conferences and workshops. Participants have been managers, academics, administrators, students and self-support groups, the latter wanting to go further than just being support groups.

As facilitator of any introductory workshop, it is important that a briefing will have been previously undertaken with the clients to determine the background of those attending, including their familiarity with working in groups, participative forms of learning and working together, and the skills that are a particular emphasis in action learning (Chapters 9 and 10). This is particularly important if the intention is to create self-facilitating sets.

Three introductory workshops

The workshop method has four phases which may be modified according to the time available. Firstly, a full-day workshop will enable all phases below to be undertaken. Secondly, it is possible to adapt the workshop to fit a minimum time of three hours or half a day. Thirdly, using a shortened workshop method, the workshop can be completed in one or one and a half hours.

First, we will assume a full day for the workshop. The phases are as follows:

1.   Introduction to action learning and triads
2.   Concentric circles
3.   Practising action learning in sets
4.   Process review and moving on.

Phase 1 aims to give a brief overview of the purpose of the day, a description of what action learning is, how it can be used and in what contexts. Phase 2, concentric circles, is the key to the workshop and the core activity that would be the basis of a workshop even with more limited time. This phase conveys to the whole workshop the nature of action learning through *doing* it. Phase 3, practising action learning in sets, gives all the participants a more direct experience of action learning by running sets concurrently for part of the workshop. Phase 4, process review and moving on, enables all participants to review the workshop and reflect upon the potential of action learning. We will detail the activities within each phase. The phases for a full-day workshop are shown in Figure 3.1 and for a half-day workshop and a one-hour workshop on pages 63–4.

Phase 1: Introduction to action learning and triads

This phase includes a description of what action learning is, how it can be used and in what contexts it is appropriate (Chapters 1 and 2). Further, an outline of the structure and purpose of the workshop will enable participants to clarify what they wish to achieve.

The workshop starts with introductions and a useful warm-up activity that is appropriate for the group. The warm-up is designed to create an environment that contributes to developing trust and support. The activity will ensure that everybody gets to know each other, their first names, roles – if appropriate, their expectations of the workshop and something about themselves that the group do not know about 'me' that I am willing to share

PHASE 1
Introduction to the day: Purpose, structure and format
Working in triads
Plenary debriefing and reflection on triads

PHASE 2
Concentric circles
Plenary process review
One-to-one reflection on the process

PHASE 3
Practising action learning in sets

PHASE 4
Process review
Moving on
Ending

Figure 3.1 *Full-day introductory workshop*

with the group. This is just one format for starting the workshop. There are many others. This is followed with an outline of the purpose and structure of the day. Here it is emphasized that we will be experiencing individually and collectively action learning and related activities. To undertake the experiential activities effectively requires an atmosphere of confidentiality and trust in a safe environment. Through the remainder of this chapter we aim to convey the kinds of conditions that facilitators and participants can follow to ensure those requirements. Each phase and activity needs to convey the conditions for creating safety, confidentiality and trust appropriate to that activity.

We follow the brief warm-up with a small group (three-person) activity known as 'triads'. For participants with little experience of interpersonal skills training or group activity, we find this is a valuable entry to action learning work, enabling each participant to present an issue with another giving attentive listening. Triads take about one and a half hours and are very effective in introducing participants to the process of enabling individuals to work to some purpose on their issues or problem as well as heightening participants' sensitivity to the skills of presenting, enabling and observing which occur in an action learning set. The triad process is a 'safe' activity because, as its name suggests, three people work together for the designated period before working in phase 2 in a larger group. The triad is a stepping stone to the next phase as it enables participants to use and acknowledge the skills in a small group as well as creating the conditions for trust to be engendered.

Participants in triads say how unusual it is to have such undivided attention for what is a very limited period. To be really listened to as a presenter is an important ingredient of action learning, as is the complementary capacity to listen on the part of the enabler.

The workshop participants are each given a written description of the triad activity as well as having it described by the facilitator. The description is in Box 3.1 below. Participants are divided into groups of three (or four where there is not a multiple of three). The groups can be self-selecting, with a suggestion that participants work with those whom they least know or do not know. Alternatively, the facilitator can, with agreement, count round the group to divide them into the smaller groups. Sometimes, this 'random' approach makes it easier for participants who are little known to each other. They are then invited to engage in the process set out below.

Ground rules for the activity are essential to agree before the activity commences. Confidentiality is the most significant. By confidentiality is meant that each participant in the triad agrees that the content of each other person's issue and their feelings will not be disclosed outside the triad. This agreement encourages trust and greater disclosure. The participants in the triad are also asked to maintain their own timekeeping to ensure that all have the opportunity of each role. The times given are broad indicators. A triad may find that one or two of their number may require more time to consider their issue, in which case they can negotiate the allocation of time between them. Participants, when observers, are also asked to give specific feedback (see Chapter 8 on giving and receiving feedback). This feedback is given within the triad group and is confidential to the members of the triad.

Box 3.1   *Introduction to action learning*

Working in triads: presenter, enabler and observer

For this activity, choose your role from the three above – descriptions of each role are given below. The presenter and enabler are in dialogue for 15 minutes and the observer gives feedback and discussion for 5 minutes. Check out confidentiality. Plenary session to discuss process issues only.

Presenter

Identify a current or emerging issue that is significant to you in your professional role. With your enabler, spend 15 minutes in dialogue with a view to coming to clarification, some resolution and/or first steps towards action.

The presenter should speak directly from his or her own experience, using 'I' statements and disclosing as much as seems appropriate. The background and details should lead to a clear statement of the issue. The presenter is supported by an enabler but retains responsibility for the outcomes of the dialogue.

Enabler

The enabler's purpose is to enable the learner to engage in a challenging and reflective dialogue about the presenter's issue, exploring it from a variety of perspectives, enabling the presenter to move towards an outcome, which may or may not be final.

The enabler should listen first until the presenter stops or reaches clarification, and then summarize. The enabler should question and summarize in turn, offering empathy where appropriate, and using open or probing questions. The enabler should encourage the presenter to move towards closure, be it action or intent, without taking away the responsibility for the potential outcome, which remains with the presenter.

Observer

The observer's purpose is to offer feedback to the enabler primarily, about what skills enabled the presenter most effectively. The observer should offer constructive feedback to the enabler in the last 5 minutes. The observer does not act as another enabler, but reports only the process he or she has observed, and how the dialogue was enabled. Further points the observer may wish to consider in the observation may include:

- Is the enabler providing solutions for the presenter?
- Is the presenter focusing on what he or she can do?
- is the presenter avoiding resolving the problem?
- is the presenter's proposed action specific enough?

Review of the process

The triad may wish to discuss the observations and review those skills in the process which were conducive to enabling the presenter to reach his or her outcome. The observer is asked to record conclusions that the triad wish to convey to the plenary group.

Take 15–20 minutes between presenter and enabler. After the session and a pause, the presenter and enabler convey how the experience was for them. The observer then gives feedback for 5 minutes to the 'enabler' on how his or her behaviour aided the presenter, followed by 5 minutes to the presenter, and then the presenter and 'enabler' may wish to add their comments. Change roles in order that each person can take the role of enabler and presenter.

During the triad activity the facilitator may go round some of the groups and give feedback from observation that may not have been already covered by the observer to the presenter and enabler.

At the end of the activity, when all participants have experienced each role, the workshop participants are invited into a plenary circle to reflect on what they have gained from the activity and how it felt doing the activity. Each person should be given time to convey his or her thoughts and feelings. The facilitator can draw on the reflection to make comparisons with the process of action learning.

The round of reflection is useful to enable participants to understand the value of the process of the triad, the skills that are being harnessed and that the activity embraces some of the skills and roles that are found in action learning. As presenters, participants gain experience in having specific time given to an issue or problem that is relevant and of concern to them. Presenters may be very clear about the issue being raised or start with only a tentative idea or a feeling about something. Nevertheless, their issue is given undivided attention. The key here is that the enabler is able to attend to the presenter without having a vested interest in the presenter's issues. The enabler gains experience in the act of attending to another person and is given feedback on his or her skills in listening, questioning, empathizing, challenging and confronting. Participants here state how rare it is to get feedback on their use of these skills. They also convey in the plenary reflections how difficult it is not to try to provide the presenter with solutions! As observers, participants gain experience in a role which is rarely exercised in this form. In normal circumstances of interaction with others they are not usually 'detached' from the interaction.

Following the plenary reflection using triads, we can now move to phase2.

Phase 2: Concentric circles

This phase conveys to the whole workshop the nature of action learning through *doing* and experiencing it. This is the key to the workshop and the core activity that would be the basis of a workshop even with more limited time.

This phase commences with a verbal and, if helpful, a flip chart description of the way in which the concentric circles work and how participants can prepare themselves for the activity. The concentric circles consist of an inner circle of participants who work as an action learning set with a facilitator (the facilitator), with an outer circle of participants acting as observers of the action learning process taking place in the inner circle.

In Figure 3.2 are the concentric circles. The inner circle is for the 'set' with a spare chair left vacant. The outer circle is for observers of the process and content. Participants as observers in the outer circle have the opportunity to take the spare chair when appropriate, but only briefly.

At this point it may be helpful to explain the reasons for using the circles method. Action learning requires to be experienced in order for each participant to get near to understanding its potentiality. If there are more participants than can be accommodated in a single set, the use of circles can enable some of the participants to experience working directly in a set while the other participants can observe the process.

The participants are then asked if some will volunteer to work in the inner circle. Four to six volunteers are invited from the whole group, who

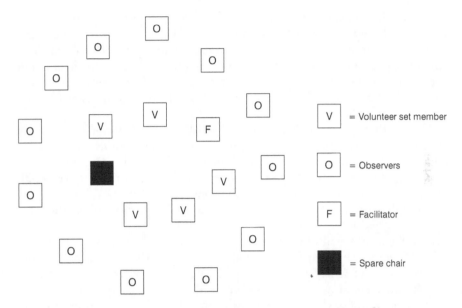

Figure 3.2   *Introducing action learning with concentric circles*
Source: McGill and Beaty, 2001

will form the 'set' with the facilitator of the workshop as facilitator. Volunteers are asked to think of an important, unresolved but real issue/problem/opportunity that has no obvious solution which they are willing to talk through in the 'set' and with the outer circle of participants observing the process. Depending on time, the volunteers are also informed that we may only be able to take one or two of the 'set'.

Those who form the outer circle are asked to observe the content of the set discussion but, more important, to observe the *process*. The content is the presenter's issue or problem. The process is what is happening in the set while the set is dealing with the issue – the *how* of action learning. The prior triad session provides a useful introduction to the role of observers in this session.

The volunteer set members can also be asked if they are willing to receive personal feedback from a participant who is acting as an observer in the outer circle. As facilitator, it is usual, in inviting this additional form of feedback, to suggest that the set member request feedback from someone from the outer circle who are observers of the process. That person may be someone they know or do not know that they feel comfortable with. All observers then observe and make notes of the process and content, and some observers additionally observe one person in particular in the set. It is emphasized prior to the action learning activity that the observer will give the feedback to the set member on a one-to-one basis privately after the plenary feedback on the whole process. This enables a safer environment for the set member to receive feedback.

Two circles of chairs are formed for the 'set' and observers. In the inner circle an additional chair is left for any of the observers in the outer circle to occupy, for a moment only, in order to pose a question about content or to convey a process observation that may enable the 'set' to progress. The vacant chair is a useful device for it usually commits the interest of observers without losing sight of their main role. We will return to this type of intervention later.

The set then proceeds like a normal set. Ideally, two facilitators run the workshop, one of whom will take the role of facilitator in the inner circle, and model the role of facilitator as outlined in Chapter 11. The other facilitator joins the outer circle as one of the process observers. If there is only one facilitator, he or she should take the role of facilitator. In this chapter we only emphasize those particular tasks for the facilitator that enable the set to operate in this 'unusual' context.

The facilitator will aim to relax the volunteer set members who may initially feel some natural anxiety about being in the middle and under observation. Our experience is that once we get going, that concern reduces significantly. Again a warm-up is beneficial to allay that concern and also help the forming of the set. One particular activity here that does not take too much time is called 'Trauma, trivia and joy' and is set out in Box 3.2. This is a very useful activity for it enables the members of the set to convey how they are feeling with an informal immediacy.

Box 3.2   *Trauma, trivia and joy*

Each person in the group is asked to convey briefly an event or incident, one of which could be termed a trauma, another a trivia, and one a joy that has happened to them in the last day or so. Each member of the set takes a turn describing their events, including the facilitator who may start and therefore model the activity.

There is no discussion of the events. Other set members usually convey their empathy and feelings with the occasional word or feeling, the effect of which is to create a warm and supportive atmosphere, relax the set members and help the set to get to know each other a little. Set members are asked not to invent events if they have not actually occurred. If a set member has just a joy and a trivia, that is fine. If a set member wishes not to be included in this activity and 'pass', that is also legitimate. Most participants find the activity light and energizing. Moreover, the activity may trigger an issue that a set member wishes to address and/or the event may unwittingly become a key part of the issue.

The activity will take about 5 to 15 minutes depending upon the numbers participating. It is important not to rush an individual but to convey the idea that it is a brief 'warm-up' to get us going.

With the warm-up completed, set members are then asked to describe, in cameo or headline form, the issue that they would like to bring to the set. This is an important moment. As facilitator, it is necessary to remind the set members that we will only have time for one person's issue or two at most. Asking each person to convey the issue he or she would like to bring to the group is important in two ways. Firstly, it conveys to the set and the outer circle of observers the range of issues that the volunteer members of the set would like to bring to the set. This immediately conveys to all present what individuals consider they could bring to the set that could be useful for them. In terms of conveying the potential of action learning, hearing examples of what could be brought to a set is instructive. Secondly, hearing the issues that could come before the set enables the set members to help make up their minds which person's issue they would like to consider. A set member may decide that another's is more pertinent than the one he or she raised. Describing the issues also conveys some significant openness and courage to all those listening. Examples of issues that volunteer set members might bring forward could be:

- organizing my time over the day (week or any period) at work;
- balancing my priorities of work with the rest of my life;
- deciding whether to register for a postgraduate qualification;
- how can I ensure that my 0.5 job share stays at 0.5 and does not become a near full-time job?
- being new to the post, how can I get support without conveying the impression that I am not 'up' to the job?

Note that the issues are critical to the person conveying them. What is brought to the volunteer set will depend on the degree of trust and therefore safety the volunteer feels towards the people in the circles. It is appropriate for the facilitator to emphasize that volunteers only bring issues that they feel safe to bring to this unusual situation, particularly in organizational settings. Once a normal set is in operation, the safety is usually enhanced and the trust enables more openness and disclosure of more sensitive and personal issues.

It is important that the facilitator lets the set members come to agreement about whose issue is considered. In the event of stalemate when the set members cannot agree whose issue should be taken, the facilitator may have to resolve it. In our experience this has only happened once. At the suggestion of the facilitator, it was amicably resolved with the toss of a coin! This, incidentally, ensured that the facilitator was not steering what should be discussed and who would bring their issue, only the process of moving on.

Guidelines for the 'set' members

Here we give only a brief textual indication of the main guidelines for a set in the workshop as full details are given elsewhere (Chapters 1 and 4). When facilitating a set in the workshop, we aim to minimize the verbal description of the process.

Once the set has agreed who will volunteer, the facilitator re-emphasizes briefly that the presenter has 40 minutes in total as her time, the initial period of which is for the presenter to take, say, 10 minutes or so to convey his or her thoughts on the issue to the set as listeners. Following her introduction to her issue, the set members and adviser can ask questions that seek to clarify what she as presenter has conveyed and to check out their understanding of her thoughts and feelings. The facilitator also emphasizes that the questioning should be supportive of the presenter in enabling the latter to focus on the presenter's issue. The interaction should be supportive yet challenging for the presenter. The interaction is not an interrogation!

The aim of the set is to enable the presenter to reach her own solutions, not for the other set members to present their solutions to her. This is the key to the whole process of interaction between the presenter and colleagues in the set. This enables the presenter to begin *taking* responsibility for her actions.

During the time taken by the presenter, she may say something like: 'I ought to do this because…' It is often very helpful to ask the presenter what she means by 'ought'. This enables the presenter to distinguish between 'oughts' and 'wants' and can be very helpful in enabling the presenter to clarify her thoughts and feelings on an issue. Complementary to this is drawing the attention of set members to the danger of 'oughts' hidden in questions that may be designed to be helpful to the presenter but are actually solutions they wish consciously or unconsciously to impose on the presenter.

Further details on the operation of the set are set out in the next chapter. However, as facilitator of the introductory session and as acting facilitator, it is important to convey to the 'set' and the observers just sufficient to get started. Otherwise there is a danger of the facilitator doing the very thing he or she wishes to avoid, namely just talking about action learning as opposed to giving participants experience of the process of doing it. The above indicators by the facilitator are therefore the minimum to get the set working and to minimize inadequate outcomes in terms of the learning about the potential effectiveness of action learning.

As the volunteer presenter nears the end of her issue, she is asked to convey how she would like to take her issue forward following the meeting and possibly to 'contract' with another person on the workshop to ensure action occurs. The contract is simply an agreement to contact the other person within a given period of time (say, a month) to convey the presenter's progress on action she agreed in the set. Undertaking a 'contract' of this kind replaces the usual arrangement set members have between one meeting and the next – a crucial aspect of set activity which the workshop cannot replicate.

The volunteer will have taken about one hour, when combined with the initial activity. It is important to judge the total length of time so that there is sufficient range of the action learning process without losing the attention of the observers.

The process review: reflection on the process by the participants

Before completion of phase 2 it is necessary for the workshop to reflect on the process of the inner circle or set. This is a crucial part of this phase. The workshop participants then form one circle. Following a short break, it is important to enable the inner circle 'set' members to start by conveying their initial feelings about the process. We usually suggest that the presenter(s) is last in this part of the reflection. The presenter should also have the option to opt out of this, like all the inner circle, by being able to say 'pass', should she wish to. This is simply to recognize that the set members and particularly the presenter may well have become very engaged in the process and have feelings and emotions that they wish to lighten gradually but are not yet ready to reflect upon.

Going round, each person in the outer circle who observed the process then relates his or her description of the process. It is in this reflection stage that participants gain their understanding of what action learning is really about. There is a tendency for the observers from the outer circle to re-engage with the content as opposed to conveying their feedback about the process observed and what was significant in that process. It is unhelpful for the presenter to have the content 'opened up' after she has agreed her actions. The only qualification here is if a reference to the content is necessary to make a point about process.

The facilitator may wish to follow up the process discussion by highlighting the main points on a flip chart for reflection.

Following the plenary reflection on the process observed by the outer circle, those observers who additionally observed, by prior agreement, a set member, give feedback in confidence to that person on a one-to-one basis.

Phase 3: Practising action learning in sets

Phase 3 gives all the participants an experience of action learning by running sets for part of the workshop concurrently. This part of the workshop will depend upon the number of participants and facilitators and the experience of the participants. Sets are created with five or six participants per set. Participants can be facilitated with facilitators if there are enough for the number of sets required, or there can be a combination of facilitated and self-facilitated sets (see Chapter 2).

Facilitators and participants in sets in this part of the workshop will again be constrained by time. The same process as for the inner circle in phase 2 will be applied. One or two volunteers will be invited, following an appropriate warm-up and brief summaries of each person's issue described to the set. The major difference in this stage is that all participants are engaged as direct participants in the sets without external observers. In this phase all participants integrate the role of observation into their role as set members.

Timing of the set is left to the facilitator with an indication of when the sets will come back into plenary for the final reflection. Time available will determine whether there are one or more presenters. Ten minutes or so are appropriate at the end of the set session to enable each person in the set to convey within the set how the process felt for them.

Phase 4: Process review: reflection on gains from the day and moving on

With phases 1 to 3 completed, the workshop can conclude with an overall reflection on the day. The purpose of this stage is to enable participants to reflect on what they have gained and learnt individually and collectively. Before engaging in the reflection it is appropriate to use a short period for any factual clarification by participants of any aspects of the action learning process and the potential uses of action learning.

How can this important stage be organized for maximum effect for each participant? Participants can be asked a range of questions that enable them to reflect upon the workshop with a view to its relevance and future use for them. Working individually, then in pairs, participants could be asked to reflect upon the following questions:

- What have I gained/learned from the workshop today:
  - for myself;
  - in my work (if applicable);
  - in relation to my colleagues and friends?
- What personal changes will I undertake/implement myself and with colleagues?
- Where do I/we go from here?
- What actions am I going to take:
  - from my work in the 'set' (if the participant had this opportunity);
  - to enable me to influence the forming of a set and/or create a set?

The responses to the above questions will depend upon the nature of the relationship of the participants at the workshop. For example, if the workshop is organizationally based in, say, a company, the focus may be on a structured response to the creation of sets for staff and management development purposes as outlined in Chapter 2. The manager responsible for staff development can then move on to devising a programme of development using action learning sets with the knowledge of those who wish to engage in this approach to management development.

If the workshop has been organized around individual responses to attending, then the questions may require participants to assess how they may get sets going in their work, amongst voluntary groups or with colleagues and friends. Sets may also be based on gender or ethnicity to enable participants to work on issues common to them.

Following the pairs work, participants can then share their ideas and feelings in a final plenary. This ensures a cross-fertilization of the ideas and can act as an energizer for each participant. The workshop can then conclude with an appropriate ending, such as a single phrase that sums up the day for each of the participants.

A cautionary note

Facilitators of workshops should exercise care in using concentric circles in an introductory workshop. In the prior discussions with the clients, the facilitator should check out the degree of likely receptivity for such an event by participants. Where there is likely to be a high degree of scepticism or even hostility to such events, using concentric circles is probably unwise. Much will depend on the culture prevailing within the organization. Where participants have made a definite commitment to action learning, the use of concentric circles is more likely to be a useful precursor to the process – its advantage being the ability to engage a larger number in action learning than could engage as a single set. Alternatives are given in Boxes 3.3 and 3.4 which also allow for different time schedules

As mentioned above, the workshop format can be adapted for a half-day workshop and the phases are given below.

Box 3.3   *Half-day introductory workshop*

PHASE 1
Introduction to the workshop: Purpose, structure and format
Working in triads
Plenary debriefing and reflection on triads

PHASE 2
Practising action learning in sets

PHASE 3
Process review
Moving on
Ending

Alternatively, the workshop method can be adapted to a one/one and a half-hour session which does not include working in sets, and the phases are given below. This workshop would only allow for one round of the triads.

Box 3.4   One-hour introductory workshop

PHASE 1
Introduction to the session: Purpose, structure and format
Working in triads
Plenary debriefing and reflection on triads

PHASE 2
Process review
Ending

Where a one-hour/one and a half-hour workshop is chosen, facilitators may need to emphasize to participants that the triad format is a microcosm of the set, using the same skills but with more people acting as enablers.

We are now ready to examine the life of a set in its initial meetings.

Chapter 4

Starting a set: the first and second meetings

We can now examine how a set can organize its first meeting. It is assumed for the purposes of this chapter and subsequent chapters that the set is to be facilitated. All necessary arrangements have been made (see Chapter 2) and the set members have agreed, with their facilitator or through the organization sponsoring the set, to meet for a whole day from, say, 9.30 am to 5.00 pm with breaks for refreshments and lunch.

Preliminaries

The facilitator usually arrives first to ensure that the room and facilities are appropriate for the set to work effectively. We will attend to this issue later in the chapter. The set members sit in a circle of comfortable chairs with the facilitator. We will assume that set members do not know each other or the facilitator. This is quite common in cross-organizational sets or those from different business sectors. Even if some set members are acquainted, it is still appropriate to follow a format that ensures everyone has some sense of each person's background and motivation for joining the set.

A useful way of overcoming any initial caution in the meeting and to start to create the culture for effective set work is for the facilitator to introduce himself and ask each set member to consider and then respond to the following enquiries:

1. who I am and what I do;
2. something that is keeping me out of this room and which I would like to leave in an imaginary suitcase outside the room;
3. what it is that I have and would particularly wish to bring into this set so that the set can work well;
4. (optional) something unusual about myself that no one else in the room knows about me that I am willing to share with the group now.

The facilitator may wish to model the tone to be set by offering to go first. This can be useful in setting an example about the degree of openness and disclosure appropriate at this early stage in the life of the set. Even if the facilitator does not go first, it is important that he also responds to these enquiries in order to set an egalitarian tone to the proceedings. We discuss the value of early facilitator disclosure in Chapter 11.

Enquiry 1 above is basic and important in conveying initial biographical details about each person. Enquiry 2 enables the set members and facilitator to unload any preoccupations they may have (including cautionary feelings about being in the set). Examples of responses to question 2 include:

- I have left a pile of work on my desk and I know I really ought to be attending to it.
- The journey here was hell, with the train late on arrival, and had threatened to be worse at one stage but at least I am here now.
- I want to be here but I am not sure that my boss does, even though he approved of the time and the funding to support it.
- My child was up all night with nasal congestion and I got precious little sleep.
- I am just glad to be able to leave my work behind.
- I have been in a set in the past and it was not a good experience and I hope it will not be repeated here.
- I feel absolutely great being here and don't have any baggage I need to leave outside.
- I am not used to working in groups and am very cautious about being in this one.

Thus it is possible to identify a wide range of preoccupations set members may have on arrival at their first set meeting. Further, set members may also be cautious about disclosing and they may have other fears about being in a set amongst others whom they may or may not know prior to the set meeting. On the other hand, anonymity can be an advantage in sets as members may feel less constrained in a new environment.

Enquiry 3 enables set members to convey to the set something positive that they have to offer the set. It is also a valuable enquiry to convey the degree of motivation and will they have in initially joining the set. Responses can include:

- I have a lot of experience from my work which I wish to contribute to the set.
- My work is now very routine to me and I wish to move on – I hope to be challenged by this group.
- I am totally committed to this way of working and wish to bring my enthusiasm to the set.

- I am not sure what it is I have to offer, not knowing quite what to expect here. However, I am willing to learn.
- I am just glad to be away from work to experience something I believe to be totally different.
- I have experienced facilitating sets in the past and am pleased to be a set member this time so that I can bring my issues. I hope to be able to support the set on the basis of my experience in the past.
- I want to share my lengthy experience of the medical profession along with other set members who share a similar range of experience.
- I want to be in a set where we all have different backgrounds and can each bring our contribution to each other.

Optional enquiry 4 is designed to enable set members to offer examples or incidents that reflect in some way their life as well as inviting a degree of self-disclosure early in the life of the set. Examples include:

- I am learning to fly and have just had my first solo flight which was hairy and exciting.
- I spend all my spare time with horses and dressage.
- I love long-distance walking and have just completed the coast-to-coast walk across England.
- I love being a secret couch potato.
- I am a naturist when I holiday in Europe.
- I support Peterborough United football club.
- I play the saxophone in clubs at weekends.
- I walked the Himalayas last summer.

Question 4 often elicits humour as well as awe at the unusual nature of what people get up to in their lives.

Once this round has been completed, it is necessary for the whole set to get to know each other much more in order that the set can fulfil its task of ensuring effective learning and development for all set members. We begin the process by seeking the set's agreement on ground rules.

Ground rules

It is necessary for the set to create its own ground rules that frame the way in which the set will work over the cycle of meetings. It is useful for the facilitator to emphasize that the set may return to the ground rules at any time, once determined, in order to review their effectiveness and if necessary to add to or amend them. Set members are invited to develop the ground rules themselves with the support of the facilitator. This ensures a greater likelihood of commitment and ownership by the set if they have shared in their creation. The facilitator is party to the ground rules as well. The ground rules below are typical for a set. Where necessary, the ground rules will be explained to ensure clarity.

Confidentiality

This is crucial and is regarded with great significance by set members. Any trust that develops in the set will depend on adherence to this rule. It needs elaboration, however. We distinguish between content and process. By content is meant the material and issues that set members bring to the set. By process is meant how the set works. Each set member is able to take his or her own content away from the set and work with it elsewhere. Indeed it may well be essential in order to take action outside the set. However, other set members' content remains in the set meeting. So set members do not disclose any matters outside the set relating to other set members.

Set members are free to relate process issues outside the set. This is important. The way in which a set works may have valuable implications for ways of working outside the set and set members may wish to use the set as an example or resource. A good example here is the use of questioning to enable a person to take responsibility for resolving a problem rather than a set member saying: this is what you do or I can solve your problem. Set members frequently assert how they have changed from being problem solvers for their staff to enabling staff to work through a problem themselves.

One qualification needs to be made regarding confidentiality and process. Say a set member has a tendency to give advice to other set members rather than keeping in questioning or challenging mode. It is appropriate for another set member to discuss this in other contexts. However, it would not be appropriate to mention by name the set member who has this tendency. That would be a breach of confidentiality about the person. Process issues can be shared elsewhere without implicating other members of the set.

Responsibility

Participants in sets are responsible for their own learning, feelings and actions. Responsibility is shared throughout by the facilitator and set members, though the facilitator has the primary responsibility for the maintenance of the set. Set members' responsibility is to share from their own experience and to get from the set what they need and want.

Being non-judgemental

Set members and the facilitator refrain from disapproval and approval both verbally and non-verbally. The set simply accepts the story being told by a presenter.

Discriminatory remarks

Any member of the set has a right to challenge any discriminatory remarks made by another, should they occur. All set members share their wisdom in the group. Recognition of diversity will enable this wisdom to emerge.

Making 'I' statements

This means that set members phrase their stories in terms of 'I'. Thus: 'I found the work difficult to carry out' rather than: 'One finds this work...' or: 'You find this work...' or: 'People find this work....' The use of the word 'I' has two benefits. Firstly, it clarifies that the person speaking is the person who is experiencing the behaviour. Secondly, it ensures ownership of the statement in the person saying it rather than creating an 'out there' vagueness or ambiguity about to whom it refers.

Commitment to the set

This means that set members commit to attending all the set meetings and giving the set a priority in their diaries. At the first meeting it is quite common for the set to agree all the set meetings that follow in the cycle.

Time-keeping

Primarily this is the responsibility of the facilitator. It is important to model keeping to times determined by the set.

One person speaks at a time

Obvious but really necessary in order that there is only one dialogue being pursued at a time. This also extends to one presenter at a time. This means that the other set members give their attention entirely to the presenter – the space belongs to the presenter. Any personal material belonging to other set members is excluded from that space. Therefore other set members do not give personal anecdotes, eg how it is in my organization.

The main criterion here for set members is not to draw attention to their own personal agenda away from the presenter's space. It is the latter alone who holds the focus.

Silence is OK

This is important and useful to be in the ground rules. Set members early on in the life of a set frequently have many interventions and questions they wish to pose to presenters. There are two issues here. Firstly, a rapid firing of questions can make the dialogue feel more like an interrogation and put the presenter on the defensive. Secondly, a presenter may pause in response to a question, and need time to reflect upon it, particularly if feelings are involved. Thirdly, the presenter may be pausing because she is 'stuck' or on the edge of some recognition about herself or her situation. Interrupting with a comment or question from another set member may divert the presenter from the pregnancy of the pause. Letting silence prevail is useful for the presenter.

Really listen to each other

This is often asserted as essential to the effective working of the set and is often a rule which set members refer to when talking about the attributes of their set once a few meetings have been completed.

Constructive feedback

Presenters often request feedback and we discuss constructive feedback in Chapter 10. In order to be useful, feedback should be specific, relevant and balanced.

Naïve questions are legitimate

Set members may come from different backgrounds and organizations unfamiliar with the profession or expertise of each other. This may not be a disadvantage and enables set members to pose naïve questions which help the examination of assumptions that a set member may have had about his or her work/life.

Admitting need is legitimate

A corollary of the preceding ground rule is that a set member can, where it is safe, disclose ignorance, admit weakness and ask for help. Indeed, it is likely that only in such conditions will it be possible for a presenter to learn at sufficient depth to develop.

Attention to process

Attention to how the set is working and acknowledging the feelings of set members is integral to the effective operation of the set.

As mentioned above, ground rules will vary from set to set. The above are typical ground rules.

Getting to know each other: introductory activities

We can now progress to an introductory activity that enables set members and facilitator to get to know each other better. There are any number of ways of enabling the set to get to know each other and for trust to be engendered at this early stage. The example offered below was first introduced by the late Roger Gaunt. As authors, we never had the privilege of knowing or working with him personally. However, he probably comes closest to the way we work and this understanding is based partly on his writing (Gaunt, 1991) and partly on our work with colleagues who experienced him as a facilitator.

Self-portrait

'Self-portrait' is designed to be undertaken by all set members and the facilitator working individually for 20–30 minutes and then sharing the results in the set. Each person in the set is given a sheet of flip chart paper and asked to create their own picture based upon 10 points (see Box 4.1). Set members are asked to convey as much as they can in pictures without needing to be experts in drawing or to be artistic. Most have a combination of words and pictures. The result is often very open, disclosing, usually stimulating, sometimes surprising and nearly always has the effect of bonding the set. The set is then ready to do some real work.

Box 4.1   Introducing ourselves – a self-portrait

For 20 minutes, create your own self-portrait based on the following 10 points for creating your portrait. Place your name in the centre of the flip chart. Share only that which you wish to share.
  The 10 points of the portrait are:

1. *a significant date:* eg birth, marriage, first house, job, divorce, celebration, event etc;
2. *a place of importance* – eg birth place, present home, holiday place, place of peace etc;
3. *a learning experience* – eg at school, college or training event or an event that had crucial and significant effect upon how you saw or see the world, ie a critical experience as well as a possible structured event;
4. *a heroine/hero or anti-hero/heroine living or dead* – historical, fact or fiction, a role model or source of inspiration;
5. *two significant people* – to whom I am now close, who are important to me;
6. *an example of unresolved conflict* – a personal issue in present experience, as yet unresolved, at home or at work;

---

7. *a present job focus/concern* – not a full job description, but a specific part of present work, which is a source of opportunity, difficulty or particular interest;
8. *symbol or picture* – some visual representation of myself: character, interest, present commitment;
9. *bits of personal history* – up to 6 selected items of personal history that represent your life to date, eg birthplace, school, children, significant people, jobs, travel etc;
10. *an example of good support network* – some place where I felt or feel understood and supported.

Each person in the set takes 10–15 minutes (the actual time dependent upon the overall time of the set meeting and whether the facilitator and set wish to commence the actual work of the set at the first meeting) to tell their story as conveyed by the words and pictures while the others listen without comment. On completion, time is given to enable set members to ask questions that clarify or illuminate the picture further.

When all participants have told their story, the facilitator may ask the set what they have gained and learnt from the experience.

Other introductory exercises that convey set member backgrounds using imagery rather than words are given in Boxes 4.2 and 4.3.

Box 4.2   Life line (Silverstone, 1993: 53)

Purpose: To get to know each other more

Each participant is given a large sheet of paper and a variety of coloured felt tip pens are made available.

Instruction: Please draw your story, your life line, in images, however you want.

Timing: 20 minutes to draw, 10 minutes each to explain what the images mean.

Box 4.3   Exercise: Life shield

Purpose: To share more of ourselves

First modelled by facilitator who produces a shield completed earlier.

My life at work	My life at home
My life with friends	My hopes and dreams

Each participant is given a large sheet of paper and a variety of coloured felt tip pens are made available.

Timing: 30 minutes for drawing, 15 minutes each to explain the images.

Beginning the work of the set

The facilitator needs to make a decision about the length of the introductory phase. The whole of the first day could be used for this activity. Such a decision has to be set against the extent of the whole cycle. If the set has a relatively short life, say 6 meetings over 6–10 months, it will be worth while making a start on the main purpose for which the set has been created. The introductory activity can be completed by lunchtime, leaving the whole afternoon for one or more presentations.

Following one of the above introductory activities, set members new to action learning will wish to find out what it is really like to engage in the process. So to make a start the facilitator invites set members to consider presenting even if there is time for only one or two persons present at the first meeting. Engaging in the actual work of the set will help support the deepening of commitment to the set.

How do presenters volunteer to present?

There are a number of potential approaches here, requiring sensitivity on the part of the facilitator to ensure that the feelings of presenters about bidding for space in the early life of the set are acknowledged. It is important to ensure that all set members have the opportunity of saying whether they do or do not wish to volunteer at that first meeting:

1. The facilitator invites set members to present by asking if anyone would like to volunteer. Volunteers wishing to present will vary in numbers. Usually at least one or two seek to present, but it can be more.
2. On a continuum from presenting or not presenting, where do you place yourself? This is a useful way of prioritizing who will present.

3. Going round the set inviting each person to convey a headline of what would be their issue if they were to present.

The facilitator then asks the volunteers to agree who will present, given an estimate by the facilitator as to how many may be fitted into the afternoon. Timing is important. It is critical that if, say, the facilitator considers there is time for two presentations, then the time has to be allocated accordingly, leaving some time near the end of the afternoon for a reflection on the day. Thus if it is 2.00 pm when two volunteers have agreed to present, the facilitator should allocate an amount of time for each. Set members tend to under-represent the amount of time they need, but 1¼ hours each should be allocated to allow for the reflection at the end. This is a broad indication. If a presenter ends naturally before that time, the set can move on to the next presenter. If the presenter is likely to run up to the designated time, the facilitator should indicate to the presenter that he has, say, 15 minutes left so that he can begin to reach some resolution for that day, with the possibility of returning to it at the next or subsequent meeting.

Presenting

When presenting, the presenter has the opportunity to tell his story however he wishes. It may be one that has been prepared and is in the presenter's mind already. It may be unformulated and incomplete, even somewhat incoherent. It is important to reassure set members that a presentation does not have to have the character of a completed picture. If it does, so be it. What is more likely is that the presenter has a mixture of feelings and ideas that may be muddled and unclear. Bringing those feelings and ideas to the set is part of the purpose of creating coherence and perhaps new understandings about an area of the presenter's life.

An example is useful here. The presenter, a senior member of staff in an English local authority, expressed unease about one of his colleagues for whom he had managerial responsibility. In essence, the presenter resented his colleague because he was totally detached from his work and expressed hostility whenever the presenter as manager confronted him, but the initial presentation, which took about 10 minutes, was expressed in an unsure and muddled way. The hostility to the colleague slowly emerged as he conveyed a picture of him as indolent, resentful and impervious to any shift in his negative approach to work. He concluded his opening story and appeared relieved to have got it off his chest. Further, he had not shared this with anyone else to date.

Following clarifying questions as to how long they had both worked in the department and the nature of their work, the presenter was asked if he had ever asked the colleague how he felt about his work. This evinced surprise on the part of the presenter who was visibly shocked by the question and later admitted it had not occurred to him to ask such a question for as far as he was concerned the colleague had a working brief and job description. The presenter himself slowly realized that he had never considered his colleague from the latter's perspective. It took some time and some silences before the presenter eventually said that he would find time to seek out his colleague and try getting into a dialogue that enabled the colleague to express his feelings and thoughts about his work.

The following set meeting enabled the presenter to report back on his progress. He had managed to find time and let his colleague just talk about his work. What transpired was that the colleague had recently divorced and this had affected his whole approach to his work, including the lack of apparent initiative in the post. The presenter told the set he had asked his colleague what would help to enable him to be more committed to the work. The colleague said he would get back to him later in the week. He did so, and came up with suggestions as to how he could embark on a new area of work which he had neglected in the past but which was still part of his brief.

This example also emphasized the initial lack of clarity about the issue which the presenter displayed. It may also have been a caution about disclosing such negative feelings early on in the set's life. What became clear, however, was the strength of feeling and the emerging clarity of resolution with the support of the set. Moreover, the presenter later admitted that looking at a person's work from their perspective was not something he had ever done before as a manager, let alone as a senior manager. This was not simply an improvement in the way the senior manager undertook his role, but represented a transformational shift in outlook which enabled him to see his work quite differently.

Ending the first meeting and day

The first day is completed with a review or reflection on the day by each of the presenters as well as by the facilitator. This can be open-ended without narrowing down the nature of the reflection. A process review on how the set worked may also be used. This could be phrased by the facilitator with questions like:

- What is it about how the set works that you would like to describe and emphasize?
- What has gone well and what could have been done better?
- How do you feel about how the set is working?

Next meeting(s)

Unless the meetings have been prearranged, it is important for the set to determine its subsequent meetings with diaries. This is easier when all are at the first meeting. If possible, the set may be able to arrange all the subsequent meetings in the cycle. If the set has not had full attendance at the first meeting, it may be possible for concurrent phone calls with the absent set members to fix the next meetings. If that is not possible, the facilitator can offer to take some dates for the next meeting and offer these to absent colleagues following the meeting and confirming by letter or e-mail the date chosen.

The second set meeting

The second meeting will have been arranged at a time after the first to allow for participants to set in train their actions and to have some reflections on their initial presentations (for those who had a presentation). This is usually 4–6 weeks following the first meeting. A cycle of six to eight meetings can then be held over a period of six months to one year, depending on the contract agreed prior to the commencement of the set.

At the second meeting it is assumed that the whole set will have met at the first meeting. Occasionally it happens that one or two of the set will not have been able to attend the first meeting.

It is important to enable all of the set to frame themselves for the ensuing meeting. One way of doing this is for the set to engage in a warm-up activity which enables set members to convey how they are feeling with an informal immediacy. The exercise 'Trauma, trivia and joy' considered in Chapter 3, page 58, is a useful initial activity. The activity will take about 5 to 15 minutes, depending upon the numbers participating. It is important not to rush an individual but to convey the idea that it is a brief 'warm-up' to get us going.

Alternative forms of conducting an initial round include:

- What's on top
- Mad, bad, sad and glad
- What have I left behind?

'What's on top' asks set members to spend a few moments making a statement about what is on their mind. It may be that what is on top may lead into what the individual wishes to bring to the set. Again, the set listens to each set member but without comment or questions. If the set member does follow through into a presentation, then that will be the point for set members to pick up their story.

'Mad, bad, sad and glad' invites set members to share feelings about recent events under each heading. This is run on the same lines as 'Trauma, trivia and joy'.

Another example for a starting round in the set is: 'What have I left behind?' followed by: 'What do I bring with me?' and 'What do I want from today?' The last statement, what do I want from today, may well elicit the number and form of the presentations for the day.

Integrating set members absent from the first meeting

Occasionally, set members may not be able to attend the first meeting but are able to attend the second meeting. It is important to ensure that they are integrated into the set at the second meeting. Before the normal work of the set commences, the set is asked to attend to this. Aware of the absence at the first meeting, set members are then asked, following completion, say, of the self-portrait activity, to remember as much as they can about each other for the next set meeting.

At the second meeting, the set members who attended the first set meeting, taking one person at a time, are asked to convey one thing they remember about that person. The set continue until they have exhausted their memories. The person selected is then asked to add one more thing about themselves that they did not express at the first meeting. They then move on to the next person until everybody has experienced the brief summary of their self-portraits, including the facilitator. Then the new set member is asked to present her self-portrait (having been asked to complete it prior to the meeting).

The integration is achieved by the new set member first hearing about everybody else before disclosing her own portrait about herself. The process is endorsing of all and inclusive of the new set member.

Presentations

Once the set has concluded this activity, the facilitator then asks who would like time today, given that those who presented last time may wish to report back on any actions they may have taken in the intervening period between the first and second meeting. When we started action learning we tended to ensure that every member of the set had time for a presentation at each set meeting. We no longer hold that view unless the set is very small or the purpose of the set is such that it is appropriate that all take time to progress a specific project. Rather we are disposed to set members having sufficient time to ensure a depth of reflection, challenge and support from the set. Thus over the course of a set meeting of, say, one day of 6 hours, there may be 2–4 presentations in addition to the reporting back of those who presented at the last meeting. Over the course of the set cycle the set members are assured of a number of presentations as well as the learning that is assured by attending to each other. Six hours' working time, allowing for about one hour for initial rounds, process reviews and end of day reflections, leaves five hours for presentations. If a set consists of, say, 8 people plus the facilitator, and all are to present, dividing by 8 means that each person would have about 35–40 minutes. We have found this to be rather short if the presenter is to have adequate time to present, followed by reflection in depth with the set and time to determine any action(s) that may follow. One and a half to two hours is more likely to enable the presenter to explore the issue in real depth. Presentations and set member involvement follow the form suggested earlier in the chapter. The key here is that the set clearly negotiates who will take time to present at the set meeting.

Process review

Following the presentation, the set is recommended to engage in a process review about *how* the set worked while the presentation was taking place. This presenter review is considered in detail in Chapter 13. An important consideration here is that the set and facilitator must endeavour to ensure that the set is not tempted to return to the content of the presenter's issue.

Review of the day

Finally, the facilitator asks the set to conduct a review of the day, also considered in detail in Chapter 13.

An alternative approach[1]

This handbook has taken the approach where set members can devote at least half a day, preferably a whole day, to each set meeting. However, we should recognize that not all organizations and individuals can devote the time suggested. While the approach taken in this book is regarded as the optimum, it is important to acknowledge situations where time is a constraint and where action learning for improvement is seen as being feasible but for transformation less significant. In such sets, task resolution will be significant and in organizational contexts this may be regarded as appropriate. The approach below is a viable example and assumes 5 set members and a facilitator.

The set allocates 2½ hours to a set meeting, with an allocation of time to stages as follows:

1.   Opening the set: 5 minutes. A quick round of what's on top for each set member.
2.   Presentation and analysis of issues: 15 minutes each to present and be in dialogue with set (75 minutes in total). What to present is usually prepared in advance.
3.   Draft action plans: 10 minutes. Undertaken individually.

4. Presentation and analysis of plan: 10 minutes per set member to deliberate on and finesse action plans with the set (50 minutes in total).
5. Review of the set meeting: 10 minutes.

At subsequent meetings set members return with the implemented actions and report back on progress to date with a new presentation on the next phase of their task:

- what I did;
- what happened;
- what was different from what I expected;
- what I did not do – what I did instead;
- what I learnt from this;
- what is the issue now;
- what actions I can take now;
- what specific action I should take.

This approach is useful where there are severe time constraints.

NOTE

1. A thank you to Brendan Harpur for this format of action learning.

PART II

Understanding action learning

Chapter 5

Dialogue and collaborative learning

This chapter is designed to show how action learning promotes dialogue that is conducive to and promotes learning. We aim to show how action learning represents a new paradigm of learning with recourse to the theoretical frameworks that underpin the paradigm.

The theory set out below and in the next chapter provides the underpinning that justifies action learning as a valid and relevant approach to learning and development. However, the theory can tend to be 'out there' and abstract. The first aim in this chapter is to show how dialogue itself contributes to learning and development. The second aim is to distinguish learning that can lead to improvement from learning that leads to a transformation of one kind or another. Here we refer to critical learning, which we will explain later. But first we wish to convey the distinctiveness of action learning from other forms of interactive dialogue.

A key feature of action learning is that it is a group experience where any learning and development that may take place is with others in dialogue. It is important to explain the particular meaning we give to dialogue and how the dialogue in an action learning set can differ from other forms of interaction.

What do we mean by dialogue?

Firstly, we distinguish dialogue that takes place between people from internal dialogue within individuals. Internal dialogue is important but it may not lead to the kind of learning and development to which we will refer.

Dialogue does occur quite naturally between people. Dialogue where the speakers' intentions are to hold forth didactically *at* one another in order to convey their position or knowledge on or about a subject is a form of dialogue that is unlikely to lead to some new understanding. This didactic form of dialogue is often characterized by one party claiming to be expert in interaction with other(s) who may not be. Indeed the *Shorter Oxford Dictionary* in its primary meaning defines didactic as 'having the character or manner of a teacher; characterized by giving instruction', of which the lecture, where the transmission of knowledge and ideas is the purpose, is a good example. For the receiver, what is received may be significant, but the mode is primarily one-way.

Dialogue can be among any number of people, not two as may be implied from the first syllable, which means 'through'. The second syllable means 'the word'. As Bohm (1996) conveys: 'this derivation suggests... a *stream of meaning* flowing among and through us and between us. This will make possible a flow of meaning in the whole group, out of which may emerge some new understanding. It's something new, which may not have been the starting point at all. It's something creative' (1996: 6, original italics).

Bohm contrasts dialogue with the word 'discussion'. For him discussion really means to break things up:

> It emphasizes the idea of analysis, where there may be many points of view, and where everybody is presenting a different one – analysing and breaking up. That obviously has its value, but is limited, and it will not get us very far beyond our various points of view. Discussion is almost like a ping-pong game, where people are batting the ideas back and forth and the object of the game is to win or to get points for yourself. (Bohm, 1996: 7)

This is a useful point at which to introduce the notion of 'separated' and 'connected' knowing, originally set out in Belenky *et al* (1986). Here we draw freely from, and acknowledge the writing of Tarule in Goldberger *et al* (1996), a sequel to Belenky et al (1986). Separated knowing leads to: 'a kind of dialogue that values the ability to pronounce or "report" one's ideas, whereas [connected knowing] values a dialogue that relies on relationship as one enters meaningful conversations that connect one's ideas with others' and establish "rapport"' (Goldberger *et al*, 1996: 277).

Separated knowing is very similar to Bohm's didactic discussion. Connected knowing is that which suggests the creation of that flow of meaning suggested by Bohm. It is appropriate here to introduce the work of Belenky *et al* (1986), who are central to our concepts of learning and development.

Stages and perspectives of learning

Belenky *et al* wrote *Women's Ways of Knowing* in 1986. The original research behind their book was undertaken to bring attention to the 'missing voices of women in their work on how people learn'. Prior to their work, the only scheme of personal epistemology and development in adult and higher education years was conducted by Perry (1970) and he only recorded the results amongst men. Belenky and her colleagues argued that this represented a major failure in not examining closely women's lives and experience. Their project was both an extension of Perry's work and a critique of his scheme.

They undertook research with a group of 135 women of different ages, ethnic and class backgrounds from urban and rural communities and with varying degrees of education, not just higher education. They included high school dropouts as well as women with graduate or professional qualifications. This was itself a breakthrough given that most research in this area at the time was restricted to white, middle-class groups, often male. They intentionally sought a diversity of backgrounds in order 'to see the common ground that women share, regardless of background' (1986: 13). They did not seek, because of the relatively small sample and the qualitative research methodology, to look at differences amongst the women in respect of class, ethnicity or other social distinctions. They simply said: 'Let us listen to the voices of diverse women to hear what they say about the varieties of female experience' (Goldberger *et al*, 1996: 4). Five perspectives emerged[1]:

1. *Silence* – a position of not knowing in which the person feels voiceless, powerless and mindless.
2. *Received knowing* – a position at which knowledge and authority are construed as outside the self and invested in powerful and knowing others from whom one is expected to learn.
3. *Subjective knowing* – in which knowledge is personal, private, and based on intuition and/or feeling states rather than on thought and articulated ideas that are defended with evidence.
4. *Procedural knowing* – the position at which techniques and procedures for acquiring, validating, and evaluating knowledge claims are developed and honoured. Within this sub-head they also described two modes of knowing [which are crucial for our purposes – authors]:
    –   *separated knowing* – characterized by a distanced, sceptical, and impartial stance toward that which one is trying to know (a reasoning against) and
    –   *connected knowing* – characterized by a stance or belief and an entering into the place of the other person or the idea that one is trying to know (a reasoning with).
5. *Constructed knowing* – a position at which truth is understood to be contextual; knowledge is recognized as tentative, not absolute; and it is understood that the knower is part of (constructs) the known. In their sample of women, constructed knowers valued multiple approaches to knowing (subjective and objective, connected and separate) and insisted on bringing the self and personal commitment into the centre of the knowing process (Goldberger *et al*, 1996: 4–5)

Perry (1970) interviewed students throughout their college years at Harvard and identified five stages of development. Although women were interviewed, the resulting scheme is based only on the male interviews. The consistency of context (ie Harvard) and the relative homogeneity of the sample enabled a clear linear sequence to appear. His research uncovered four epistemological 'positions' through which students gave meaning to their learning experience. Students progressed from *dualism*, through *multiplicity*, to *relativism subordinate* and ultimately *relativism*. The dualism position took students from the basic, right or wrong absolutist position, through uncertainty or guessing the right answer, to an acceptance of uncertainty or no answer yet available. The multiplicity position found students realizing that everyone has a right to their own opinion, a recognition that all knowledge is relative, and a crisis of personal commitment. The relativism position implies commitment to a position, the implications of such a commitment and the development of mature approaches to it.

Silence did not appear at all in Perry's scheme; the power of finding their voice is a particular characteristic of the women's group, and confirms the influence of gendered power relations on learning. For instance, women respondents reported being unable to speak after an academic 'put-down', as well as the silencing through culturally and socially determined difference, with its implied disparities of power. As Perry's group were college men, the likely silencing of less privileged men does not appear in the results. It is possible to compare Perry's stages of learning and development with the categories given above (Belenky *et al*, 1986; Goldberger *et al*, 1996) and two of his stages of development, dualism and multiplicity, exactly match the categories of received and subjective knowledge identified for the women's group. Although the Belenky model (Belenky *et al*, 1986) appears as stages, the research established that some learners may engage in the categories in a non-linear fashion. Nevertheless, we show the equivalence of the two schemes below:

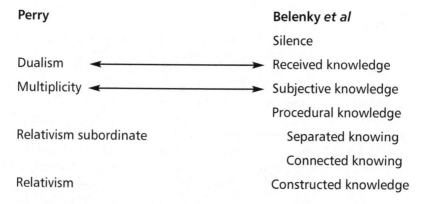

Perry	**Belenky *et al***
	Silence
Dualism ←——————→	Received knowledge
Multiplicity ←——————→	Subjective knowledge
	Procedural knowledge
Relativism subordinate	Separated knowing
	Connected knowing
Relativism	Constructed knowledge

The stage described as procedural knowledge was realized in two forms: separated and connected. Researchers found the connected mode was more typical of female conditioning, while the separated mode was akin to the men's stage entitled 'relativism subordinate'. When Perry's men move towards an understanding that all knowledge is relative, they are thought to adopt a strategy, also found among college women, entitled separated knowing. The separation strategy, known as 'the doubting game' or even 'critical thinking', is characterized by the objectification of the other (Elbow, 1998). A powerful account of relationships based on such objectification can be found in Buber (1994), where seeing the other as a thing-to-be-used is characteristic of an I–It orientation, while an aspiration to connect with the other as a person reveals an I–Thou orientation. Academics in universities tend to engage in separated knowledge, as they conduct adversarial interactions, putting concepts on trial in order to attack them, and 'it's not personal' is something to be proud of. The adversarial jousting has been called 'ceremonial combat' and is a style peculiarly attractive to men, as to many women it seems silly. Indeed the feminist Adrienne Rich declares that 'rhetoric is a masculine adversary style of discourse' (Rich, 1979: 138).

Connected knowing builds on subjectivist knowledge and, known as the 'believing game' (Elbow, 1998), it is learnt through empathy, without judgement, and coming from an attitude of trust, quite the opposite of separated knowing. Connected knowing differs from simple subjectivism as it is 'the deliberate imaginative extension of one's understanding into positions that initially feel wrong or remote' (Belenky *et al*, 1986: 121).

Separated or connected knowing prepares learners for their next stage of development, the adoption of constructivist approaches to knowledge. For the constructivist, 'all knowledge is constructed, and the knower is an intimate part of the known' (Belenky *et al*, 1986: 137). In this category of learning, we are informed that there is passion and participation in the act of knowing (Polanyi, 1958) and the stance is beyond the narrow objectivism of academia, which, as the philosopher, Sara Ruddick knew only too well: 'instead of developing arguments that could bring my feelings to heel, I allowed my feelings to inform my most abstract thinking' (Ruddick, 1984: 150).

Such a stance alters one's orientation to experts, as 'an expert becomes somebody whose answers reflect the complexity... the situation holds' (Belenky *et al*, 1986: 139), and constructivist learning is characterized by empathy and connectedness, so relationship is a key ingredient in what is a completely holistic stance towards knowledge and learning. We acknowledge the components of constructivist knowledge as those that lead to a recognition of relationship in learning, ie connectedness to others, empathy and awareness of feelings.

For Belenky *et al* the use of the terms 'separated knowing' and 'connected knowing' is intrinsic to their work. In the sequel to Belenky et al (1986) the terms separate (not separated) and connected are used (Goldberger et al 1996). We want to explain these terms more fully for they are a valuable way of understanding action learning, based as it is on particular forms of dialogue. In addition, the forms of dialogue represented in action learning underpin the values in the approach as well as promoting reflective learning.

The terms separated and connected knowing, as introduced earlier in this chapter, are also valuable in providing us with an alternative theoretical perspective based upon epistemology, ie the theory of knowledge. By going to the root of how we discourse with each other we can offer a *raison d'être* as well for action learning and why it can be justified as an appropriate format for learning and development.

Knowing: separate and connected

It is not possible to examine the terms separate and connected knowing without explaining why these writers use the word knowing. Why did they not use the words *believe* or *think* or *feel*? (Clinchy, 1996) sums it up well:

> we wanted as much as possible to hear the women in their own terms and 'knowing' seemed to come closest to what most of them meant. We rejected 'thinking' because, given the dichotomy in this culture between cognition and affect, we were afraid that 'thinking' might imply absence of feeling, and for many of the women, feeling was intimately involved in 'knowing.' We rejected 'belief' because although some of the women we interviewed distinguished between believing and knowing, others did not... we relied on connected knowing. (1996: 212)

We can now return to the terms connected and separate knowing using the context of action learning. Connected knowing means set members suspending judgement in an attempt to understand the presenter's ways of making sense of their experience. In the words of Elbow (1998), set members 'play the believing game.' Questions like:

'What do you see? ... Give me the vision in your head.' (Elbow, 1998)
'That's an experience I don't have. Help me to understand your experience.'

The other set members are seeking to understand where the presenter is coming from and what it means to the presenter as 'knower' of that experience.

In contrast, when conducting a dialogue through separate knowing, the set members will relate in a different way to the presenter. They will, in Elbow's words, 'play the doubting game' (1998), looking for flaws in the presenter's reasoning, examining the person's statements with a critical eye, and insisting that the presenter justify every point they make.

With separate knowing the dialogue is about testing the validity of propositions or statements or stories against some objective criterion and/or my view of the world. It tends to be an adversarial stance – the mode of discourse is argument. With connected knowing the dialogue is about understanding what the person is saying – their experience. The mode of discourse is 'one of allies, even advocates, of the position they are examining' (Clinchy, 1996: 208).

Clinchy does not wish to set up separate and connected knowing as dualistic opposites where we have to take sides. Each has their value in context. In addition, she does not wish to pose extremes to represent differing validities. For example, at the extreme, separate knowers are sometimes perceived as stubbornly attached to their own opinions and deaf to the views of others. Connected knowers can also be perceived as excessively open-minded or as having no minds of their own, rather like 'over-empathizers' or flotsam. Clinchy suggests that each of these pictures should be seen as caricatures distorting their 'mature forms' (1996) which are more appropriate in their contexts.

The key for us is the context. Action learning is a particular context where understanding where the presenter is 'coming from in their experience' is significant in enabling the set members and facilitator to work with that experience. '"Playing the believing game" becomes a *procedure* that guides the interaction with other minds. It is not the *result* of the interaction' (Clinchy, 1996: 209). In other words, I do not necessarily have to agree with the person's stance, but I suspend my judgement in order to understand that person's stance.

Connected knowing as a procedure

Clinchy refers (1996: 205) to connected knowing as originally a serendipitous discovery when they undertook the research leading to their publication, *Women's Ways of Knowing* (Belenky *et al*, 1986): 'Connected knowing was originally a serendipitous discovery. We did not ask the women we interviewed to tell us about it; they did so spontaneously, and from their comments we constructed the procedure as a sort of "ideal type"' (1996: 205).

Similarly, when we started working with action learning we found that the interactions that endeavoured to understand the presenter's experience, rather than attempt to 'knock it', actually worked, and presenters shifted their understanding of their worlds without having to be convinced by the 'rational' arguments of others. A very ordinary example will be given here.

In an early (when starting action learning) set, one of the authors heard a presenter wishing to sort out her work priorities. To this end, she brought a long list of things she was attempting to do currently in her work. As (with hindsight now) separate knowers, we would have challenged the list and no doubt sought to get her to order the list according to some logic and criteria. In fact the set listened to her explanation of what she was doing, not doing, frustrations, blockages, and feelings toward her work. There was a seeking of clarification by us but it was simply to ascertain what she found important and how she felt about it all. At the end of the first meeting she had done some sorting but there was a sense of the unfinished about it. Slowly, at subsequent meetings the list became a recognition of something wider and deeper – her recognition of a shift in potential direction of her career. The set could not have foreseen this and it would have been inappropriate at an earlier stage to have drawn that conclusion.

As our experience with action learning developed, we realized that getting into the presenter's world was not only effective from their standpoint, it was also, in Clinchy's words, a useful *procedure* to adopt to enable the presenter (and the set) to understand her world and to work from there.

Procedure as a culture change

What we again only slowly realized was that the procedure we were adopting for action learning was also a shift in culture by moving away from our prevailing ways of discourse in the worlds of work that we lived in – academia, business and training. In action learning there is an explicit aim through the process to get into the presenter's world. This does not mean a subjective immersion in the presenter's world. Simply it is to try to understand where the other is coming from. The emphasis here is on the word try. It is not easy or natural. Clinchy quotes the anthropologist, Clifford Geertz (1986), here:

> Comprehending that which is, in some manner or form, alien to us and likely to remain so, without either smoothing it over with vacant murmurs of common humanity,… or dismissing it as charming, lovely even, but inconsequent, is a skill we have arduously to learn and having learnt it, work continuously to keep it alive; it is not a natural[2] capacity, like depth perception or the sense of balance, upon which we can complacently rely. (In Clinchy, 1996: 209)

In early meetings, near the commencement of a cycle of meetings, in some of our sets, set members do endeavour to get into the presenter's world. However, there may be a temptation to make assumptions about that world and to base interventions upon those assumptions without checking if they are accurate. Having made assumptions about the other's world, they may then proceed to ask questions that detract the presenter from her world on the basis that the set member now knows her world. In fact the dialogue may be detracting into the set member's world, not the presenter's.

We should emphasize that getting into the presenter's world through connected knowing does not mean that the set members are acritically accepting that world. This would mean a subjectivism which would suggest that the listener accepts whatever the presenter says as a valid view of the world. The point for the connected knower is to understand the presenter's world, not necessarily to accept it. Understanding what the presenter expresses as what she knows doesn't mean set members have to think the same thing. Geertz (1986) explains this as: 'understanding in the sense of comprehension, perception and insight needs to be distinguished from "understanding" in the sense of agreement of opinion, union of sentiment, or commonality of commitment... We must learn to grasp what we cannot embrace' (Clinchy, 1996: 217). For Clinchy, 'from the connected knowing perspective, of course, we must first try very hard to embrace it' (1996: 217).

To be really heard in an action learning set in connected knowing terms is to be affirmed and validated. It is not because she, the presenter, has been told she is right. By 'swinging boldly into the mind of another' (Clinchy, 1996: 218), two perversions of connected knowing are prevented. The first, known in the USA as the 'Californian fuck-off', typified by a response like: 'Well, given your background, I can see where you're coming from', is simply patronizing and is a totally negative response. The second is like the assumption-making above, with a quick response like: 'I know exactly how you feel', when in fact the speaker has little idea or quite the wrong idea.

The relatedness that arises when connected knowing occurs has echoes in a story we have of a recent international visit where we were invited to spend a week introducing action learning to senior personnel staff in the civil service. Following the first day, when we arrived at the start of the next day of the workshop (and each day thereafter) we would ask the participants for their overnight thoughts. The purpose of this was to address any concerns or reflections about the previous day and was useful in grounding the workshop at the beginning of the day. We asked on the third morning for overnight thoughts. We were working in consecutive translation, that is, our translator converts to English after we listen to the participant speak in their own language.

One of the participants told a story to us and his colleagues. Prior to his contribution, the overnight thoughts that day were fairly low key. The response to his comments as they unfolded (which we observed but could only pick up the non-verbal clues) became very animated and drew much appreciation from the others. He had telephoned his partner late the previous evening and she had relayed to him her upset at how she had been treated very negatively by her manager that day, despite undertaking all that had been required of her. Our storyteller asked many questions, essentially about what had happened and how she felt. She worked through on the phone her feelings about the event and created her own picture about the interaction with her manager. The participant smiled as we heard the translation (his English was really very good), particularly when we had conveyed to us that this was the first time he had ever done this with his partner. Usually on hearing her woes he would have launched into giving her solutions. He was surprised by his change in behaviour, which he attributed to the work he was doing at the workshop. He had swung boldly into the mind of his partner without being judgemental and endeavoured to understand her world of work and the relationship with her manager, a good example of connected knowing.

We can now summarize the story so far. In action learning we enter into a dialogue with the set member who is currently working as presenter. The dialogue that we engage in can be termed one of connected knowing, that is, we endeavour to enter the presenter's world in order to understand where she is coming from. It is a procedure to enable the presenter to understand her world too, and possibly to learn from it as well. The form the dialogue takes represents a cultural shift from that prevailing in many work situations. We can now introduce more widely known theoretical frameworks to explain the theory behind action learning.

NOTES

1. This summary of the five perspectives is drawn from Goldberger *et al* (1996) rather than the original (Belenky *et al*, 1986).The summary is essentially the same, except that the later version is probably intended to be more accessible to the reader. In Goldberger *et al* (1996), the original authors and invited contributors explore how the theory introduced in Belenky *et al* (1986) has developed and shifted over the years.
2. In the original quotation, Geertz uses the term 'connatural'. We take this to mean the same as 'natural'.

Chapter 6

Action learning as a reflective process

In this chapter we incorporate the notion of reflection and reflective practice into action learning. This chapter is not essential to being able to engage in action learning. However, as this is a handbook and therefore aims to be comprehensive in scope, we include this element. To our knowledge, no other writing on action learning has included the relationship of the action learning process to reflective practice and reflective learning.

This chapter takes forward the idea of action learning being about dialogue and interaction between set members. What is added is the relationship of that dialogue to reflection and how reflection can take different forms.

What does it mean to engage in reflection? What do we mean when we engage in reflective practice? When can we refer to ourselves as 'reflective practitioners'? How can reflective practice encourage the deeper levels of learning to which people aspire?

We will make the journey through development of the notion of reflective practice as a means to convey our meanings. Before embarking on this journey we make a further note about the chapter for readers. We wish to explain the ideas on reflective practice as clearly as possible. In doing so we realize that we are using a cognitive, analytical and fairly rational means in order to make the explanation as accessible as possible to readers. In the description we may inadvertently convey the idea that, once cognitively understood as a concept, reflective practice is a straightforward and rational process. A cognitive understanding of reflective practice is a step towards what is in practice a complex and more holistic endeavour.

Barnett (1992a: 185) uses the phrase, 'We're all reflective practitioners now'. By this is meant a continuous search for knowledge in propositional knowledge and knowledge derived from practice – there is no endpoint. We would add that the conscientious practitioner engages in this as a matter of course, as the criteria by which we practise require to be evaluated continuously. We need to be aware, therefore, of our actions in order that we may evaluate them. The capacity to engage in reflective practice becomes one of the means of enhancing the quality of our work and of promoting our learning and development. Action learning is an apt vehicle for achieving some of that learning and development.

Engaging in reflective practice means developing the capacity continuously to engage in critical dialogue about professional activity individually and with others in *all* they think and do. It is a reflexive process in that it is constant, iterative and continuing. The learning and developmental outcome to be desired is that of the reflective practitioner. It is an outcome that set members can achieve when they bring their practice to the set.

It is necessary now to go to the origin of the contemporary meaning of reflective practice. Schön's writing (1983, 1987) made a major contribution to the idea of reflective practice as a means of enhancing a person's critical and reflective abilities. We offer an adaptation of our reading of Schön as a basis for reflective practice in the context of action learning.

Schön's reflective practitioner

Schön, in developing the notion of 'reflective practice', drew largely upon applied areas of study where students were receiving an education designed to equip them directly for professional occupations. Those teaching disciplines were in the business of creating and promulgating largely propositional knowledge (knowing that, knowing about/something). Schön suggested that such propositional knowledge, on its own, is of limited value for the emerging professional, eg lawyer, social worker, physician etc. Propositional knowledge is limited because it does not take into account the realities of professional life and practice.

Yet emergent professionals go into practice and are effective 'despite' their professional training. They develop *practice experience* and professional knowledge and excellence. That practice experience includes the propositional knowledge (knowing about, knowing that) they acquired in order to qualify, but is also more than that. So what is it that is more than propositional knowledge that nevertheless enables the professional to engage in their practice effectively?

Schön unpacked the means by which professionals *enhance* their practice while they *engage* in it. He referred to this as professional artistry, where professionals deal with the unique, the unanticipated, the uncertain, the value conflicts and indeterminate conditions of everyday practice for which there is no 'textbook' response. Whatever our profession, we come to the point early on when we cannot rely simply on the propositional knowledge we acquired in our education and training. The response of the practitioner to untested situations is the development of professional artistry. As a consequence, over time, professional artistry embodies earlier propositional knowledge, making it past experience, that is, tacit.

However, it is not much help to refer to it only with this term, professional artistry. Colloquially, it is like asking a person how he does something who then replies, 'Oh y'know'. Schön, not satisfied with this apparently intuitive means of learning, set out to describe tacit knowledge (Polanyi, 1967). Schön looked to those institutions concerned with vocational education where reflecting in and on professional practice was an intrinsic part of the professional's training.

In such institutions Schön found that professional artistry meant that the teachers and students engaged in *reflection on* emergent practice that was to underpin their learning and therefore enhance their practice. Putting it more simply, students learnt by listening, watching, doing and by being coached in their doing. Not only did they apply what they had heard and learnt from lectures, books and demonstrations but when they did an action that was part of their future profession, eg using a scalpel, they also learnt by reflecting themselves, and with their tutors, how the action went. They *reflected on* their practice immediately following the action or event. In addition, they would 'take with them' that reflection as a piece of 'knowledge' or learning when they went into the action the next time. Thus in the next action they would be bringing all their previously acquired understanding and practice and be able to *reflect on* the action as they did it, particularly if a new circumstance came up.

Thus for the moment we have built up a meaning for reflective practice as reflection-on-action and reflection-in-action. We also adopt Schön's use of the hyphen to suggest two things. One is to convey interaction between action, thinking and being. The second is to suggest an immediacy inherent in reflection and action. This is particularly apposite in relation to reflection-in-action where the professional may well be 'thinking on her feet', as we say.

Reflective practice

We will now extend and deepen the meaning of the terms we are using in order to convey the significance of reflective practice in action learning. We will explore in more detail what we mean by reflective practice. Here we define our terms and, in doing so, also set out some of Schön's category of terms to construct a vocabulary that enables a professional to be a reflective practitioner and for us to converse with our readers. Key terms include:

Knowing that...
Knowing-in-action and knowledge-in-use
Reflection-in-action
Reflection-on-action

We will consider each in turn:

1. *'Knowing that...'* This is another way of defining propositional knowledge and is that which the professional student acquires in the main-

stream part of their professional study at university. This may also be referred to as *textbook knowledge* or *'knowing about…'*.

2. *'Knowing-in-action and knowledge-in-use'*   That which comes from professional practice. Schön refers to this kind of knowledge as *knowledge-in-action*, a description or construction of that *knowing-in-action* that is tacit, spontaneous and dynamic. Knowing-in-action is hyphenated by Schön probably to emphasize that 'the knowing is *in* the action' (Schön, 1987: 25). Knowing-in-action becomes knowledge-in-action when we describe it! Until we describe it we just do it – intelligent knowing-in-actions that we perform in all manner of situations, from sawing a piece of wood in a straight line, to riding a bicycle, to a surgeon making an incision. Once we know how to do these actions we do them spontaneously, without putting words to them. 'The knowing-in-action is tacit… yielding outcomes so long as the situation falls within the boundaries of what we have learnt to treat as normal' (1987: 28). So describing our knowing-in-action brings us to our knowledge-in-use which we can then use when we reflect-in-action.

3. *Reflection-in-action* happens when we are in the midst of an action and in the doing. We are, for example, asking ourselves:
   – Something is happening that surprises me – it is not usual.
   – Is what I am doing appropriate at this moment?
   – Do I need to alter, amend, change what I am doing and being in order to adjust to changing circumstances, to get back into balance, to attend accurately etc?
   – To check with myself that I am on the right track.
   – If I am not on the right track, is there a better way?

An example may be useful here. One of us was helping a friend reinsert a door frame on to its hinge after trimming the base of the door to prevent it from scraping on the floor as it closed (neither of us had professional joinery skills). The two hinges on the door slid on to two hinge butts on the door frame. We were trying to lift the door sufficiently to enable the door hinges to fit exactly onto the frame hinge butts. We were unable to lift the door high enough without misaligning the door and not achieving a fit. I said, 'Have we something we can use to lever the door from the floor?' My friend went to the garage and returned with a long, thin, rigid piece of metal. He lifted the door slightly while I inserted the lever under the door. We were then able to lift and balance the door to enable us to place the two hinges accurately on the hinge butts. The realization of the use of the lever as we undertook the task was an example of reflection-in-action. In this instance it was a better way to achieve the result, but it was also not an earth-shattering revelation and did not mean much thought – it just made that job much easier. But it was also a reflexive process – the application of knowledge-in-action to a new (for us) situation, becoming reflection-in-action.

For Schön, what distinguishes reflection-in-action from other forms of reflection 'is its immediate significance for action... the rethinking of some part of our knowing-in-action leads to on-the-spot experiment and further thinking that affects what we do – in the situation in hand and perhaps also in others we shall see as similar to it' (Schön, 1987: 29). To the outsider and even for the skilled individual engaged in the act it will appear a smooth act without apparent hesitation or thought. This meaning signifies reflecting while the action *is* happening – a kind of checking function, and if there is to be any modification arising from the reflection-in-action, adjustment will take place to resume normal service!

4. *Reflection-on-action.* This is the act of reflection *after* the action has taken place and will be considered below in greater detail.

Reality and reflection-in-action

It is useful at this point to refer to how Schön fits reflection-in-action into ways of seeing reality:

> Underlying this view of the practitioner's reflection-in-action is a *constructionist* view of the reality with which the practitioner deals – a view that leads us to see the practitioner as constructing situations in practice, not only in the exercise of professional artistry but also in all other modes of professional competence... In the constructionist view, our perceptions, appreciations, and beliefs are rooted in worlds of our own making that we come to *accept* as reality. (Schön, 1987: 36, original italics)

We discuss how action learning relates to constructionism in Chapter 7. Here Schön is recognizing the subjective construction of reality. This is close to Belenky *et al* (1986) in relation to women's experience of higher education, where they note that the individual learner comes into her own when she is able to be in a position of constructed knowledge where knowledge is seen as contextual and created by the person valuing both the subjective and objective.

As we have seen in Chapter 5, Belenky *et al* (1986) recognize that there is an earlier stage of coming to know, that is, a stage of procedural knowledge where some women apply objective procedures for obtaining and communicating knowledge (separated knowledge). This stage is akin to Schön's position about technical rationality which rests 'on an *objectivist* view of the relation of the knowing practitioner to the reality he knows. On this view, facts are what they are, and the truth of beliefs is strictly testable by reference to them. All meaningful disagreements are resolvable, at least in principle, by reference to the facts. And professional knowledge rests on a foundation of facts' (Schön, 1987: 36, original italics).

An additional category (connected knowing) was more characteristic of the women studied by Belenky *et al*, leading naturally to constructed knowledge as above. Belenky *et al* (1986) undertook their research in relation to women's experience of higher education in the USA and identified constructive learners in their sample. However, our experience suggests, and we have no reason to doubt, that it can apply to men as well. The implication we are making is that propositional knowledge (knowing about) really only comes to have internalized and real meaning as knowledge when the receiving learners begin to apply that propositional knowledge to themselves by relating in some way to their experience, as part of developing a constructivist orientation to learning and development, where the practitioner as actor creates knowledge, in collaboration with others.

More specifically, if as a practising professional I am to bring the propositional knowledge into a reality for me, then by immersing myself in a task that employs that knowledge, I will internalize it and make it have meaning when I bring it to bear with my existing knowing-in-action and emerging reflection-in-action.

Reflection-on-action

Having investigated some of the components of reflection-in-action, we now need to consider what happens when our professional engages in reflection-on-action in order to encourage reflective learning as well as encourage critically reflective learning. By reflective learning we mean learning that results in improvement. By critically reflective learning we mean the possibility of learning that is transformative.

What does the term reflection-on-action mean? What detailed meanings are subsumed within reflection-on-action? How can the conditions be created to enable reflection-on-action to happen?

We will take initially Schön's reference to reflection-on-action. It is significant to his main thesis of developing the professional practitioner. The capacity to reflect-on-action is significant for continuing professional development and, as it happens, for effective action learning. 'Clearly, it is one thing to be able to reflect-in-action and quite another to be able to reflect *on* our reflection-in-action so as to produce a good description of it; and it is still another thing to be able to reflect on the resulting description' (Schön, 1987: 31, original italics). Here is the recognition that there will always be some aspects of action where explanation after the event in words will not be possible, for example in music by virtue of its nature. Given this, there is much that can be unravelled and described in words that can then be used for reflection. This is significant for action learning, given the key notion of reflection on actions after the event.

We will take the situation of a presenter in a set relaying to the set an issue or an action in the recent past as a reflection-on-action. The capacity of a presenter to reflect-on-action is significant in developing critically reflective learning. But we need to unpack Schön's statement by treating this as think-ing, feeling and doing at a number of levels and incorporating propositional knowledge and that which occurs in the action as considered earlier.

Drawing upon Schön, we can start at the bottom, level 1, with the action, shown in Figure 6.1.

Level 1 is the action or event that the set member is presenting, which has embodied in it *knowing that; knowing-in-action; knowledge-in-use*. Level 2 is any reflection-in-action which is also, strictly speaking, embodied in the action or event. Level 3 is the presenter's description of the event, including any reflection-in-action. Level 4 is the presenter's reflections on the description of the event. These will include her thoughts and feelings as well as the ques-tions, insights and feedback of other set members and facilitator.

We prefer to show the levels as dimensions as in Figure 6.2. Levels imply a hierarchy and implicitly that which is at the 'lower' level is less important. Further, levels can imply separateness between levels. As dimensions they are related, overlapping, and experience-in-action is just as important as reflection-on-action. Each and all interrelate just as thinking, feeling and doing fuse and intermingle.

Strictly speaking, dimension 2, reflection-in-action, happens within the action, dimension 1, but because it is reflection-in-action is somehow differ-

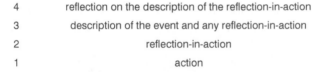

4	reflection on the description of the reflection-in-action
3	description of the event and any reflection-in-action
2	reflection-in-action
1	action

Figure 6.1   *Hierarchy of reflection*
Source: Brockbank and McGill, 1998

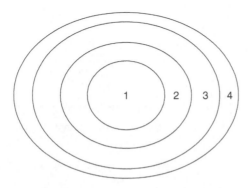

Figure 6.2   *Dimensions of reflection*
Source: Brockbank and McGill, 1998

ent from that taken in the past and therefore modifies the action, we will delineate it as dimension 2. We have here, following Schön's description, dimensions of thought based in and on an action (applying here to thinking and feelings about past and current doings). Within dimension 1, action, we would include any propositional knowledge *(knowing that)* brought to the action but now probably embedded; knowledge-in-use brought from previous experience; and current knowing-in-action as well. These are all in harness, working together. So Figure 6.1 can now revised as in Figure 6.3.

For the learner to go into reflection-on-action mode on dimension 4 requires, on dimension 3, a description of dimension 2: the reflection-in-action and the action, as recalled on dimension 1. We would also add that describing some of dimension 1, in particular, as knowing-in-action may also be novel at dimension 3. For the reflector the act of describing is sometimes to name that which may have been previously unnamed. This leads to the common difficulty of a skilled practitioner (Schön, 1987) being able to articulate what she does in action, and *differentiates the teacher, facilitator, coach or mentor who may be able to articulate their actions by modelling their behaviour and articulating the model as well.* Our italics are to emphasize the importance of naming the process and the importance, in dialogue, with someone who has the skill initially (and therefore to be modelled for the set members), to identify these dimensions of reflection.

Obviously, reflection-in-action is within the action of the person engaged in the action and therefore part and parcel of the action. Reflection-on-action can be undertaken by the person individually after the action. This

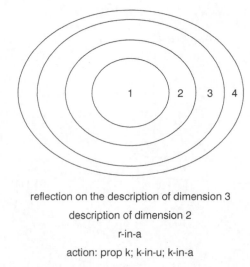

4	reflection on the description of dimension 3
3	description of dimension 2
2	r-in-a
1	action: prop k; k-in-u; k-in-a

Figure 6.3 *Four dimensions of reflection*
Source: Brockbank and McGill, 1998

personal (on their own) reflection-on-action is important in the continuing internal dialogue about their practice and may influence their future action and reflections-in-action. However, while this form of reflection is necessary and desirable it is not necessarily sufficient for reflective learning.

Reflection-on-action with another(s) in dialogue which encourages reflection about the actions a person has undertaken will be more likely to be effective in promoting critical reflective learning. Without the interaction brought about by dialogue, critically reflective learning may not happen. Hence our emphasis on conditions we recommend to enhance the quality of that dialogue (Chapters 4 and 5).

The presenter brings to any action all her accumulated propositional knowledge (and we include that which has become tacit), knowledge-in-use as a result of her prior experience (again now likely to be tacit), knowing-in-action and reflection-in-action. At the point of reflection-on-action, all the aforementioned come into potential play.

Thus returning to our question about reflection-on-action, we have a reflection at a meta level on which the presenter is able, initially to describe or name what has happened and then reflect on, and work with, the material that is before her. Schön describes the 'levels of action and reflection on action as the rungs of a ladder. Climbing up the ladder, one (*the presenter with the set members and facilitator*) makes what has happened at the rung below an object of reflection' (Schön, 1987: 114, our italics). We have preferred to use the notion of dimensions in order to mirror the idea of permeability across dimensions and to prevent the demotion of experience against reflection. We will take an example.

A presenter was engaged in a project which was in draft report stage (current action completed, or levels 1 and 2). With the set, the presenter is reporting upon her progress to date. The presenter, in reporting upon her progress, describes her journey to date (level 3). Within dimension 3 she struggles, but describes the difficulty that she had in writing an early section but nevertheless pursued working on that section before moving on with the next section sequentially. The set then go into dialogue with her about her experience in writing up the project. (We distinguish dialogue from discussion in Chapter 5.) At one point a set member asks what is the reason for writing the sections sequentially. The presenter is surprised by the question and at first replies 'but that is how I have always done it'. Questions follow that pose why such a procedure is necessary. Gradually, the presenter realizes this is a habit (knowledge-in-use) she has applied up to now without questioning it. Recognition becomes apparent to her that she could have adopted alternatives to writing up the project. She realizes she could work on a section where she is not 'blocked' and where she has energy and will, or she may undertake a section that appears at the moment 'easier'. Here we have reflection at dimension 4 for her but also for the set, amongst whom this notion appears novel and potentially useful.

Thus through the dialogue which enabled reflection-on-action in the set, our presenter has learnt about her process (of compiling the project report), as well as, potentially, providing food for thought for some of the others in the set. Moreover, we have the possibility that had she reflected on her action (after the writing) on her own, she might not have realized that potentiality. Therefore the dialogue, necessarily with others, *enabled* her to reflect upon her actions and move towards improvement or transformation. We discuss the significance of these terms in more detail in Chapter 7.

If we stand outside the four dimensions given above and consider the whole process, we can see that the presenter is engaging in reflective practice *and* is also becoming aware of doing reflective practice. She is also learning about some aspects of the way she is learning – meta-learning or learning about learning. She and the set are working in another dimension, dimension 5. Again the outcome may be improvement or transformation, here in relation to how she learns – again, see Chapter 7.

Dimension 5

Returning to the dimensions, we can refer to another – inherent here – dimension 5, where the set reflects on the reflection-on-action process. On this dimension, set members are working on the significance of reflection itself, that is, learning about how they learn! Thus in reflective dialogue on this dimension there may be learning for the individual that derives from the interaction in the set. In Figure 6.4 we will refer to dimension 4 as reflection-on-action and dimension 5 as reflection on reflection-on-action.

In summary, we would suggest that reflection of a presenter's practice may take place *within* actions and *following* actions. The reflection can be a conversation with oneself during the action and/or with others engaged in it through but not necessarily via dialogue – it is possible to communicate by non-verbal means. It is also possible to engage after the action by oneself and/or with others. Indeed the ability to reflect after an action is critical to the potentiality of future actions and events. We are also arguing that reflection-on-action after the action with other(s) in dialogue (as in action learning) is important, for the actor may not be able to *see* herself without some self-deception, thereby limiting her range for potential reflection (here reflection is an act as well as the past action being reflected upon).

The key for us is how best to engage in reflection-*on*-action to attain critical reflection, that which is potentially transformative and/or results in a paradigm shift. An action learning set is at its most effective when this is achieved. It is necessary, briefly, to return to a further aspect of Schön's reflection-in-action.

For Schön, reflection-in-action has an additional meaning: 'a critical function, questioning the assumptional structure of knowing-in-action. We think critically about the thinking that got us into this fix or this opportunity; and we may, in the process, restructure strategies of action, understandings of phenomena, or ways of framing problems' (Schön, 1987: 28).

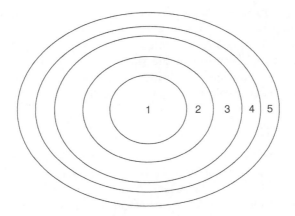

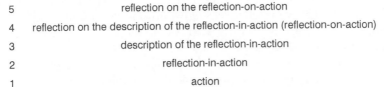

5	reflection on the reflection-on-action
4	reflection on the description of the reflection-in-action (reflection-on-action)
3	description of the reflection-in-action
2	reflection-in-action
1	action

Figure 6.4 *Five dimensions of reflection*
Source: Brockbank and McGill, 1998

This latter meaning of reflection-in-action is very different from the earlier examples yielding improvements. It has been called a paradigm shift as it is transformative in character. As Eraut (1994) has suggested, this is more difficult to 'fit' into the more intuitive reflection-in-action posited by Schön, and in Eraut's view this is because Schön tends to be less clear about the time scale in which reflection-in-action may occur. For Eraut it all depends upon how the action is defined in terms of time and what is determined as the action: 'is the action a scene, an act or a whole play? Or is it reflection-in-action while the actors are on stage and reflection-on-action when they are not?' (1994: 147).

This raises definitional problems of when our practitioner is reflecting-in-action or reflecting-on-action. In action learning it is more important that the set draw out the paradigm shift whether or not it has been explicit for the presenter. If the significant shift occurred in-action then the set may well enable the presenter to articulate and learn from the shift. The key contribution of Schön is his emphasis on knowing and knowledge as constructed in and out of practice, not only derived from propositional knowledge derived from the training manual or from the lecture hall.

To summarize to this point, knowing-in-action and reflection-in-action are integral parts of the task or event. They happen during and in the event, not after the event. Each supports the other. The distinction between the two is that the former follows accustomed practice, the latter enters when there is a surprise occasioned by the unaccustomed, a change in the usual circumstances or an emergent critique of the way of doing something that gives rise to a modification in the way the action will be undertaken in future. It is now important to consider in more detail the idea of a paradigm shift and how this contributes to critical reflective practice and learning.

Paradigm shift

It is useful to draw a further potential effect of reflection across the five dimensions referred to above. We have already referred to the effect of dimension 5 in learning about learning. We can also consider the idea of reflection-on-action that takes place within a paradigm and reflection that enables a move(s) out of an existing paradigm. This is another potentiality and links with what we refer to as single and double loop learning considered in greater depth in Chapter 7. In single loop learning the presenter may be endeavouring through reflection at level 4 to understand and take 'corrective' action from the reflection in order to make future action more effective. The presenter's reflection-on-action becomes her potential knowledge-in-use. With double loop learning through reflection, particularly with others in dialogue, the presenter may:

1. recognize a paradigm that she been in without realizing it;
2. recognize/realize that there is another paradigmatic framework other than the one she is in;
3. shift her paradigm;
4. understand and work across paradigms.

An example of 1 would be recognition of the discrepancy between my espoused as opposed to my in-use notions of sexism – what I espouse perhaps being very different from my actions and my being made aware of the incongruity. An example of 2 above would be recognition of the idea of Einstein's relativity in relation to the mass of a body, in contrast to earlier ideas of mass as constant. A change in attitude to gender issues would be an example of 3. Scientists now working in both Newtonian and Einsteinian paradigms is an example of 4.

We are aiming in action learning to convey through reflective dialogue, and a range of applications, a process by which reflection can occur. Our aim is to create the conditions for reflection that promote and encourage critical learning. This incorporates thinking, emotion, and in-the-world action that a person undertakes, while recognizing the social and political context and values within which the person lives.

The deliberate process of reflection on action may lead to a reframing or reconceptualizing about actions or situations, the potential result of which is the presenter, with the support of the set, being able to move into a different paradigm from that previously; to engage in meta-cognition (Eraut, 1994); to engage in critical dialogue (Barnett, 1997). Schön's contribution is that this meaning of reflection can happen in action as well as after action.

Reflection as a concept has emerged from the rationalist tradition in the dualism of the mind/body divide. Definitions of reflection are therefore prone to privilege the rational and cognitive over the physical, that is, in such definitions reflection is an activity of the detached mind, using reason as its tool. Alternative approaches to reflection which avoid the mind/body split have been described as a reintegration of 'cerebral ways of knowing with thinking through the body' (Michelson, 1996: 450). We assert a more holistic definition which values the senses, recognizes emotion and draws in personal experience through dialogue.

We thus define reflection in two senses: firstly, as a process by which experience is brought into consideration, and secondly, deriving from the first, the creation of meaning and conceptualization from experience and the capacity to look at things as potentially other than they appear, the latter part embodying the idea of critical reflection and potential paradigm shift. When experience is brought into consideration it will include thought, feeling and action. Moreover, some treatments suggest a static, separated quality, as if reflection-on-action can be, after the event, totally separated from the previous experience. The reality is that the presenter and set will, where the reflection is intentional for promoting learning, bring that action into the dialogue. This point further explains our circles as dimensions of the totality of experience.

In terms of reflection as part of reflective practice and, within this, reflective dialogue, the integration of mind and body (emotion/feeling and action) means that in the act of reflection we bring to that act our cognitive and affective experience.

Reflexivity

Finally, we can link the above to reflexivity. The capacity in non-traditional societies to reflect on one's condition becomes part of the discourse which yields emerging meaning. Working in action learning sets enables participants to engage more intentionally in a process where reflection on a condition can bring about new meaning and action. For example, Giddens (1992), in relation to, for example, understanding human sexuality in modern society, cites Foucault: 'Foucault is surely right to argue that discourse becomes constitutive of the social reality it portrays. Once there is a new terminology for understanding sexuality, ideas, concepts and theories couched in these terms seep into social life itself, and help reorder it.'

The meanings we give to describe our lives 'routinely enter and transform it... because they become part of the frames of action which individuals or sets adopt' (Giddens, 1992). Thus ideas about relationships between men and women have been profoundly influenced by, and influence, relationships in a way that was unrecognized in more traditional societies. The voicing of the implicit affects the explicit and becomes part of a reflective discourse.

In this chapter we have developed the notion of reflection by identifying five dimensions of reflection. We now consider the importance of social context in action learning.

Chapter 7

The social context of action learning

In this chapter we explore some of the theories that underpin our concept of action learning and how these influence the approach we recommend for reflective learning. In particular, we identify the social factors that influence learning and the context in which action learning takes place. We begin with learning theory about single and double loop learning, examine the philosophy that underpins the action learning approach, and discuss how this impacts on the power relations and politics in organizations.

How does action learning enable reflective learning for improvement and transformation? Learning theory helps us here as we turn to the idea of single and double loop learning.

Single and double loop learning

The terms single and double loop learning were first used by Argyris and Schön in 1974 to distinguish between learning for improving the way things are done, and learning that transforms the situation. They based the idea on the concept of feedback loops in control engineering, cited in *Design for a Brain* (Ashby, 1952). Single loop 'instrumental' learning, while it achieves immediate improvement, leaves underlying values and ways of seeing things unchanged. Improvement learning may involve reflection on the given task but is not likely to change it. Double loop learning is learning where assumptions about ways of seeing things are challenged and underlying values are changed (Brockbank and McGill, 1998). Double loop learning, in questioning 'givens' or 'taken-for-granteds' (tfgs), has the potential to bring about a profound shift in underlying values by cracking their paradigms or 'ways of seeing the world' (here 'world' is used to denote the realities of an individual, group or organization). This we are defining as reflective learning for transformation.

Single loop learning or day-to-day maintenance learning, for improvement, meeting goals and altering practice on the basis of experience, enables progress to be made. The concept of effective single loop learning has been described graphically in a well-known diagram by Kolb (1984), where goals are set on the basis of theory, action is taken and, on the basis of this experience, and reflection, a new action or plan is devised. For day-to-day learning the loop is productive and the learner gains competence and confidence, ie this is reflective learning for improvement. The process is illustrated in Figure 7.1.

In action learning terms, the presenter starts by telling the story from their experience, engaging in reflection and coming to some new insights (generalization) which can then be tested in action following the set meeting. The cyclical nature of learning illustrated here is rarely realized in practice, as typical training and development programmes talk about the cycle but are actually an engagement in a linear process *with the ends joined up* (Hawkins, 1994). Hence even single loop learning with a reflective element is not always achieved.

We refer now, with permission, to Peter Hawkins' original diagram to illustrate double loop learning in Figure 7.2.

The arrows in the lower circle indicate day-to-day functioning in single loop learning. When conditions are favourable, assumptions or taken-for-granteds are questioned, and the learner may swing out of lower circle orbit and begin to traverse the upper circle in double loop learning mode. The learner has 'come outside of their box'. The option remains of returning to the single loop when appropriate, perhaps to test a new theory in the time-honoured way, and continue to achieve improvement with a new understanding. The single loop orbit is contained and can be traversed within, say, a development project, setting goals within a given cycle of activity or achieving a level of understanding within a professional field. The double loop orbit would occur when reconsidering the whole project with a view to major change, or even reconsidering an organization's purpose, structure or culture, ie learning for transformation.

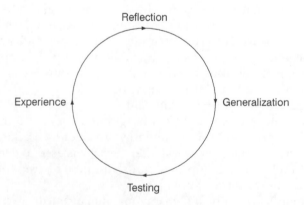

Figure 7.1   *Single loop learning*
Source: Brockbank and McGill, 1998

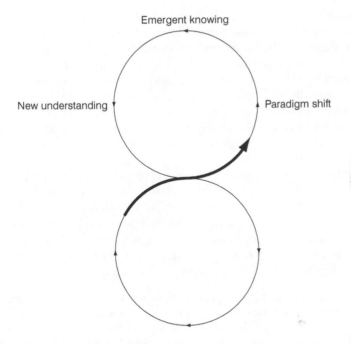

Figure 7.2   *Double loop learning*
Source: Adapted from an original idea by P Hawkins, 1997, in Brockbank and McGill, 1998

What is needed to enable the learner to shoot out of the single orbit, and traverse the exciting and potentially disturbing orbit of double loop learning? If we were to pursue our analogy of orbits and rocket science, the answer suggests that what is required is *energy* to fuel the 'burn' of a changed trajectory. Where is the source of this energy to come from?

Emotion and action learning

The evidence suggests that 'emotion and motivation are inherently connected' (Giddens, 1992: 201) and that double loop or transformative learning can be triggered by strong emotion, through trauma or 'peak' experiences (Brookfield, 1987: 7). The language used to describe such learning indicates the strong emotive content in comments such as 'passion to learn', 'hunger for truth', 'thirst for knowledge'. In addition, the process of questioning and challenging the taken-for-granteds can stimulate strong emotions, disturbance, distress and also joy and exhilaration (Brookfield, 1987: 8). We are told that a certain degree of energy or excitement is necessary for learning to occur, so that a crisis may generate organizational learning. However, research suggests that stress is a major block to learning, and an organization where fear is rife and staff are operating under pressure is unlikely to engage in transformatory learning (Brundage and Mackeracher, 1980). So there is a fine line here between reflective learning, which stimulates emotional energy and transformation, and stressful situations which inhibit learning. Individual learners may judge where their own fine line exists and this will be different for everyone. Feelings of boredom are a sign that no learning is taking place and it has been said that 'all progress in business life comes from kicking a habit, from doing something new and refreshingly different. Because if you do what you've always done, you'll get what you've always got' (Browning, 1998).

Learning and development does not take place in a vacuum. In action learning we emphasize the emotional and social as well as the cognitive context. Set members can benefit from interaction with others through dialogue and the structured synergy that can be available to an action learning set. This structured process is often conducive to enabling a set member to learn, develop and change. Vince and Martin (1993) capture this aspect of action learning:

> One of the most powerful aspects of the Action Learning model is the clarity of roles, structure and timescales it provides. Its highly structured format often provides containment for the anxiety that is generated in the learning environment. The managers we work with appreciate the model because it is an approach that creates familiarity and trust while promoting practical reflection on management practice. The model therefore makes it possible for managers to stay with their uncertainty about taking risks, about their struggles. (Vince and Martin, 1993: 211)

The idea of 'containment' has been explained by French and Vince (1999) as a method of engaging with a range of unconscious and conscious organizational processes. Action learning can provide a temporary container for learning from experience, in the here and now, exploring what is happening in the moment. 'Such exploration stimulates perception and interpretation by all involved, of the feelings they have, the projections that are in play, and the issues that are at stake' (French and Vince, 1999: 5). We discuss these terms in detail in Chapter 8.

Vince and Martin (1993) suggest that traditional approaches to action learning emphasize the rational, task-orientated aspect of learning, in, for example, the learning cycle. We have emphasized the importance of process as well as structure and the interaction of emotion and feelings in working with personal issues that enable learning and change. In this chapter we are stressing the need to make explicit issues of power that exist in set members' working context as well as being represented in sets themselves. We support the view of Vince and Martin that the emotional and political (power) aspects of action learning need to be made explicit.

Emotions and feelings will surround the action learning process for a variety of reasons. A set member may be; anxious about sharing an issue with the set; unused to taking responsibility for her learning; not used to speaking out or challenging another set member. There are two possibilities:

1. The anxiety created may be redressed by the trust and confidentiality within the set. In such a situation the set will be able to encourage the learning of the presenter or set member through the stages: uncertainty → risk → struggle → to insight → a new way of seeing the(ir) world and, ultimately, empowerment.
2. On the other hand, if the conditions are not appropriate, the anxiety may lead to flight or fight (Bion, 1961), ie withdrawal or aggression expressed in some form, denial or avoidance, defensiveness or resistance, each of which or in combination 'creates the right conditions for his or her own willing ignorance' (Vince and Martin, 1993: 210).

When facilitators make explicit these two possibilities, one which enables learning and empowerment, the other which inhibits learning and empowerment, set members are likely 'to make sense of processes of change, both personal and organizational' (Vince and Martin, 1993: 211). If the set can make explicit the emotional aspects as well as the task-orientated aspects of work in the set, this is likely to encourage the set member to address the emotional aspects at work where previously these may have been ignored. Attending to feelings is a key characteristic of our approach to action learning. Traditional learning prioritizes knowledge over action and emotion, while action learning allows set members to learn in all three domains of learning (Brockbank and McGill, 1998). Action learning attends to what presenter and set members are feeling, as well as what they are doing and saying.

So what other barriers are there to prevent double loop learning for potential set members?

Defensive reasoning

The tendency to overlook the obvious, the taken-for-granteds (tfgs), is supremely human. Some of the tfgs form quite powerful defences, known as defensive reasoning, which are difficult and painful to dislodge.

As learners, the prospect of really looking at what is taken for granted in our work, and analysing our defensive reasoning (Argyris, 1991), is threatening on four counts:

- We may lose control.
- We may not win.
- We may not be able to suppress negative feelings.
- We may not be rational.

For chief executives, senior managers and directors, trained in the Western rational system, such threats are real and powerful, even in comparison to external pressure from their shareholders. Leaders resort to defensive reasoning in order to protect against these threats, maintaining comfort and, in the process, cloning another generation of managers in their own image. For leaders to engage in reflection, they need to be confident in themselves and able to tolerate doubt and uncertainty about their decisions. It has been said that leaders are traditionally insecure, power-hungry and not prone to self-analysis, and this works against them engaging in reflective learning. (Coopey, 1995, quoting Kets de Vries, 1991).

Leaders who can face up to the possibility that they might have so-called irrational feelings, and express them, are prepared to display their vulnerability. To engage in double loop learning calls for a degree of vulnerability in those at the top of the organization that seeks to learn, and learning will be nurtured in organizations where defensive reasoning is undermined, with the chief executive in the lead. This is done by naming what is taken for granted in the work context, and staying with the discomfort that may be engendered by such naming. An example is the recognition by senior staff that a punitive appraisal system is demotivating employees and a commitment to replace it with a developmental programme. Needless to say, such moves can lead to differences in the organization, and this may lead to conflict. Where conflicts arise, the political process in organizations rarely offers facilitation for resolving differences, so how is the organization to learn?

A programme of action learning sets in an organization offers opportunities for double loop learning for both individuals and the organization, if the conditions for reflective dialogue and reflective learning are present.

What approach to action learning will provide these conditions? We now look at the conditions for reflective learning.

Conditions for reflective learning

First we revisit our definition as given in Chapter 1:

> Action learning is a continuous process of learning and reflection that happens with the support of a group or 'set' of colleagues, working on real issues, with the intention of getting things done. The voluntary participants in the group or 'set' learn with and from each other and take forward an important issue with the support of the other members of the set. The collaborative process, which recognizes set members' social context, helps people to take an active stance towards life, helps overcome the tendency to be passive towards the pressures of life and work, and aims to benefit both the organization and the individual.

On the basis of this definition, our action learning philosophy suggests that the set's activities will:

- maintain the role of relationship in the development of the person rather than adopting the modernist belief in individualism;
- recognize that, as learners, we share in the construction of our world, rather than believing in the idea of objective reality;
- acknowledge the power of discourse rather than the denial of power relations.

We discuss these terms below, and how the action learning methods we promote can address them.

Modernity and individualism

Drawing on Fetherston (2002), we may define modernity as: a set of interrelated discourses which generate a 'regime of truth' from social and historical circumstances which gave rise to industrialization and capitalism. This regime of truth involved the organization and control of employees, requiring them to perform specific and regulated roles. An important consequence of modernist thinking is the cult of individualism, where the individual is identified as the source of disorder and the only resource for curing it, making the individual solely responsible for outcomes in the workplace. While recognizing the importance of individual responsibility at work, the dogma of individualism may lead to a work environment where set members feel helpless, confused and stressed. Why should this be?

Where individualism is the only theory available, the social context, with its power nexus, is largely ignored and kept invisible, particularly to those who are powerless. This is known as a power horizon (Smail, 2001: 67) and is kept in position by offering a version of objective reality as truth, known as the prevailing discourse, a version which maintains the sources of power invisible. The arch-proponent of individualism was Margaret Thatcher, who famously declared that 'there is no such thing as society'.

The idea of a power horizon which is always just out of our sight suggests a prevailing discourse which maintains it in position, not unlike the unfortunate hero in *The Truman Show* who was unaware that his life was actually a TV show. The power horizon divides our real-life experience at work, the nearby power effects on an individual, from the distant power effects exerted by larger political and social factors, keeping the latter invisible (Smail, 2001: 67). The individual's power horizon, through the prevailing discourse, ensures that distant power effects are out of sight, leaving the individual no option but to concentrate on closer agents who are often themselves powerless and held within their own power horizon. An example of this is a set member's perception of her manager as 'difficult' when he makes demands, while the manager is himself struggling to meet targets set by his superior, who is responding to board-level panic, a consequence of share-price insecurity. The set member's power horizon ensures that she attends primarily to her manager, without 'seeing' the more distant causes of her difficulty. How does action learning help her?

The collaborative nature of the action learning process has the potential to expand the power horizon for individual set members, enabling them to see, often for the first time, where the source of their difficulty or frustration lies. This is achieved in action learning by recognizing and challenging the prevailing discourse

The prevailing discourse and objective reality

The idea of a prevailing discourse comes from social constructivist ideas which depart from traditional approaches to personal development, by challenging the presumption of objective reality, and focusing on language or discourse as the medium through which learners construct new understandings (Burr, 1995). Such a stance holds that our realities are deeply influenced by our life experience, past and present. Thus learning contexts, like action learning, are themselves socially constructed, so that 'we create rather than discover ourselves' and we do this through engagement-with-others, using language in discourse (Burr, 1995: 28). The powerful role of language and discourse lies in its taken-for-granted nature. The prevailing discourse in any system is invisible to its users, being beyond the power horizon (Smail, 2001). For learners the context is defined by the concepts and 'givens' of the prevailing discourse. An example of an invisible prevailing discourse is the executive washroom, where only those above certain grades are admitted and this is accepted without question by those excluded. How does a prevailing discourse become established?

The prevailing discourse is defined as 'a set of meaning, metaphors, representations, images, stories, statements etc that in some way together produce a particular version' of events, person or class of person (Burr, 1995: 48). Examples of how such discourse is used can be seen in terms like 'attitude problem', downsizing', regulating, on-message, globalization, unionized, eco-warrior and, as above, 'executive washroom'. Hence as learners we exist in a system or paradigm which is not value-free, where power is exercised that can influence our progress and affect our development. If we accept that our context is defined by the prevailing discourse, this has implications for our understanding of self. Existing in an ever-changing social context, the self is ever-changing, responding and influencing its environment, being constructed continuously through interaction with others. Smail (2001) maintains that 'our environment has much more to do with our coming-to-be as people than we do as authors of our own fate' (Smail, 2001: 23).

Action learning, through collaborative reflective procedures, which we describe in detail in Chapter 5, seeks to offer learners an alternative discourse. Such a paradigm shift has the potential to challenge the taken-for-granted assumptions of the prevailing discourse in which each set member is embedded. The action learning model, where each set member has dedicated time to work with his or her issues, in a context of acceptance and challenge without judgement (itself an alternative prevailing discourse), allows the presenter to reconsider some of the givens of his or her situation.

It is important here to recognize that we are not proposing an either/or argument, but we do say that action learning allows for environmental influences to be acknowledged and their subjective effects given voice. In an action learning set, the recognition that 'the self' can take an infinite variety of forms enables set members to access their potential and challenge what constrains their learning.

Action learning is at its best when the set is able to challenge the dominant paradigm in which set members are living and working. An example of this is 'presenteeism', the practice whereby employees believe that working long hours over their working day makes them more productive and will get them promotion. In action learning the subjective experience of set members is recognized and valued, giving them the option to seek improvement or transformation. Where set members are struggling with their work/life balance, the realization of 'presenteeism' as nothing more than a paradigm may lead them to transform their approach to work.

How action learning promotes double loop learning

Action learning supports both reflective learning for improvement and reflective learning for transformation (Brockbank *et al*, 2002). Cox (1981, cited in Fetherston, 2002) has identified the limitation of moves towards change that seek only improvement of existing practices. Such learnings, he maintains, are 'discursively bound' and knowledge outcomes from them are rational, efficient, controllable and fixed. We concur with this view but accept that such learning for improvement is part of the larger picture of learning. We have discussed reflective learning for improvement and reflective learning for transformation elsewhere (Brockbank and McGill, 1998; Brockbank *et al*, 2002) and recognize the value of both. Cox (1981) maintains that to achieve transformation, there needs to be a learning process which addresses the subjective world of the learner, challenges the tfgs (the taken-for-granteds which maintain the power horizon) and thereby problematizes the dominant framework, rather than the individuals within it.

Such reflective learning for transformation through action learning can offer alternative paradigms with the potential to transform institutions and social meanings. Set members who engage in such transformation have been able to see beyond, above, below and beside the taken-for-granted assumptions, and the outcomes may be threatening to the status quo, as they often choose to leave. Organizations which aspire to be 'learning organizations' are likely to cope with such challenges and benefit from them. The concept of learning as additional insight is replaced by learning as 'outsight' where the learner has identified the environment, beyond their power horizon, as part of their difficulty/frustration (Smail, 2001: 8–9) and this might enable people to 'live their lives as themselves, and understand their own experience as valid' (Smail, 2001: 8–9).

Action learning, power and organizational learning

For effective organizational learning there is a need to recognize power relations rather than power as a 'given' commodity, which leaves the individual feeling helpless. All social and personal relationships, including work relationships, have a power element and the action learning set is no exception.

Action learning sets have a political dimension, in that they represent, interpersonally and in the set, the sense of power and powerlessness that is found in any other group or organization. Individuals can feel a sense of power or powerlessness *vis-à-vis* others. This can also be innocent in the sense that an individual may not be aware of their position or role but nevertheless live it. Issues of power can be implicit across the set as well. A set that is aware of power issues within the set and works explicitly with these politics will, as Vince and Martin express it, recognize that: 'The political nature of action learning is expressed through the strategic choice available to learning groups to move in a direction that promotes learning, or a direction that discourages learning. In other words, movement towards either risk or denial/avoidance is often a political, as well as an emotional, act on behalf of the individual' (Vince and Martin, 1993: 213).

Examples of power differences in a set could include: a white male set member unaware that the issue he brings to the set and his use of language inadvertently puts down women; a set member who dominates a set to the exclusion of others; a facilitator and/or set members who recognize (or not) an example of racism by a set member but who do not challenge the set member (or are unaware of the racist nature of the statement).

The set may move to challenge the set member and (if necessary) the facilitator. If the conditions are appropriate the set can help the person and the set in a direction that promotes learning and empowerment for the set and the set member. We have again a potential for anxiety in the person wanting to take the risk to raise the issue and challenge the behaviour as well as possible anxiety on the part of the receiver of the challenge and possibly other members of the set who hear the challenge and await a response.

Take one of the behaviours above (eg the behaviour exhibited by the white male set member). Confronting, however appropriately, the behaviour means that the individual challenged and perhaps the person expressing the challenge may nevertheless feel vulnerable and anxious. The set that is aware of these political dimensions is, despite the uncertainty felt and the risk taken, potentially more likely to move into the process described above, leading to insight and new learning that is empowering. Working implicitly without recognizing this political dimension may mean that the set colludes with power relations that limit the effectiveness of the set. Furthermore, if sets implicitly replicate power relations elsewhere, the opportunity to work on the 'external' power relations will also be limited as the set will simply mirror that which is often implicit in organizations. Providing this political perspective in the action learning process gives set members the opportunity to reflect upon the 'personal and institutional significance of different managerial (or other set member) experience (eg black/white, female/male, disabled/able-bodied, gay/straight) for the very practice of change within their work' (Vince and Martin, 1993: 214, parentheses in original).

It is important to acknowledge the interrelationship between emotional feelings and political power in a set. Emotions promoting or discouraging learning are affected by the internal politics of the set as well as the emotional. In our example above, if the set did not disturb the 'innocence' of the set member about his sexism, the set member(s) who wished to but did not confront him is likely to experience feelings of resentment and anger that remain silent or are expressed in another way. The set moves into the limiting mode of learning and the politics remain as they were.

Let us examine briefly the term 'innocence' used above. There is still a tendency to make assumptions in organizations about 'the way things are done around here'. Managers and staff fit into implicit norms of behaviour that actually represent and reflect the power of those who run organizations. Our society is still in transition in this respect – some organizations are endeavouring to acknowledge and work with difference to the benefit of the previously disadvantaged, while other organizations are still living innocently with the assumptions of the past. This has been referred to as 'the power of innocence' (James and Baddeley, 1991: 115):

> People's personal positions are arrived at and sustained by being in a group of people whose understanding of the world is similar to their own. Thus their position is both sustained by other group members ('That's the way the world is') or even attributed to the group ('If you're a manager this is what you think'). The last thing the fish discovers is water. Innocence derives its power through being comfortably and unreflectively surrounded by others of like mind. From this stance individuals cannot see themselves colluding with the larger flow of institutional direction and its consequences. [parentheses in original]

'This is the way things are done around here' is being replaced by the acknowledgement that those who created the world in which such a condition could prevail are having to reflect upon those norms and share power with those who previously did not share power with them. An obvious example is where women are increasingly finding but challenging the 'glass ceiling' above them and white men are discovering the 'innocent' power they have held as being untenable. That ceiling is, for some men, unwittingly applied at the personal level but is also institutionally discriminatory. A similar position applies in respect of race and disability as well as age and sexual orientation.

The key is to overcome the discriminatory practices without resorting to scapegoating or blaming of those who have held power traditionally as well as enabling opportunity for those who have not shared power. For both groups the result can be empowering and create a necessary pluralism. 'As the cloak of hegemony is discarded the individual can re-centre,... rediscover themselves and build their own connections, relationships and identity. This may involve a personal crisis but losing one's innocence need not entail an enduring loss of personal power' (James and Baddeley, 1991: 117).

This re-centring is further enhanced by the explicit recognition of the emotional and political aspects of learning and development in organizations. Where action learning procedures recognize such power relations, through recognition of the discursive context, this may enable set members to transform the dominant paradigm, the tfgs in which they are embedded. Set members may set a political agenda for change if that is what they desire (Townley, 1994). We note here our use of the term political, often perceived as negative, and consciously wish to draw attention to the way that discourse itself promotes particular power relations, by naming and then silencing unwelcome voices as 'political'. Where the learner becomes aware of the reality of such discourse and identifies practices which dominate relationships in the workplace, through action learning, there is hope of personal and organizational transformation. The importance of a learning context which addresses the power of an embedded discourse has been recognized by others (Reynolds, 1997a) and action learning is recommended as one way of enabling the critical approach needed to realize its existence.

Many writings on learning and development, particularly management development, treat that development in an individualistic and decontextualized manner. In other words, the idea that individual managers are responsible for their own development suggests that their progress is a product of their own motivation, commitment and drive. Some of the tools for enabling managers to determine their progress, eg learning styles, assume a neutral context, as if the manager was somehow the same gender, class and race and that the notions of diversity, status and relative opportunity did not exist. There is also a tendency to ignore the impact of discourse, culture and ideology on learners.

The factors of class, race, gender, role, identity and relative opportunity impact on learning. In addition, the organization is not neutral territory. Organizations have their formal and informal power structures and relationships in which employees are actors, as well as organizational agents and respondents. Engaging in reflective learning and development, through action learning, which challenges the dominant discourse, may impact upon those structures and relationships, particularly if development is related to promotion as well as operational effectiveness. The organization will learn to the degree that 'it can reconcile individual and organizational needs to release and support the inherent energy and creativity of its individual members' (Pedler *et al*, 1990: 172). The assumption that individual and organizational learning goals are compatible has been questioned and the complexity of negotiating within the tension explored. Antonacopolou (1999) has identified the positive and negative attitudes of managers towards the need to learn. Her findings illustrate how the interaction of personal and organizational factors create conditions that affect individuals' receptivity to learning, and are situation-specific, so that individuals respond differently depending on the situation. The managers in her survey reported that they were more significantly affected by organizational culture and the attitude of top managers than personal barriers to learning. Also, the way that the interaction between personal and organizational factors was perceived by managers was identified as one of the issues that determine an individual's attitude towards learning. These findings should alert us to the danger of assuming that responses to learning are, like the concept of 'learning styles', simplistic and uniform (Reynolds, 1997a).

This brings us to the essential tension that exists between organizational purpose and self-development. How the organization generates its purpose may influence the commitment of its members. There will be difference and conflict in any organization, particularly about its purpose and chances of survival. The inevitable conflict between individual need and corporate purpose has been noted by John Heron as follows: 'what makes an organization enlightened is that it has built-in procedures for acknowledging such conflict and working constructively with it' (Heron, 1977: 7).

The political process of learning from difference, challenge and conflict is unfortunately dubbed as 'politicking' and viewed negatively, an example of how discourse can silence voices. The power of discourse lies in its connection to how an organization is run. A discourse is so embedded in our discursive culture that it is invisible and hidden from us, beyond the power horizon (Smail, 2001). Therein lies its power. As Foucault put it, 'Power is tolerable only on condition that it masks a substantial part of itself' (Foucault, 1976: 86). The challenge of embedded discourse is the 'uncovering' of its taken-for-granted status, often by drawing on alternative discourses, considering multiple meanings and others' stories. These processes are typical of action learning activity.

Where the embedded discourse is resistant to challenge, the organization will be unaware of its culture, convinced of the 'truth' or validity of its position, and this ideological belief will be enjoyed by many of its members. Organizations that seek culture change and transformation are seeking to dislodge the prevailing discourse and generate a new 'view of the world'. The difficulty is that the very structures and procedures that maintain the prevailing discourse may work against the prospect of transformation. French and Vince describe this paradox as 'that organizations espouse and want learning and change at the same time as they prevent themselves from embracing them' (1999: 18). For example, judgemental appraisals and a blame culture will resist openness and honest debriefing as too risky. Additionally, it can be argued that discourses are really powerful when they are not perceived and, therefore, not perceived as a problem. Under these circumstances there would be no intention to change them, and hence they continue to be 'natural' or 'the only way to do things'. Action learning, in revealing them as not the only way, may open a Pandora's box for organizations. If individuals and groups are encouraged to challenge existing ideologies then they may become aware of some of the other realities of their corporate system. Those enlightened organizations which have the courage to open up their culture to critically reflective learning will be taking a risky step towards transformation and future survival.

How action learning promotes critical reflection

The humanistic values of action learning are married to some ideas of critical theory to promote critically reflective learning. Action learning adopts the humanistic values as follows:

- A belief that people are driven to grow and develop rather than stagnate.
- A person is a whole person, not just the part that is doing the job.
- Goodwill is how most people operate.
- People are abundant rather than an assumption that they are in deficit.
- People have spiritual dimensions in their lives.

The humanist values above are recognized within the structure of action learning, and are usually recorded within the ground rules agreed by set members at the start of a cycle of set meetings. Examples of such rules are given in Chapters 4 and 8. The values above have been described as person-centred (Rogers, 1983). Person-centred means that the learning approach recognizes every set member as unique, whole and having the resources they need to learn and develop. Rogers' conditions promote a person-centred climate in a set, thereby making possible the release of the individual's capacity for learning and development. His person-centred conditions are:

- congruence – genuineness, being real, sharing feelings and attitudes rather than opinions and judgements;
- unconditional positive regard – acceptance and 'prizing' of the other;

- empathy – understanding the other's feelings and experience, as well as communication of that understanding.

These three conditions are described in detail in Chapter 8. Rogers also gave some interesting insights into 'conditions of worth' as part of his model of personality.

Rogers' model of the person

Rogers' model of the person stipulates that we are influenced by how we are nurtured from the day of our birth. He maintains that every human being is reared under 'conditions of worth', so that their self-concept is based on conforming to behaviour which is 'approved of' by the significant others in their life (usually a parent or parent-substitute). This socially acceptable self, formed for fear of losing the love of parent, is often in opposition to the true 'organismic self' which is suppressed by conditions of worth. The struggle to live up to this idealized self is carried forward into adult life. In action learning the idealized self-concept is revealed in the 'shoulds' and 'oughts' and 'got to's' which may appear in a presenter's story. The use of 'should' suggests that the presenter may be speaking under conditions of worth – rather than from her true organismic self (Rogers, 1992). In action learning, when Rogers' three conditions above are met, such conditions of worth are undermined, allowing the presenter to access the energy of her organismic self. (Note: the presenter may well choose to follow the path of her 'should' but has made the choice herself after reflecting on it.)

Carl Rogers in his book *Freedom to Learn for the 80s* emphasized the importance of relationship in learning: 'the facilitation of significant learning rests upon... qualities that exist in the personal *relationship* between the facilitator and learner [our italics]' (Rogers, 1983: 121) and that this is not an easy option: 'the person-centred way... is something one grows into. It is a set of values, not easy to achieve, placing emphasis on the dignity of the individual, the importance of personal choice, the significance of responsibility, the joy of creativity. It is a philosophy built on the foundation of the democratic way, empowering each individual' (Rogers, 1983: 95).

A full understanding of Rogers' thought suggests that any learning approach should include a recognition of the social, cultural and political contexts (mentioned above) as part of empathy and unconditional positive regard. However, the usual interpretation of Rogers tends to leave out the significance of the sociopolitical context and this has been critiqued as lacking the 'bite' of a more radical version of his humanistic thought. Such a radical version would include critical theory and reflective awareness of the social context, described above, where power relations may affect the individual's ability to act. We discuss below how the action learning process can incorporate such critical reflection with humanistic values and practice.

Critical reflection

Reynolds (1997b) and others have drawn on the idea of a critical theory as put forward by Habermas (1972) to identify critical reflection. A critical theory can be defined as 'a reflective theory which gives agents (*learners*) a kind of knowledge inherently productive of enlightenment and emancipation' (Geuss, 1981: 2, italics added). This is based on Habermas' idea that 'reflecting on the social and political forces which affect and often distort communication between people can lead to more authentically democratic relationships' (Reynolds, 1997b: 313).

In order to achieve the reflection needed for this emancipatory activity, Hindmarsh (1993) and Kemmis (1985) offer three types of reflection:

1. instrumental – concerned with achievement of goals/solutions eg improvement;
2. consensual – questioning ends as well as means, eg culture change programmes;
3. critical – challenging assumptions and the prevailing discourse.

The recommended type is number 3, critical reflection, which Alvesson and Willmott (1992: 435) suggest 'seeks to encourage the questioning of taken-for-granted assumptions' (1992: 11) so as 'to reflect critically on how the reality of the social world, including the construction of the self, is socially produced and therefore open to transformation'. Reynolds (1997b) gives us the characteristics of an approach which promotes such transformation:

- questioning the tfgs;
- analysing power relations;
- collaborative learning;

and notes that action learning offers the necessary conditions.

The word critical is difficult in a humanistic setting. How is a set member to critique a colleague while adhering to humanistic principles as given above? A critical theory approach recommends a dialogue where validity claims can be investigated, hence enabling set members to assess the prevailing discourse. In using the critical theory approach above, set members are able to highlight the political nature of seemingly neutral techniques appearing in the workplace, like portfolio working, call centre systems, performance-related pay, reward and appraisal, teleworking etc.

How does the critical theory approach work in action learning?

- By exposing unequal power relations – previously hidden behind the power horizon (see above).
- By challenging what is deemed 'natural'.

- By accepting the reality of conflict through dialogue.
- By appreciating the power of language and the prevailing discourse.

So a humanist approach, which includes potential challenges to embedded power relations through revealing a prevailing discourse, is how action learning enables reflective learning for set members. The process of action learning offers opportunities for set members to reflect with others for both improvement and transformation. As meaning is created in relation to others, reflection is part of the process and meta-reflection is possible as an additional dimension of reflection. We discuss dimensions of reflection in Chapter 6.

In this chapter we have visited some of the philosophies and theories which underpin our approach to action learning. We move now in Part III to how action learning can be facilitated.

PART III

Facilitating action learning

Chapter 8

Group dynamics in action learning

In this chapter we draw on a range of psychological theory to see how group dynamics relates to action learning. It has been one of our intentions to take away any mystery there may be about action learning and about how sets work. This chapter may be of interest to aspiring facilitators who are curious about the way their group behaves, as well as possibly being worth while for set members with some experience of action learning sets who would like to explore what is happening in terms of group dynamics.

Action learning is a particular form of group working that is highly structured and supportive of participant set members. The structured way in which the set works is particularly important in the early life of a set when participants may be apprehensive about working in groups. Yet with practice and some continuity it can be a challenging and non-collusive environment beneficial to its members. Chapters 1 and 4 describe the basic processes of a set meeting. If these procedures are broadly adhered to, the set can begin to work safely. Set members may like to refer to Chapters 9 and 10 for a discussion about being effective in a set either as presenter or as set member.

Group psychology

The action learning structure, while primarily humanistic in philosophy and intent, utilizes ideas from the psychodynamic and existential fields, as well as behavioural concepts. The psychodynamic approach to group behaviour emphasizes:

- the significance of past (childhood) experience on present behaviour and feelings in an action learning set;
- the existence of unconscious feelings and motives in the set;
- the potential for transference within the set – we explain what this means below.

Action learning adopts the *psychodynamic* principle of a 'holding' environment, through firmly agreed boundaries, particularly in the early stages of the set's development (de Board, 1978). In addition, action learning facilitators will benefit from an understanding of defence mechanisms in groups, another concept from the psychodynamic field, and 'containment', particularly at the 'storming' stage (Barnes, Ernst and Hyde, 1999). We discuss these psychodynamic ideas in more detail below.

The *existential* approach confirms our social constructivist stance, discussed in Chapter 7, by emphasizing the importance of relationship in action learning, where members explore issues of choice, identity, isolation, freedom and responsibility. The basic assumption here is that set members create and construct their own worlds and are therefore, as intentional beings, responsible for their actions. Action learning strives to avoid 'rescue' or 'blame' and recognizes the human condition of 'angst' or anxiety as part of living. An existential stance accepts that an action learning set will experience an active life, what has been called the 'performing' stage, and will ultimately end, the mourning stage of development (Yalom, 1995; Van Deurzen-Smith, 1997). We explore these existential ideas in more detail below.

The *behaviourist* approach is represented in action learning by a recognition that habits and beliefs are learnt and therefore can be unlearnt by set members if they so desire. In addition, the idea of imitation and modelling is how set members develop their managerial and facilitation skills by being in the set. Action learning incorporates behaviourist principles in its recognition of the power of modelling in that facilitator behaviour can be imitated by set members and skilled behaviour can be learnt by imitation (Bandura and Walters, 1963). We discuss how this happens in a set below.

Action learning adopts the *humanistic* principles of abundance in personal resources and experience, rather than deficiency of them; a belief in the human potential to grow and develop as a whole person; and a positive attitude to human endeavour in all its forms (Rowan, 2001). These principles inform the action learning structure where each set member has protected time, where the set's resources are at their disposal, and set members work without judgement but offer challenge and support in equal measure. We discuss the way action learning uses the humanistic approach to groups in more detail below.

In our discussion below, we draw on all four sources to make sense of individual and group behaviours in an action learning set.

Our philosophy

As discussed in Chapter 7, we take a social constructionist view of learning, so that set members are assumed to be active creators of their realities and these realities are deeply influenced by their life experience. The set is a learning context which is socially constructed in which set members are invited to 'create rather than discover' themselves, through engagement-with-others (Burr, 1995: 28). For reflective learning, the recognition that 'the self' may take an infinite variety of forms, that our conceptual space is created from our language, and that our context is defined by the prevailing discourse enables set members to access their potential and challenge what constrains their learning. The prevailing discourse is defined as 'a set of meanings, metaphors, representations, images, stories, statements and so on that, in some way together produce a particular version' (Burr, 1995: 48) of events, person, or class of person. Each action learning set is likely to develop its own prevailing discourse during the life of the set.

The social contructionist stance described in Chapter 7 gives action learning its particular values, ie a critical stance towards taken-for-granted knowledge, the potential of humans to self-develop, a resistance to objectivism, and a focus on social activity. The social nature of action learning offers opportunities for the set members to reflect upon their learning not only by themselves, but with others. As meaning is created in relation to others, reflection and the creation of meaning is inevitably a social process. The action learning set in which such reflection occurs is also a group and we now turn to the nature of the group process.

Group working has inherent characteristics which differ markedly from traditional ways of learning such as lecturing or directive training. The significance of group work for learning and development has been explored at length elsewhere (Hartley, 1997; Luft, 1984) and here we simply recognize that, when we arrange a group in the way described in Chapter 4 and facilitate communication within it, group effects, known as group dynamics, affect the individuals in the group and the group as a whole. A group behaves rather like a person, with distinctive and recognizable characteristics, as well as having a significant impact on the individuals within it (Bion, 1961; Egan, 1977; Foulkes, 1975).

First, we explore the psychodynamic concepts of boundaries, a holding environment, containment and defence mechanisms, ideas borrowed from psychodynamic psychology (Stafford-Clark, 1965; Fordham, 1982; Winnicott, 1965; Bowlby, 1979). Thereafter we identify the humanistic approach to group dynamics, including existential ideas, and we complete our exploration with a brief comment about how behaviourism plays its part in action learning.

Psychodynamic concepts in action learning

The most dramatic effect experienced by individuals in groups is feelings of fear and lack of safety, and we recognize that the degree of these feelings will vary with membership of the group, and between individuals. This effect exists in everyday social groups, though not articulated, and accounts for some of the discomfort experienced in some social situations, committee meetings and work groups. Defensive forms of behaviour in groups are usually triggered by anxieties, either anxiety triggered by being-in-a-group or archaic anxiety with its roots in the past (Heron, 1999). Anxiety about being-in-a-group may take the form of 'self-talk' such as: Will I be accepted, wanted, liked? Will I understand what's going on? Will I be able to do what's required? Archaic anxiety is the echo of past distress and comes from the fear of being rejected or overwhelmed. These anxieties are real for anyone who takes part in a group where all members are given voice, as in action learning. The casual comment or joking aside may cause hurt as it can trigger damaging self-talk as described above.

Taking account of this knowledge, in order to facilitate learning using a group format, the facilitator may need to accommodate the fears of group members by establishing, very early, an atmosphere of trust and safety, so that learners can contribute and all can benefit. The boundaries provided in an action learning set go a long way towards providing safety for set members. At an early stage (see Chapters 1 and 4), in order to establish boundaries, the group should be invited to agree on ground rules for working in a group. Why is this necessary?

A 'holding' environment for action learning

When set members are arranged in group format, and are offered the possibility of being congruent (discussed in Chapter 9), it is necessary also to protect them from psychological harm. By this we do not mean nervous breakdowns or the like, but we do recognize the potential for group dynamics to trigger the hurt child in every human being (Miller, 1990), and this may include the facilitator. Nitsun (1989) has compared the dynamics of early group formation with early development in infancy, where the group, like a newborn infant, is endeavouring to integrate. The effort to 'form' as a group may trigger anxieties from the past. The set can be provided with a 'good enough' environment using the concept of 'holding', ie taking care of set members, through boundaries and ground rules (Winnicott, 1971). In addition, these ground rules provide what has been described as a 'secure base' in which set members can feel safe enough to develop themselves (Bowlby, 1979). Hence, when launching an action learning set, the facilitator begins by discussing the model of learning she proposes, gaining agreement to it, and establishing with group members a series of ground rules for group behaviour. We are aware of a variety of versions of such guidelines and below we list some of the items that may appear when a set is invited to contribute (usually in brainstorming style) to the question: 'What conditions would you want to have in place while working in this set?'

Clearly, set members will need to understand what the action learning style of working is, and we assume this has been established, including clarifying that responsibility for learning lies with the set member rather than the facilitator, and this can be a revealing moment for everyone. Some set members may want to be passively fed, while others are familiar with experiential group learning techniques. The brainstorming process, where all contributions are accepted, after discussion, should produce some of the following ground rules (and this list is not exhaustive):

Typical ground rules for set meetings (see also Chapter 4, Starting a set)

Confidentiality
One person at a time
Listen to others when they speak
Be honest and open
Don't attack others
Challenge constructively
No compulsion to speak
Feelings may be expressed
Feelings not dismissed
Awareness/acceptance of diversity
Observe time boundaries

A number of these items will require discussion to agree their meaning in the set. Taking a humanistic stance, there is no right or wrong meaning. Providing persons are respected, difference is recognized and context is articulated, then whatever the group decide is the meaning to be observed; this conforms to the person-centred model we recommend.

The set may need to get used to a different style of working to the fast-paced wordy interactions of the typical workplace or meeting. Facilitative methods seem slower at first and the set may wonder if anything is happening at all. Whatever they are, the ground rules provide what has been called a 'good enough' holding environment for the set, and will become a 'secure base' from which they can develop. The facilitator's role is to hold the boundaries agreed by the set in their ground rules even when the set is pushing against them, thereby ensuring the psychological safety of the set.

Bion's two groups

The nature of group dynamics was explored in depth by Bion (1961) and he established that any group operates at two levels, the basic assumption group (unconscious) and the work group (conscious). When operating in the unconscious, basic mode, group members behave as if they hold basic assumptions about the life and purpose of the group, which are quite different from the declared purpose of the work group. There are three basic assumptions which the group may adopt, as follows:

- Dependency: The group believes that security lies in a powerful leader usually identified as the facilitator – and failing that, the group will generate a fantasy leader. The effect of this assumption is that group members deny their own competence, preferring to place all their hopes (and therefore blame) on the leader.

- Pairing: The group unconsciously shares the assumption that an ideal couple or pairing exists within the group and that this will produce a messiah who will be the group saviour. The effect of this is that group members focus on a fantasy future rather than the present and may be preoccupied with a potential romantic coupling within the group.
- Flight/fight: The shared group assumption is that the group's survival will be achieved if its members fight or flee from someone or something. The effect of this assumption is that group members behave as if the group is being attacked by a fantasy 'enemy'.

Bion's work, developed by others (de Board, 1978: 37–9), established that any group flips continuously between the basic assumption group and the work group throughout its life. Lengthy committee meetings are a mixture of both. How does Bion's work apply to action learning sets?

If the set remains strictly in work mode it is deprived of warmth and power, whereas if the set remains strictly in basic assumption mode, set members may not pursue their goals. When the set is in basic assumption mode the effect is revitalizing even if it may feel catastrophic to members. Skilled facilitators often move a group or set into basic assumption mode in order to access its energy, by responding to expressed (but not verbalized) feelings. When the emotional charge in the set is put into words by the facilitator (or indeed a set member), the group is able to access its energy, process the feelings and move on to address their task in work mode. This process is known as 'containment', and described by French and Vince as 'the ways in which emotion is experienced or avoided, managed or denied, kept in or passed on so that its effects are either mitigated or amplified' (1999: 9).

When a set is able to function effectively in work mode, the members are able to assist each other to achieve their goals, address reality, and develop or change. The same set may operate in basic assumption mode, using its energy to defend itself from fear and anxiety, without achieving any task. The tension between the basic assumption group and the work group is believed to be essential for transformation (de Board, 1978: 44–8; Barnes, Ernst and Hyde, 1999). For action learning the set takes energy from its basic assumption mode and pursues action within its work group mode. The action learning structure allows the set to move freely between both modes. For example, the presenter may find that her issue uncovers some strong feelings about her work and the set may tap into its basic assumption mode by waiting for the facilitator (its fantasy leader) to 'rescue' the situation. Where the emotional reality is articulated by the facilitator or set members, the set can move off into work mode as the presenter focuses on what she actually wants to do.

We noted above the impact of group dynamics on the feelings and behaviour of those in the group, as well as the facilitator. While a full treatment of group dynamics is beyond the scope of this book, we do recognize that set members and facilitators may wish to have some idea about the unconscious forces at work in their action learning set and we introduce the basic concepts below. The idea of a part of each person which is unconscious and inaccessible is a key concept in psychodynamic thought, and the unconscious works for the person to maintain an image of self which he or she finds acceptable. We discuss how a person discovers what is acceptable in Chapter 7 under 'conditions of worth'. Suffice to say that the unconscious uses defence mechanisms to keep the self-image in place, and plays its part in maintaining the psychological health of the individual.

The group dynamic is dominated by feeling, and group behaviour is ruled according to 'habeas emotum' (Luft, 1984: 154), which is a version of the legal term 'habeas corpus'. Habeas corpus means, literally, 'you shall have the body', where the person is protected from illegal custody, having the right to a fair trial. Habeas emotum refers not to physical freedom but to the psychological freedom to have emotions and express them. The facilitator needs to be aware of emotion in the set as potential energy for learning or potential blocks to learning if unexpressed. We discuss managing emotion in Chapters 9 and 10.

Defences in an action learning set

The unconscious forces within a group or set, often called defence mechanisms, include projection, projective identification, transference, countertransference and other dynamics of group behaviour. We define these terms below.

The facilitator of an action learning set does not need to 'work with' these dynamics as an analyst would, but she will feel more confident when she understands what is happening in a group when these unconscious forces are at work. For example, it is quite common, in a group where freedom of expression is granted, for members to attack the perceived leader or authority figure. Indeed a leaderless group will create such a figure primarily for the purpose. This is an example of Bion's 'dependency' assumption above. The tendency in an action learning set for the presenter to address most of his 'story' to the facilitator is a sign of the presenter's identification of the facilitator as some sort of leader. A skilled facilitator will be aware of how this may affect her response, and monitor her own response to the situation (Egan, 1976; Foulkes, 1975; Bion, 1961). Hence facilitators may attract aggression or adulation from set members and these feelings are part of the group dynamic.

As part of a group, set members may *project* their own feelings onto others, especially if they are uncomfortable feelings like anger or sadness. 'Projection is a process whereby the person defends against threatening and unacceptable feelings and impulses by acting as though these feelings and impulses only exist in other people, not in the person himself or herself' (McLeod, 1998: 43). For example, set members may find themselves feeling angry about the way the presenter is being treated at work, while the presenter remains as cool as a cucumber! When the projection is 'taken in' by the other person(s), ie they swallow what has been sent unconsciously to them, as the set member did above, and it becomes a recognizable part of self-awareness, this is called *projective identification.*

Projective identification has been defined as a normal psychological process which is a transaction across the boundary between two people, ie between what I am and what you are. Let us look at this idea more closely.

The presenter P is projecting some feelings of anger about her manager onto another set member, S. P has unconsciously learnt that angry feelings are unacceptable to have and she pushes them away from herself by 'seeing' them in others. This means that the presenter is not conscious that her anger is really part of her own self, having learnt in the past that being 'good' was being 'not angry'. The set member, S, 'takes in' the feeling of anger unconsciously projected at him, experiences it as real, and may feel impelled to express it. Hence what set member S is feeling in that moment is really part of the presenter P but appears to both P and S as part of S. 'Projective identification occurs when the person to whom the feelings and impulses are being projected is manipulated into believing that he or she actually has these feelings and impulses' (McLeod, 1998: 43), eg the set member feeling angry above.

What happens if a set member projects feelings onto the presenter? The clue to projection is the strength of feeling which the set member may have about the part of himself he perceives in the presenter, as theory suggests that this is how he really feels about himself but defends against this knowledge by projection. This is why taking back projections is incredibly illuminating. The perceived aspect of the presenter, say a lack of confidence, which the set member reacts to strongly, suggests that lack of confidence is something that clearly has importance for the set member concerned. This is why projection has been called 'a gift in the present from the past' (Neumann, 1998). So when a set member feels *strongly* impatient with a presenter's perceived weakness in dealing with her manager, psychodynamic theory suggests that his impatience is a clue to how he himself feels about his own weakness, projected onto the presenter. If, through processing the feelings, our set member is enabled to 'take back' his projection, and accept his own weakness, he has a chance to know himself better.

We must not underestimate the fearful nature of some of our projective material – it is being sent out to another in order to lessen the pain or fear which we would experience if we 'owned' it properly. Hence where projection may be identified by the facilitator or set members themselves, in a set, great care is needed if we call attention to it, and we advocate a gentle and non-jargonistic observation with no pressure on anyone to respond or recognize what is being suggested. Such an observation also releases other set members from 'carrying' the projection without making a huge fuss about it. This frees set members to deal with their own material rather than feeling weak and helpless.

Another form of projection is the defence known as transference. Where feelings experienced in the past are 'transferred' unconsciously into present relationships, the term transference is used (Jacoby, 1984). These feelings are not just memories; they are alive and can deeply affect current relationships. 'Transference repeats and relives the love, hatred, aggression and frustration experienced as an infant in relation to his parents' (Jacoby, 1984: 17). In addition, they may not be all negative, and can take the form of undiluted admiration *or* hostility. The emotions and feelings involved are repetitions of the original ones (de Board, 1978). Transference can be seen as an entirely normal occurrence in any relationship and may have archetypal contents (Jacoby, 1984), ie the ideal father or perfect mother. If this seems a fanciful idea, the concept of projection was applied to everyday living by Ferenczi (1916; see de Board, 1978), who suggested that people are continually transferring their own feelings onto other people. For instance, when a presenter focuses all her attention on the facilitator, almost ignoring set members, it may be that the presenter has 'transferred' feelings of undue deference onto the facilitator.

Set members or the facilitator are type-cast or propelled into the matching pre-prepared script, and may respond in role, as if they are actually the source of the transferred feelings, and this is called *counter-transference*. Counter-transference is a particular case of projective identification, where emotions are felt in response to the projected transference feelings. Counter-transference may draw on ideal archetypes just as transference does, so the set facilitator may enjoy a sense of being god-like, the ultimate healer, the good parent, etc in response to the presenter's deference described above. The presenter's transferred feelings of over-deference, as above, may give rise to corresponding god-like and all-powerful feelings in the facilitator. We suggest that when facilitators begin to experience such feelings, they may call attention to what is happening by being congruent, eg 'I am feeling rather over-important here – I wonder why?'

The task for an action learning facilitator or indeed set member is to disentangle what may be their own feelings from what is being unconsciously projected onto them by others. For instance, where the facilitator or set member feels an urge to rescue the presenter – surely not an appropriate feeling between adults – this may alert them to the possibility that the feeling is counter-transference. They are feeling the urge to rescue in response to the presenter's feelings of helplessness, transferred and projected onto others. Either set members or facilitator may choose to mention their 'rescue' feeling and discuss whether it is appropriate to the presenter's situation.

The facilitator needs to be aware of the effects of defences in an action learning set. As mentioned above, there is no need for the facilitator to 'work with' any of the psychodynamic issues raised by anxiety (as a therapist would); her awareness of them is sufficient. When appropriate, she may use non-technical language to point gently to what is occurring in the set. For example, the facilitator may observe that the set is in flight from the task by means of distraction, as they are moving away from the presenter's agenda, or projection, avoiding an uncomfortable feeling of anger or weakness by perceiving it in others. She may note that there is conflict between certain individuals in the set, and open up the issue in the process review. Alternatively, the facilitator may simply live with the unconscious projections in the set, observing that members are demonstrating dependency by waiting for a lead from the facilitator, or transference behaviours by offering the facilitator over-deference or hostility. The facilitator may deal with her own counter-transference feelings of anger or irritation, internally, without commenting on it. This is described as the facilitator acting as a 'container' for difficult or unacceptable feelings and therefore making them safe (Bion, 1961).

The facilitator can help group members to unlock these defences, usually by making possible projections implicit, eg by noting that the presenter is being badly treated at work but it's the set member who is angry about it. The set can be invited to explore why this is occurring and what might change for the presenter if *she* were to be angry for herself. Where the facilitator is part of the defence, ie transference, where set members may project feelings of resentment or anger from the hurt child within, the facilitator needs to resist the temptation to offer a punitive response. Similarly, the facilitator may need to resist being carried away by the undiluted admiration given by some set members and, alternatively perhaps, dare to reveal the cracks!

In Box 8.1 we include a facilitator's story encapsulating some of the above in a set that had been formed as a mandatory part of a wider development programme where the voluntary principle was compromised.

Box 8.1   The terrors of conscripted sets

The set were meeting for the fifth time, out of eight mandatory sessions, and a set member at session four had requested a change in facilitator or permission to self-facilitate. After consulting with fellow-facilitators, I decided to discuss with the set, at their next meeting, the skills required to facilitate action learning, and explained why I thought we should explore this.

I invited set members to express how they understood the skills of facilitation. During the process, in addition to the spoken words, there was a strong sense of unrest, even anger, and what I perceived as unwillingness. While giving their views, set members seemed to me to be sabotaging the session, passing round notes/photos, and it really felt like pulling teeth. I felt angry and abused and unsure what to do next. I felt like walking out but decided to 'stay calm, think carefully, move outside the box and make a decision'.

I remembered Berne's parent–child adult model and decided to tell the set that they were moving me towards the critical parent role that I did not want to play. I challenged individuals whom I perceived as disruptive, asking them why they chose to do this. Responses included:

- 'don't want to be here';
- 'bored';
- 'don't like someone';
- 'better things to do with my time';
- 'don't like group work';
- 'waste of time';

and the process enabled some of the angry feelings of challenge in the set to recede. I felt I now knew that the set members were responsible for the way they chose to learn, and whether they attended the set or not. I was able to shift my position from one of feeling threatened to one of resignation.

To facilitate a conscripted set demands a wide range of skills and the strength and experience to deal with heavy projections and transference from the set. The significant skill described above was the facilitator's ability to deal with her own counter-transference, and maintain her 'self' when under coded or indeed uncoded attack.

An effective facilitator will have the ability to observe, identify and, if appropriate, describe such dynamics in a set, through process comments, in simple terms, where appropriate, enabling reflection on that process by articulating it. For instance, calling attention to the set's over-reliance on the facilitator, noting where set members rather than the presenter feel angry, and mentioning the tendency to 'rescue' in the set. Process comments, if accepted by participants, are the trigger for reflection, and may be the first time the process has been highlighted for them.

In addition, in order to maximize the opportunities for full reflective learning, ie for transformation as well as improvement (see Chapter 7), the set allocates time for processing its work, at the end of each session or after a particular presentation. This process review is when the set can analyse what has occurred and why.

Humanistic concepts in action learning

The facilitator can anticipate much of the group defences by declaring the humanistic values of support, trust and safety. Action learning adopts humanistic principles as it focuses on subjective experience, the individual's view of the world and their interpretation of that world. In action learning there are no impositions or preconceptions or theoretical data. Hence the psychodynamic ideas above are given only as background to a humanistic approach. Action learning sets norms of disclosure, owning, honouring and respecting choice, and these are the conditions identified by Carl Rogers for person-centred learning which we discuss in Chapter 7.

The conditions required for human learning and growth were defined by Rogers as a consequence of his research into human development. The three key behaviours, known as person-centred core conditions, are:

- congruence, ie genuineness, realness, sharing feelings and attitudes rather than opinions and judgements;
- unconditional positive regard (UPR), ie acceptance and 'prizing' of the other;
- empathy, ie understanding of the other's feelings, experience and attitudes and communicating that understanding.

Congruence

Congruence has been defined as 'a state of being' (Mearns and Thorne, 1988), although 'a statement of being' is a good description where the set member is openly being what she is in response to her colleague. The set member is congruent when her response is what she feels and not a facade. She is real and authentic, 'freely and deeply herself, with actual experience represented by awareness of herself' (Rogers, 1957). Realness and authenticity involve some disclosure, a willingness to be and live the feelings and thoughts of the moment. Expression of feeling is culturally specific, and the UK is not among the leaders here. The continuum of expression from easy to difficult shown in Figure 8.1 offers a way of understanding how much easier it is to express a negative feeling from the past, about someone who is not present (classical gossip), rather than expressing positive feeling in the present about someone who is present (giving praise).

Unconditional positive regard

Rogers describes unconditional positive regard as 'a warm acceptance of each aspect of the other's experience' (Rogers, 1957: 98). Other explanations present unconditional positive regard as an attitude, which 'manifests itself in... consistent acceptance of, and enduring warmth towards others' (adapted from Mearns and Thorne, 1988). Additional descriptions include 'non-possessive warmth', 'respect', 'affirming' and, of course, Roger's term 'prizing'. Prizing, acceptance and trust of the learner implies a belief that the other person is fundamentally trustworthy... this means living with uncertainty.

Empathy

Rogers defines empathy as 'an accurate understanding of the other's own experience' (Rogers, 1957: 99), or an ability 'to sense the other's private

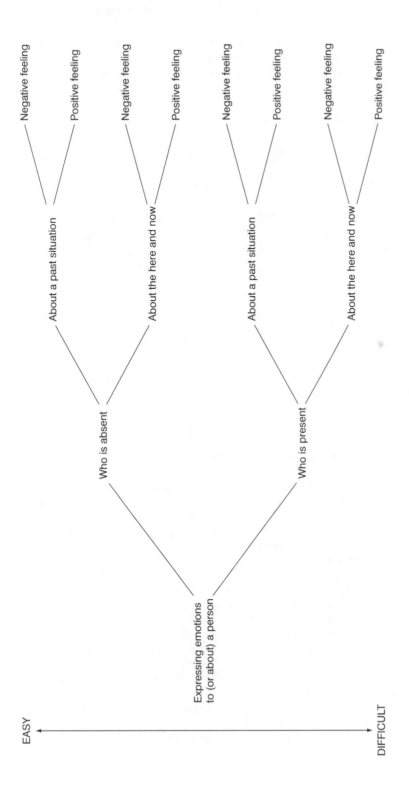

Figure 8.1 *Expressing emotion: the difficult–easy continuum*
Source: Adapted from Egan, 1977:81, in Brockbank and McGill, 1998

world' as if it were her own. Other descriptions present empathy as a **process** where the set member 'lays aside her own way of experiencing and perceiving reality, preferring to sense and respond to the experiences and perceptions of the other' (adapted from Mearns and Thorne, 1988: 39).

The set member's response can be empathic at four levels as follows:

level 0, where the set member has no understanding of the presenter's expressed feeling;
level 1, where the set member has a partial understanding of surface feelings;
level 2, where the set member shows an understanding of expressed feeling, also known as accurate empathy (see also Egan, 1990);
level 3, where the set member shows an understanding of both surface and underlying feelings, known as additive empathy or depth reflection (Mearns and Thorne, 1988: 42).

We note that the definitions of empathy encompass all aspects of experience, doing, thinking and feeling. Where one or other is neglected the quality of empathy is likely to be reduced. In addition, empathic understanding must be communicated (silent or invisible empathy is not much use).

We offer here a facilitator's story which emphasizes support and empathy. It is included here because it embraces the Rogers core conditions.

Box 8.2   Support and empathy

I recently had an experience in a set that challenged the way in which I was running the set. The group had been working together for some time and had established ground rules as a framework for agreed working together. When exploring the ground rules we had devoted quite a bit of time to unpicking principles such as trust and confidentiality. We had spent less time unravelling the complex concept of support and what this really meant to people.

At a set meeting, one of the group presented her story which was related to a future event that she was anxious about. She wanted to think about ways in which she could plan the way she would act. The group asked many questions and some were aimed at challenging her to consider possible consequences of particular actions. At the end of the session, when I asked the group to consider process issues, the presenter commented that she felt quite angry that she had not felt supported by the group during her presentation.

I felt challenged as the facilitator as these comments had implications for me. I decided not to ask her more questions about why she felt unsupported but to allow her to carry on talking about the way she felt and allow there to be silences as she was doing this. When she had finished describing the way in which she felt, I, as facilitator, acknowledged her feelings and commented about how sad I was that she felt this way. I then asked the group if they would like to say anything to the presenter. No comments were given, although there was a silence that conveyed how sorry people felt. I then asked the group to consider what this notion of support looks like and how we might give support in a group. The group came up with the following points:

- Support is not necessarily about saying you understand or giving loads of positive feedback to make the person feel good.
- Support is about owning up to how you are feeling when the presenter is telling her story. So, for example, if you feel sad or anxious or frustrated it can be supportive to the presenter to share these feelings you have with her.
- Support is about checking out with the presenter during the course of the discussion how she is feeling and what she would like from us as a group.
- Support is about paying attention to non-verbal cues and the pace of the presentation.

Everyone engaged in this discussion and came up with a clear idea to them of what support looks like. They felt positive that they could work with this and try to put it into action.

The final evaluation of the set occurred a few months after this event. All of the group spoke about how much they had learnt from this experience. The presenter commented on how she felt she had really been listened to and it would give her courage to challenge the process in the future.

I learnt that as an experienced facilitator there is still much learning to do, in particular the skill of reflection in action. I had to think and make decisions quite quickly in this instance. The decision I made was not to ask the presenter more in-depth questions about feeling unsupported as she had been asked enough questions over the past hour and had already felt in the 'hot seat'. Instead I chose to acknowledge her feelings, share how I and the rest of the group were feeling and move to using the skills within the group to learn from the experience and plan how we might look at the issue of support in the future.

The story illustrates the facilitator's use of empathy in verbally acknowledging the feelings of the presenter; unconditional positive regard is shown by the facilitator allowing space and silence for the presenter; and congruence is present in the facilitator's expression of her own sadness in response to what the presenter has said.

All three qualities call for a high degree of emotional intelligence, in that to be genuine implies a willingness to express feelings, acceptance relies on managing competing emotions, and empathy is the key skill for handling emotional material. When a facilitator holds such attitudes set members are given 'freedom and life and the opportunity to learn' (Rogers, 1983: 133) and we are told that, as outcomes of the process, set members are likely to 'learn more and behave better when they receive high levels of understanding, caring, genuineness, than when they are given low levels of them' (Rogers, 1983: 199).

The values of action learning are undeniably drawn from the humanistic field: the voluntary nature of it, the emphasis on positive outcomes, challenge as well as support, no advice, and the holistic approach to a presenter as the expert in his or her own issue.

How do these humanist ideas link up with the psychodynamic principles given at the beginning of this chapter? The humanist approach recognizes transference and offers empathy as a response to archaic feelings of anger or adoration. The counter-transference experienced in the set, usually by the facilitator, can be noted by her without intervention, or can be openly articulated by her through being congruent. The projections in the set can be recognized similarly by set members' congruence. For example, when a set member begins to feel something that doesn't seem to be 'hers', it is possible that the feeling is a projected one from another set member. For instance, if a set member finds herself feeling unaccountably angry and the presenter is talking calmly about exploitation at work, she may wonder if what she is feeling is projected from the presenter. If she can be congruent about that feeling and say she feels angry but she's not sure why, then the presenter may recognize the feeling as hers and choose to repossess the feeling. Even if the presenter chooses not to own the feeling, our set member has freed herself from the projection by her congruence. All unconscious defences are contained by a set climate which offers respect and unconditional positive regard, where the ground rules ensure that no one is attacked or over-challenged, so that fears, anxieties and perceived weakness are safely processed within the set.

Existential concepts in action learning

Action learning also draws on some ideas from existential philosophy, and examples include the way the set is structured. This maximizes the potential for individuals to take responsibility for their own issue. The dedicated time for each presenter, the absence of advice-giving and the balance of challenge and support give the presenter non-judgemental acceptance in their situation. Existential principles demand that individuals are active, not passive, in the way they conduct their life, being responsible for contributing to their own reality, and action learning seeks to enable this to happen. The individual set member is presumed to have freedom to choose and can therefore take responsibility for acting. The set member, as an existential human being, is presumed to be intentional, and hence self-responsible. However, existential principles require a balance of challenge together with support for the set member who seeks change and development. We illustrate this in Figure 8.2.

Another existential concept in action learning is the idea that development is created through relationships, in particular the I–Thou relationship

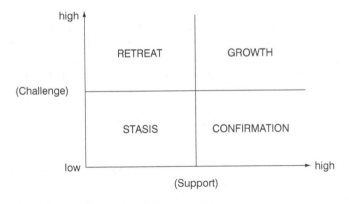

Figure 8.2   *Mutual dependence of challenge and support*
Source: B Reid in Palmer *et al*, 1994: 38

(Buber, 1994), and this has been described as follows: 'In an I–Thou relationship where I take my partner seriously, I owe him honesty; I can tell him how his behaviour affects me. I do not have to play the invulnerable one, I can react as a human being' (Jacoby, 1984: 86).

The action learning set offers members the opportunity to 'react as a human being', express their vulnerability and collaborate with fellow members in their learning. When a presenter can admit to feeling at a loss with a situation at work, and share this with the set, the I–Thou relationships in the set ensure that set members stay with the presenter, supporting her and encouraging her towards a resolution of her difficulty.

Behaviourist concepts in action learning

Action learning accepts the behavioural principle of modelling (Bandura and Walters, 1963). In a set, modelled behaviour by the facilitator is picked up and imitated by group members, consciously or unconsciously. The work of Bateson (1973) explored the phenomenon of *schismogenesis*, the tendency for humans to imitate observed behaviours, and modelling seeks to use this tendency to support learning. The old adage, 'don't do as I do, do as I say', recognizes that, as learners, we 'pick up' the implicit process and copy it, thereby imitating behaviour rather than responding to spoken instructions, so we might as well model process intentionally.

There is plenty of evidence for such effects. The power of the majority over the individual was demonstrated by the Asch (1974) research where one of the group was persuaded to change their perception about the length of a line by others disagreeing. The idea of groupthink emerged from disasters like the Bay of Pigs and *Challenger* (Janis, 1982). On the positive side, research work in group dynamics showed that learning was enhanced by group interaction, giving dramatically better results than lectures, for instance (Chickering and Gamson, 1989). Hence set members enhance their own skilled behaviour, and we give an example of this in Chapter 10.

The facilitator may encounter any or all of the above dynamics in the session itself, as well as in the process review, as described in Chapter 13.

The life of a set

The action learning set, while focused on self-understanding and change, is also dealing with action, so does action learning have 'stages'? For the action learning set the 'stages' are embedded in the structure so that the set is 'formed' by initial exercises and the setting of trust; the 'norms' are established by the ground rules; the set 'performs' within a presentation; the set may 'storm' during the process review when feelings may be expressed and 'held' by the facilitator. So the 'storming' stage is contained by the structure of the set meeting and made safe by the skill of the facilitator. The stages were first presented by Tuckman in 1965.

A later study by Tuckman and Jensen (1977) identified the termination phase of a group – adjournment, together with some typical defence behaviours which are common to the ending of relationships, and these have been described as 'mourning' the ending of the group. Set members may experience real feelings of bereavement at the ending stage and facilitators need to take account of such feelings. Action learning sets should always work to an agreed series of meetings so that members are aware of when adjournment will occur. Each set will have its own way of ending and facilitators should enable set members to complete a satisfactory ending. Note: set members may wish to continue in another set and then the whole process begins again.

How is action learning different from a T-group, therapy or counselling?

The concept of a T-group (standing for Training Group) grew from the Human Relations workshops devised by Kurt Lewin (1951) to enable members to reflect on the meaning of their own and other's behaviour in group situations. The method has been called the laboratory method of learning (Luft, 1984) and was used extensively in the UK at the Tavistock Leicester conferences (Trist and Sofer, 1959, cited in De Board, 1978: 65).

T-group principles were:

- The main agenda in a T-group was the 'here and now'.
- Mutual sharing of perceptions about what is happening in the group at the moment.

- Members were encouraged to disclose their feelings and receive feedback.

The quality of feedback was crucial to the safety of the group and there were unfortunate experiences in T-groups where the quality of feedback was not high or facilitators were unskilled.

Carl Rogers created a version of the T-group which he called the Basic Encounter Group, echoing Bion's two groups described earlier in this chapter. Rogers' intent was to provide a group experience which would enable 'normal' people to gain insight into their own behaviour in a much more fundamental way than is possible in a social or work context. The intended outcome was for individuals to be able to relate better to others, both in groups and later in everyday life. The facilitator in an encounter group has four functions:

- modelling self-disclosure, especially emotion;
- caring and support for group members;
- clarifying the meaning of group dynamics;
- executive responsibility for boundaries (time and space).

Where individuals reported positive outcomes, these were associated with a facilitator who had high ratings on caring and support, and meaning functions (Lieberman *et al*, 1973).

Our model of action learning adopts some of Rogers' encounter group ideas, but could never be described as a true 'encounter' group. The structure and boundaries preserve the action learning process within what might be called the 'normal' limits for work-related learning and development. Action learning has been described as 'an intentional strategy based on normal, but unusual effective practice' (McGill and Beaty, 2001: 12) and not something that occurs socially without intention.

How does this differ from therapy or counselling?

An action learning set is not a therapy or counselling group. Presenters can expect to be listened to and to receive questions and comments aimed at enabling them, but they should not expect counselling from either set members or the facilitator. Sets may wish to include this in their ground rules.

Therapy and counselling are activities that occur within a professional relationship where the client elects to embark on a journey of self-discovery within the safety of what is known as 'a therapeutic frame'. Such a frame includes prescribed codes of ethics, payment, confidentiality and professional liability appropriate to the nature of therapeutic work. Such codes are designed to protect the potentially vulnerable client from being exploited.

The purpose of the relationship is agreed between the parties and may change over time. The therapeutic relationship is a powerful force for learning and change, being a good example of the I–Thou relationship mentioned above (Buber, 1994). Therapeutic relationships may be one-to-one or two-to-one, and in the case of group therapy, many-to-one. Neither therapist, counsellor nor client can predict where the journey might take them, and much depends on the skills of the practitioner involved. The process may take both into uncharted waters, where high degrees of distress and pain may be experienced. Regulation of the profession is proceeding, which ensures that those in practice are suitably qualified and monitored.

Action learning is a voluntary and professional activity freely entered into by individuals who seek to learn through a repeated cycle of reflection and action, with the support of a set. Set members are there to support each individual in moving forward with their issue and they are also there to challenge each other with care. The set may provide a place where members can explore personal issues but they are unlikely to find in a set, and should not be offered, therapy for psychological problems. The facilitator's awareness of unconscious material, eg transference, should not become the material for discussion in the set (as it would in therapy), and if such matters emerge in a set, facilitators are empowered to refer the individual concerned to a qualified therapeutic practitioner.

The perceived similarity between action learning and therapeutic activity is the use by set members of skills which are associated with counselling. For example, the skills of listening with respect, congruence and empathy are needed by those who are not counsellors, ie managers. The skills, described in Chapters 9, 10 and 11, are effective in supporting set members in their reflective dialogue, while keeping a clear line between action learning and any kind of counselling or therapy.

Chapter 9

Being a presenter

In this chapter we examine in detail the skills that contribute to being effective as a presenter in an action learning set. We discuss action learning skills as they apply to the presenter in order to enable readers to focus on their current interpersonal style and possibly modify their style in order to enhance their effectiveness in a set. We identify the skills used by the presenter and we describe the relevant skills and indicate how they might be used in a set.

Being effective in a set

As a presenter, skilled behaviour begins from awareness or perception of what is happening in a set and this includes what is happening in the self.

By awareness or perception, we mean:

- Being in touch with myself, when presenting, so that I know what's going on inside me, especially what I am feeling at the moment. If a set member says to me: 'You seem angry with X' and I reply: 'Who's angry?' – I am not realizing that I am angry.
- Being in touch with others, ie picking up clues such as the use of language, non-verbal behaviour, and how that relates to what is being said.
- Being in touch with what's happening in a set, ie listening to the interaction and understanding what may be happening between set members.

Being a presenter

Being effective as a presenter has four interpersonal aspects, namely: congruence, self-disclosure, managing emotion and receiving feedback. We use a diagram known as the Johari window to illustrate the effect on the presenter of their own disclosure; a scale of emotional expression from easy to difficult; and the Zucchini model to illustrate feedback from set members.

Congruence

When taking time, the presenter can take as long as he likes, repeat himself, get mixed-up, or just pause to consider what to say next. In action learning the presenter's time is sacrosanct and he may tell his story in his own way and in his own time. However, over time in a set, the experience of presenting may alert set members to the importance of congruence.

When taking the role of presenter, for action learning to be most effective, congruence is a key skill attribute. We have defined congruence in Chapter 8 and for the presenter to be congruent means: a way of being genuine, being real, sharing feelings and attitudes as well as opinions and beliefs/judgements.

Egan (1973) has defined this kind of congruent speech as 'story' and the less congruent version as 'history'. We will identify the characteristics of both here.

Telling it like a story

'Story' is involvement. It is authentic self-disclosure – an attempt to reveal the self as a person and to reach the listener. Story involves emotion. Story is a signal of invitation – the presenter is opening the door to others in the set. It is a story if it is a description by the presenter about themselves expressed, for example, as 'I felt thoroughly undervalued by my manager when my administrative assistant was transferred without consulting me.' The defining characteristic of story mode is the use of 'I' statements rather than 'we', 'one' or 'it'.

'History', on the other hand, is non-involvement. History is a statement or message which is analytical, factual – it ticks off the facts of experience and even interpretation of these facts but leaves the person who is making the statement untouched, relatively unknown. For example, the presenter might say: 'The management takes decisions without consultation.' The presentation may be long and even boring. The presenter is detached and uninvolved, taking no risks. The presenter treats herself as *object* who is 'there and then' rather than subject who is 'here and now'. Generalities may be disguised by the use of words like 'we', 'one' or 'it'. History does not reach or engage the listener. It is flat or boring because it is divorced from the person. It is not really disclosing of the person.

Again, a story may start as a story but because the individual has worked through an issue it is no longer really an issue for her. One presenter recalls taking time in a set to discuss a matter of importance – it was about the use of time at work – and was challenged by another set member as the latter felt there was no real will or commitment about what was being described. The presenter agreed; the issue had already been resolved. The story had become history. We list below the characteristics of both modes:

Story	*History*
I	Them; it; people
Feeling; affect	Fact
Actual	Abstract
Real	Abstract; detached
Interesting	Boring; a turn-off

In other words, when the presenter is expressing feelings (the emotive or affective part of the self) as well as the knowing (cognitive) and doing (conative) part, she is likely to be in story mode and disclosing something about herself that has its basis in a real meaning that will make connections with the listeners.

Story is selective in detail – not necessarily complete in communicating fact, but complete in communicating self. The story teller is taking a risk and knows it. By so doing, the presenter requests support from set members. In a set, self-disclosure is a leap of trust – and demands dialogue 'here and now'. It is unusual not to be engaged when someone is telling their story. It is almost always interesting. The presenter may have taken a risk, made herself vulnerable in the process, but will not lose the set members' attention. The set members will seldom be bored by a story with sincere self-disclosure but they may be embarrassed.

This embarrassment can be a cultural bias against self-disclosure and the expression of emotion – seen in some contexts as a weakness at one extreme or exhibitionism at the other. Self-disclosure peaks in childhood and is seen as a passing phase that disappears with oncoming maturity. In the fullness of time we become fully locked-in mature adults! However, as human beings we do not lose our emotions; they remain in us and can be a barrier to our development or can enhance that development. Self-disclosure is often associated with the psychiatrist's couch – we must be weak and in need of 'treatment'.

Fortunately, this model (a medical model) is becoming outmoded with our increasing understanding of ourselves as having subjective feelings which impinge on our everyday lives. For example, our presenter earlier in this chapter felt undervalued by her manager and she also wanted to go for promotion. She was inhibited by a lack of confidence, and after her 'undervalued' feelings were acknowledged by set members she was able to discuss her lack of confidence about promotion, although she appeared super-confident to others. Thus telling it like a story is more likely to convey congruence between what we are saying and what we are feeling or thinking. It is more likely to create bridges of understanding than history, which takes no risk and may lead to misinterpretation.

What happens when the presenter is unable to be congruent in the set?

What if the presenter communicates in 'history' mode, with a great deal of factual material, and opinion about other people, situations and events but lacking feeling or real issues? Either the set members or the facilitator may challenge the presenter's incongruent mode, and we deal with this process in the next section. What happens if neither set members nor facilitator challenges the presenter? The action learning set becomes a problem-solving exercise, with the focus on a factual issue, distant from the set, and for which the presenter is not responsible. We discuss responsibility in Chapter 7. The set is working 'at one remove' and personal commitment to action is unlikely.

What happens when the presenter is able to be congruent?

The set members can work with the presenter immediately, responding to the 'story' (eg the presenter's account of her difficulty with her manager) in both supportive and challenging ways, and we describe these in the next section. A useful way of seeing what is happening when the presenter is congruent in a set is the model known as the Johari window.

The Johari window

A very useful insight into how we may relate to people is the diagrammatic representation known as the Johari Awareness Model or Johari's window (the name being coined from the joint authors' names (see Luft, 1984). The model, shown in Figure 9.1, rests on humanistic, holistic and psychody-namic assumptions as follows:

- Subjective factors dictate our impressions of each other.
- Emotions influence behaviour more than rational reason or logic.
- Human beings have limited awareness of self, and benefit from information from other sources.
- Change promotes the possibility of learning and development.
- Experience is fluid and ever-changing.

Interaction between two or more people depends on the extent of openness in a particular context. The square or window describes the possible forms of awareness of behaviour and feelings in a relationship and here the window represents the presenter's relationships in an action learning set. We will examine each quadrant in turn.

Quadrant 1, the open quadrant, refers to those behaviours, feelings and motivations that the presenter knows about themselves, while others also know these, having seen or been told about them. This is the window that the presenter lays open to the world. It is the basis of most interaction that is willingly displayed.

Quadrant 2, the unaware quadrant, is that which refers to those behaviours, feelings and motivations that other set members see but which the presenter does not. This is the window the presenter may display to other set members without being aware that he is displaying it. In an interaction

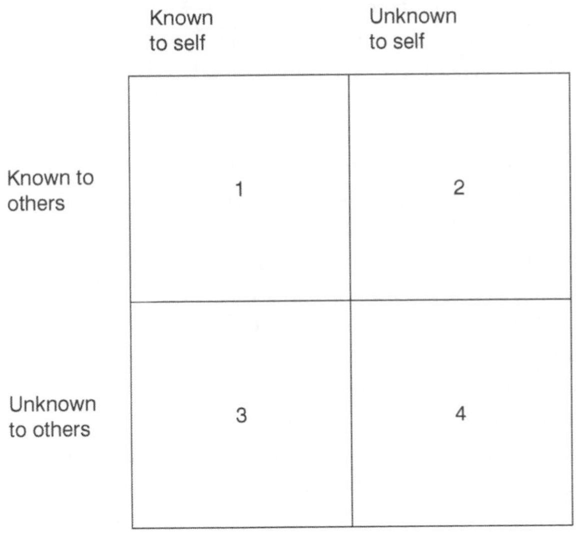

	Known to self	Unknown to self
Known to others	1	2
Unknown to others	3	4

Figure 9.1   *The Johari window*
Source: Brockbank and McGill, 1998

the presenter displays himself as quadrant 1 – his public self. Set members, to whom he displays himself, see the public self, but may also get an insight into the presenter through quadrant 2 where the presenter is unaware. For example, the presenter may comment in a sexist way, without realizing it. Only if another set member points out the remark to the presenter will he be aware of it. How such feedback is conveyed to the presenter, and how he reacts to it, will influence how the presenter gets to know that particular aspect of himself, and we deal with the skill of feedback in Chapter 10.

Quadrant 3, the hidden area, is that window which refers to those behaviours, feelings and motivations that the presenter knows about but is, currently, unwilling to convey to others. For example, the presenter may be unwilling to disclose what he feels is a weakness to other set members. For example, our presenter earlier was keeping her lack of confidence within this hidden quadrant.

Quadrant 4, the unknown area, is the behaviour, feelings and motivations of which the presenter is unaware, and is not known about by others as well. Access to this area can be found through our dreams when we sleep or even in the occasional daydream. This quadrant will contribute to the presenter's behaviour but he does not, as others do not, normally see that part of the self, and hence working in this quadrant is not appropriate for an action learning set. It is possible to gain insight into this part of the self through therapy and that is the place for it.

The total window is drawn to scale for ease of representation, although Luft (1984) suggests that quadrant 4 is much larger than displayed. Using the Johari window we can see in Figure 9.2 how disclosure works in an action learning set.

In window a) we have a starting point, say in a new set. In window b) the presenter begins to disclose some of quadrant 3, ie that which is hidden from the view of others. The result is an enlargement of the open quadrant, quadrant 1, as the material is now in the public (set) domain, and this is represented by window c) in Figure 9.3. This enlargement is likely to apply only within the set. Outside the set, in interaction with other people and groups, the presenter may return to the original window a) in his interactions, shown by the hatched line.

Clearly such a transfer is managed as a choice by the discloser and is relevant to the context. For instance, disclosure in a family situation differs from disclosure at work or with friends. In action learning the context is reflective dialogue with the purpose of enabling connected learning. Belenky *et al* (1986) have identified connected learning as very different from the separated learning that maintains a distance from the issues concerned. Belenky and her colleagues described 'really talking' (Belenky *et al*, 1986: 144) as characteristic of constructivist learners (described in Chapter 5). The constructivist approach to learning is one of sharing, as if learners 'do not articulate what they've learned, then that renders their knowledge useless if they can't share it with other people' (Belenky *et al*, 1986: 144). In addition to sharing what they know, constructivist learners also have a willingness to describe how they got there (Belenky *et al*, 1986: 145). They differentiate 'really talking' from the holding-forth style of communication, where there is no intention to share ideas, only to transmit them one-way (Belenky *et al*,

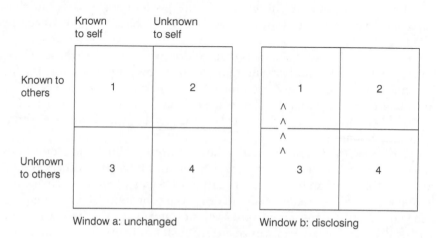

Figure 9.2   *Disclosing*
Source: Brockbank and McGill, 1998

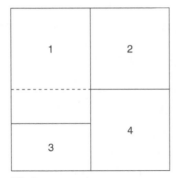

Window c: more open

Figure 9.3　*Johari window after disclosure by presenter*
Source: Brockbank and McGill, 1998

1986: 144). Really talking enables learners to engage in reflection through reflective dialogue. We shall explore below what 'really talking' means in terms of the skill of self-disclosure, as it is a key dialoguing skill.

We know that reflective dialogue involves disclosure as the presenter seeks clarification of their learning processes through sharing them with others. This sharing builds the structure for connected knowing, which enables the presenter to allow herself to be 'known' by set members. If this seems too 'personal', we need only look at the separate knowing that results from impersonal, objective approaches to learning which we discussed in Chapter 5. The presenter, in sharing the personal components of her learning in reflective dialogue, takes the opportunity for deep and significant reflection. The kind of reflection that challenges assumptions hitherto held firmly, and questions the taken-for-granteds (tfgs), the 'givens' and assumptions that we never think to question because they are there, has the potential to construct a new view of the world. In order to maximize deep and significant reflection, set members will be asked to self-disclose to each other, as appropriate. As facilitators are models here, we therefore recommend that aspiring facilitators acquire the skill of appropriate self-disclosure, so that set members are given an idea of how to proceed.

How is the presenter to be congruent?

In order to convey her genuine and real issue the presenter will need to engage in self-disclosure. In operational terms this means that the presenter will tend to make 'I' statements, owning her contribution, rather than using 'you' or 'one' or 'we' or 'it', all of which have a tendency to distance the speaker from ownership of what is being said.

Although the term self-disclosure may put people off, as it sounds exposing and like being stripped naked, in reality, in all our relationships we self-disclose, and we control how much we reveal of what we are thinking and especially feeling. How much we disclose is likely to be related to differences in culture, gender, class, race, sexual orientation or disability. It will also relate to the nature of the relationship concerned, eg:

- a loving partnership;
- a working relationship as:
  - colleagues;
  - manager and managed;
  - doctor and patient;
- woman to woman;
- man to man.

Any disclosure will be transmitted through messages between the sender and receiver and subject to some loss and potential misinterpretation. We discuss this under listening in Chapter 10. A person may also disclose intentionally or unintentionally. The messages that carry disclosure may be conveyed via:

- the body – face and parts of the body;
- the voice – how we talk;
- touch – physical contact with another;
- verbal – what we say;
- actions – what we do as a contrast to, or confirmation of, what we say and how we say it.

Appropriateness of disclosure

Too much self-disclosure is embarrassing. Too little and we may find we do not relate to others and reduce our capacity to reflect upon ourselves in the set. Quadrant 3 in the Johari window is hidden from our listeners. How far we disclose depends in part upon our values and the norms of the set. Some people value openness, others privacy. Over-disclosure occurs when the disclosure is inappropriate to the context.

The level of disclosure which is suitable to the context can be called appropriate self-disclosure. 'Appropriate' is defined by:

- amount (how much);
- depth (how deep);
- duration (how long);
- the target (to whom);
- the situation (time and place).

We all have experience of a myriad of versions of the above combinations. For example, someone who insists on talking in detail about themselves constantly and at length (duration) is deemed inappropriate, as is the over-discloser who reveals intimate details (depth) to almost anyone (target) on any occasion (situation). So we have a true sense of appropriate self-disclosure and moderately well-adjusted persons disclose appropriately for human contact and social intercourse. In addition to the above, the literature on self-disclosure reveals that women are higher disclosers than men, and that disclosure is reciprocal in effect, ie where high disclosers are present, this increases disclosure by everyone (Cozby, 1973).

The term itself holds fearful connotations for some. The fashion for over-disclosure in some groups has given the term a bad name, and horror stories abound about learners being 'taken apart' in T-groups etc. We do note that the horror stories are almost always recounted by *another* member of the group, suggesting that most of the distress was experienced by the observers rather than the learner concerned. However, we do recognize that the associations with nakedness, exposure and stripping are connotations that may concern presenters and affect their levels of disclosure.

There may be strong cultural imperatives against self-disclosure and this may inhibit the presenter's behaviour, especially in conditions where they perceive themselves to be under test. For many, self-disclosure implies weakness, rather a lopsided view as we hope to show below. The reverse-halo effect (where a weakness in one area is presumed to exist in other areas) and fear of shame and rejection are strong inhibitors, especially in a group where no trust has been established. And here we have the conundrum. A sure way to establish trust is some self-disclosure in the group, but on the other hand, group members may fear self-disclosure until they are confident of trust in the group. How can this loop be breached?

The first person to take a risk is the facilitator, who, we recommend, discloses first, and we discuss this further in Chapter 11.

Our experience of action learning sets is that set members do engage in self-disclosure as the atmosphere of trust develops between members. We have seen earlier that the development of that trust depends on the set adhering to the ground rule of confidentiality. Knowing that what is said in the set will not be repeated by other set members outside the set is crucial. Action learning sets can provide for a degree of self-disclosure that may not be available elsewhere.

Self-disclosure in a set provides a means of finding out things about ourselves of which we may not be aware. If I am more open towards other set members, I am conveying something of myself and conveying the *willingness* to do so. This willingness can encourage others to take the risk of disclosure about themselves.

Managing emotion as a presenter

We address emotion because of its key role in reflective dialogue, double loop learning and connected/constructivist learning. The expression of emotion is socialized on cultural and gender lines, eg privileging particular emotional expression to females but not to males, such as weeping. Some emotions are more acceptable than others; this is inculcated very early in life and there is no further training in the handling of emotions (Skynner and Cleese, 1983), leading to the inadequacy of emotional matters in the wider (Western) society (Orbach, 1994).

People who declare that they feel no emotion have just got the lid on tighter than the rest of us and will reveal 'leakages' in some way. Emotion in itself is a fact. We are living human beings for whom emotion is an integral part of ourselves. Facilitation offers us the chance to express feelings safely.

Being socialized to discourage the expression of some of our emotions is partially useful. I may be angry with someone. That does not mean I can hit out physically or abuse them emotionally. That is useful socialization. However, some forms of socialization may result in inhibiting the display of emotions so that we may become 'locked-in' emotionally as adults.

Jourard (1971) suggests that persons who are 'known' by others are healthier and happier than those who are not. The suppression of emotion, in Jourard's view, is a major component of stress in modern society. In our role as facilitators we have often heard a set member say that being able to give voice and express their emotions has been a major breakthrough in tackling a major task in work or in life, confirming expert findings on stress management (Cooper, 1983).

If a person does not express their emotions verbally, there will be a tendency to 'leakage' – the expression non-verbally of the emotions. Both can, of course, be expressed together as congruent behaviour. Non-verbal expression of emotion may include tone of voice, gesture and body language. Verbally emotions may also be expressed inadvertently when the words belie the stated intention, as in Freudian slips!

The root of the verb 'emovere' suggests movement and it doesn't take a lot of thought to recognize that emotion is a strong motivator. Given our cultural heritage, which leans towards not revealing our emotions, how can we deal with expression of emotion and what is its value in an action learning set?

Expression of emotion

First, emotions are part of being human, in themselves neither right nor wrong, and though we can suppress or even repress 'unacceptable' emotions they are not so easily controlled and may be released verbally and/or non-verbally. Secondly, the motivating power of emotion provides the 'fuel' for the adventure of double loop learning (see Chapter 7). Emotion is an important source of energy to support and sustain the learner through the 'dip' of the learning curve. In addition, an ability to deal with emotional material is necessary if we wish to 'unpack' the blocks to learning which emerge in reflective dialogue.

However, we recognize our heritage and seek to identify where our difficulties may lie. We discussed the difficult/easy continuum based on the work of Egan (1977) in Chapter 8 and the diagram on page 139 indicates how awkward or easy we find emotional expression, under a variety of circumstances.

We find it easier to express negative emotion and this is borne out by our lopsided emotional vocabularies which incorporate more negative feelings than positive ones. Further, we are able to express emotions about people in their absence more easily than to their face, what we call the gossip syndrome. In the light of this for the presenter, how might she express emotions appropriately?

Responsibility for emotion: owning it

We are each responsible for our emotions. If, say, a set member seems dismissive of the presenter's issue, the latter may feel angry and disappointed. What does he do with his anger? He could respond with either 'You are making me feel angry' (which may be received as an accusation), or 'I feel angry because you don't seem to be taking my problem seriously... I'm disappointed.'

With the latter, the presenter is taking responsibility for dealing with his own anger and disappointment. This is important. If he makes the former statement, the person to whom he is making it may feel accused, threatened and defensive, while the latter statement relates to the presenter alone.

Storing up emotions

Saving or storing up emotions is not helpful, for when they eventually erupt they may explode. It is better to express feelings as they arise, even if they are negative. We may need a little time to identify what the emotion is and how we feel, but that is different from putting the emotion into storage.

Knowing your own emotional states

Awareness of our emotional states enables us to express clearly in words what it is we are feeling and why. Set members and facilitators may have difficulty expressing some emotions or express them indirectly. For example, set members may feel anxious or inadequate, while the facilitator may feel frustrated or impatient; the first is likely to be revealed by the set members' lack of eye contact and drooping body language, and the second may be leaked in the tone of voice used by the facilitator.

Parking it

We may decide, having identified our feelings about an issue or person, to 'park' the feeling until the situation arises where it can be dealt with. The person concerned may not be available or the time may not be right, and emotional intelligence means judging when to deal with and when to 'park' emotion.

As noted above, feelings and emotions are basic human characteristics. They are neither good nor bad, right nor wrong. However, we may seek to control the expression of our emotions even though we may feel them. In fact, how we handle our emotions is a learnt style of behaviour. We may be socialized not to show some of our emotions, eg hurt or anger. As a consequence, we may not be able to handle it in ourselves or in others. An example of the first would be a reluctance to cry if another person makes me feel angry or hurt because it may be seen as a sign of weakness. An example of the second would be if another person is in tears, I might feel embarrassed and avoid the situation.

An action learning set is conducive to members expressing their feelings in a safe environment where the usual sanctions against displaying emotion are less powerful. Hence presenters may express anger or weakness within the set which they would never dare to show in the workplace. The action learning process is designed to give presenters the opportunity to express their needs, wants, opinions, beliefs and feelings in direct, honest and appropriate ways. This is most effective when they have an awareness of what is happening in themselves, and the ability to convey their message appropriately.

Receiving feedback

For set members who will be engaging in reflective dialogue, an important skill to develop is that of giving feedback, and we discuss this in detail in Chapter 10. As presenters, they will need to receive feedback in a way that will enable them to achieve connected and constructive learning. To understand the role of feedback in reflective learning, we look again at the Johari window, the details of which were given above and are shown in Figure 9.4.

This time, we are considering movement of information from quadrant 2 to quadrant 1, after the presenter has received feedback from set members. The presenter will, if there is trust in the set, receive information about himself from quadrant 2 which he is unable to know without the insight of others. The result may be that he discovers a new, more informed self, represented by the enlargement of quadrant 1 as shown in Figure 9.5.

The concept of feedback comes from systems theory, and the idea that systems that include individuals can be self-correcting, as a consequence of information from inside or outside the system. Action learning is an example of the latter. In an action learning set, effective feedback on our actions and behaviours is a way of learning more about ourselves and the effect our behaviour has on others. Research suggests that constructive feedback increases our self-awareness, offers us more options to how we can act and relate to others, and the opportunity to change our behaviour (London, 1997).

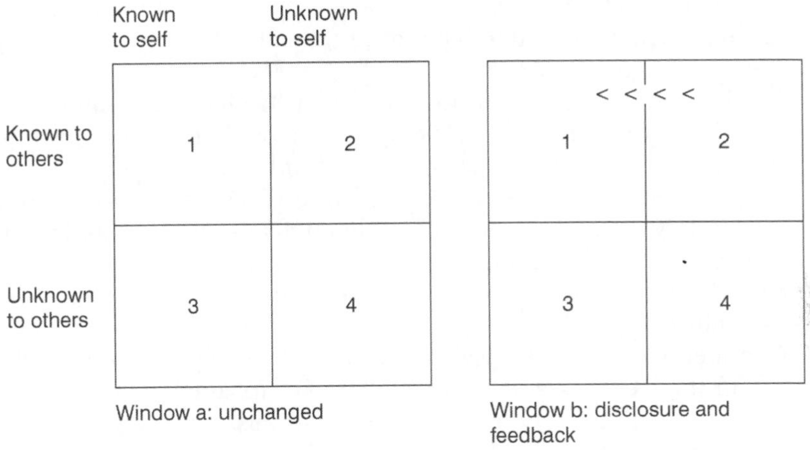

Known   Unknown
to self   to self

Known to
others   1   2   1   2

                                      < < < <

Unknown
to others   3   4   3   4

Window a: unchanged   Window b: disclosure and
                                 feedback

Figure 9.4 *Johari window*
Source: Brockbank and McGill, 1998

Known   Unknown
to self   to self

Known to
others   1   2

Unknown
to others   3   4

Window c: more open

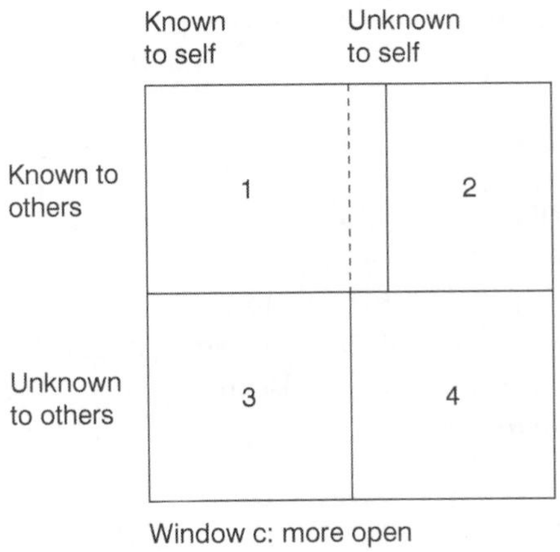

Figure 9.5 *Johari window: The presenter's window after feedback from set members*
Source: Brockbank and McGill, 1998

In order to maximize the benefits of feedback, we describe here how to receive it effectively:

1. The LAW rule: Listen And Wait – listening to the feedback rather than immediately rejecting or arguing with it.

   Feedback may be uncomfortable to hear but we may be poorer without it. People do have their opinions about us and will have perceptions of our behaviour, and it can help to be aware of these. However, having listened carefully, it is important to clarify your understanding of what you have heard.

2. Clarify. Be clear that you understand what has been said without jumping to conclusions or being defensive before responding. A useful device is to restate what it is you think you have heard, to check for accuracy. This also gives you time to consider how you will respond. A useful discipline is writing the feedback down and reading it slowly before responding, or even opting to take it away and consider it at leisure. There is no rule that says the receiver of feedback must respond.

3. Consider whether you agree or disagree. If you agree, you may like to accept the feedback and you may also wish to comment on its significance for you. Again there is no rule about this. You are free simply to accept the feedback and say nothing more. Alternatively, you may disagree and choose not to accept the feedback as it stands. Here you may choose to consider checking out the feedback with other set members.

4. Check out with others where possible rather than relying on one source. In a set, others may give another perspective and we discuss this in relation to the Zucchini connection in Figures 9.6, 9.7, 9.8 and 9.9 on page 162.

5. Ask for the feedback you want but don't get, if it does not occur naturally. Feedback is an important part of learning for the presenter. Presenters should ask to receive feedback from set members if they wish.

6. Decide what you will do because of the feedback. 'It takes two to know one' is the meaning of the Johari window, rather than relying only on our own view of ourselves, offering instead multiple views for our consideration. The presenter may also like to consider the Zucchini connection, which we describe below.

The Zucchini connection

The idea that the presenter must accept all feedback as the gospel truth does not hold up, as research suggests that all feedback is in some way flawed, or partially true. In order to explore this idea, we turn here to what is known as the Zucchini connection (Luft, 1984).

The Zucchini connection (so called because of the shape given to the self in Luft's diagrams – Zucchinis are known as courgettes in the UK) is a model developed by Joseph Luft (1984) to clarify the self-perception, self-illusion, distortions, illusions and others' perceptions of the self. The model draws on the 'six ghostly appearances' of Buber (1957: 97), Goffman (1969) and the studies of dyads by Laing, Phillipson and Lee (1966).

First, we describe the model itself and then identify the theoretical assumptions underlying it. The model starts from the belief that human interaction rests upon less-than-perfect interpersonal and intrapersonal perceptions, ie our sense of self may be distorted, inaccurate or incomplete and so is how we are seen by others. Figures 9.6 to 9.9 represent how the presenter perceives himself and how he is perceived by a set member.

The zucchini shape in Figure 9.6 is the presenter as she really exists. In Figure 9.7 the square frame shows how the presenter perceives herself. We can see that the presenter perceives part of herself accurately (the shaded area) but is unaware of some parts of herself, while she holds also perceptions which are inaccurate, ie in the frame but outside the zucchini.

In Figure 9.8 the heavier square shows a set member's perception of the presenter, some of which is accurate (labelled 2 and 3) and some inaccurate (1, 4 and 5). In Figure 9.8 we have labelled the presenter's accurate perceptions as 3 and 7, while we have labelled the presenter's inaccurate perceptions 4, 5, 6 and 8 as they lie outside the zucchini shape. Both the set member and the presenter share some inaccuracies about the presenter in common (4 and 5), while both the set member and the presenter remain unaware of part of the presenter as she really is (9).

Martin Buber describes some of these divisions within and without the zucchini as 'ghostly appearances' present in any two-person relationship (Buber, 1957: 97). Support exists in the literature for the zucchini idea in studies by Laing, Phillipson and Lee (1966), Shrauger and Shoeneman (1979) and Bandura (1978).

We are not promoting the idea that all distortion/fantasy/illusion can be eliminated, even if that were possible. The point we are making here is that in an action learning set the presenter and set members contribute to the construction of each other's reality and there are multiple sources of feedback for the presenter.

The model relies on some key theoretical assumptions which we declare below:

1. The presenter's awareness of self is limited.
2. The accuracy of a set member's perception of the presenter is partial and incomplete.
3. Imperfections in the set member's perceptions may be seen in terms of transference and counter-transference in the set, and we discuss these terms in Chapter 8.
4. The set member's perceptions of the presenter contain fictional elements and over-statements of truth as well as distortions and illusions.
5. All relationships between presenters and set members contain some illusions which are held mutually, and these resist correction.
6. Distortions and illusions are a frequent source of interpersonal difficulty.

Figure 9.6   *The presenter as she really is*
Source: Adapted from Luft, 1984: 90–1

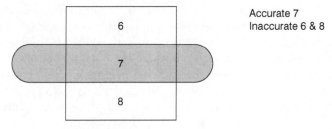

Accurate 7
Inaccurate 6 & 8

Figure 9.7   *The presenter's perception of herself – her self-image*
Source: Adapted from Luft, 1984: 90–1

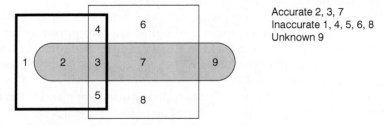

Accurate 2, 3, 7
Inaccurate 1, 4, 5, 6, 8
Unknown 9

Figure 9.8   *One set member's perceptions of presenter*
Source: Adapted from Luft, 1984: 90–1

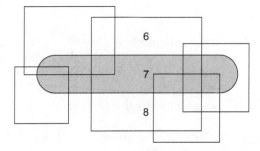

Figure 9.9   *A variety of set members' perceptions of presenter*
Source: Adapted from Luft, 1984: 90–1

To use the zucchini model productively in a set, the presenter may be offered the opportunity to hear from set members as follows: 'Would you like to hear other people's picture of your situation?', using the zucchini effect in order to enrich the presenter's assessment of her situation.

This chapter has explored the importance of disclosure by the presenter for productive dialogue and reflective learning. The Johari window illustrates what occurs when the presenter discloses and also when she receives feedback. Finally we presented the zucchini diagram to illustrate multiple feedback. We move now to the experience of being a set member.

Chapter 10

Being a set member

In addition to the presenter skills of congruence, disclosure, managing emotion and receiving feedback, described in Chapter 9, we now discuss set member skills. In order to be effective in an action learning set members will use listening, restatement, summarizing and Socratic questioning, as well as empathy and giving feedback.

Listening

When an action learning set is working effectively, the whole set is *really* listening. We regard this as one of the basic skills brought to a set. It is a basic skill but probably the most important, as the remainder of the skills we address in this chapter depend on it. By listening we mean the ability of the listener to: 'capture and understand the messages (*communicated by the presenter*), whether these messages are transmitted verbally or nonverbally, clearly or vaguely' (Egan, 1990: 108, our addition in parentheses).

People spend much of their lives listening, unless they have an impediment in their hearing. It is a very familiar activity. However, despite the significance of listening, people experience *not* being listened to. We still are surprised by the comments from set members such as: 'It really is a luxury to be listened to, really listened to. In my work I can go through the week with colleagues without them knowing what I am feeling or thinking. I suspect I am the same with them' or 'This is the only place where I have the space to be listened to. No one listens to each other in the department.'

It seems that listening is not as easy as it sounds! The difficulty and rarity of real listening was noted by one of the founders of humanistic psychology, Abraham Maslow (1969), and his comments are still relevant today:

> To be able to listen… really wholly, passively, self-effacingly listen – without presupposing, classifying, improving, controverting, evaluating, approving or disapproving, without duelling with what is being said, without rehearsing the rebuttal in advance, without free-associating to portions of what is being said so that succeeding portions are not heard at all – such listening is rare. (Maslow, 1969: 96)

Set members, when reviewing how their set has worked over a cycle of meetings, refer to how affirming it is to be listened to by other set members. Affirmation of the person expresses that person's essential worth as a human being, just as the opposite behaviour can undermine that essential worth.

It is easy to state the above, but there is a significant tendency for us to lose some of what a person has said, because we are human. We may lose a significant part of what is being said simply because the act of verbal communication is itself complex, even though we take it for granted.

We illustrate what happens when A communicates with B in Figure 10.1. When A communicates with B in five stages, accuracy may be compromised, and the message may be reduced or distorted at every stage in the process:

1. A formulates an idea and creates a message which may or may not signify exactly A's original idea.
2. A transmits the message which, in the form of sounds and visual signals, travels through space and time to B and may be distorted by external factors such as noise, light, wind etc.
3. B hears approximately 50% of the message, as B may make judgements, create arguments etc, perhaps while A is still speaking, and may miss part of the message.
4. B decodes the message, and may decode incorrectly for all sorts of reasons, including lack of understanding through different forms of discourse, which can be influenced by, for example, class, gender or culture. B may also be confused by conflict between verbal and non-verbal information.
5. B reconstructs the message to fit her cognitive map, ie B may have a negative or positive 'fix'. By the word 'fix' we mean the tendency for selective listening – only hearing what we want to hear. We often evaluate listeners as they are speaking, eg when a politician of a different persuasion to ourselves speaks, we may 'switch off' and hear only what we want to hear. Conversely, with a politician of our own persuasion we accept the speaker's message without question. The listener evaluates the message as it is transmitted, judges it and rejects (or accepts) it without critical analysis.

After the five stages of communication, how much is left of A's message?

How can we reduce this loss of what is transmitted? The largest loss occurs at the point where B receives or 'hears' A's message and this is where training and practice can improve the situation. There are records of 25 per cent improvement in the accuracy of listeners after training. But surely listening is a 'natural skill'? Weren't we born knowing how to listen? Burley-Allen suggests that the reason for our poor showing on listening lies in its absence from our education:

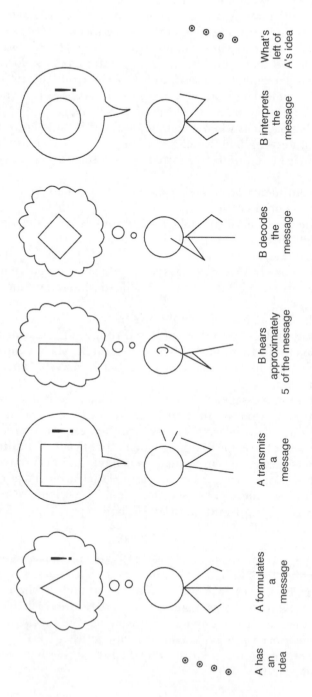

Figure 10.1 *A communicates with B in five stages*
Source: Brockbank and McGill, 1998

Mode of communication	Years of formal training	Estimated % of time used
Writing	12	9
Reading	6–8	16
Speaking	1–2	35
Listening	0–1/2	40

(Burley-Allen, 1995: 39)

So how can we ensure accurate listening? How can we reduce this loss of what is transmitted? We can reduce the loss by *attending* to the presenter, suspending our responses to enable us to reflect on the presenter's message, and checking internally that we are with the presenter in a non-judgemental way.

Attending to the presenter

In order to listen it is necessary that we first attend to the other. The reinforcement power of attending means that attending can alter another's behaviour (quoted in Egan, 1976: 96). Indeed, the withdrawal of attention has been described as psychological punishment (Nelson-Jones, 1986) and likely to damage development (Bowlby, 1969). Certainly the effects of never being listened to have been summarized in the statement: 'A riot is at bottom the language of the unheard' (Martin Luther King, 1963).

Attending refers to the way in which we can be *with* our presenter (in the context of a set meeting) both physically and psychologically. Attending is how set members are personally present, physically receptive, calm and grounded, without anxiety, ready to tune in to verbal and non-verbal messages. A feature of a set meeting where listening is happening by the whole set is the sense of the presenter being attended to. By this is meant the quality of the attention the other set members are giving to the presenter. The body stance and orientation of the set members will influence the quality of their listening, and Egan (1990) has characterized this with the SOLER mnemonic to assist set members to adopt an attentive posture in order to convey the minimum requirements for a listener to attend to a presenter:

SOLER
S – Face the presenter **Squarely**, that is, with a posture (usually seated) that conveys involvement, reflects the presenter in a positive manner and indicates that you wish to be with the presenter. This is in contrast to a posture that turns away from the presenter or appears disinterested. The square posture shows that you are not distracted and ensures stereophonic reception.
O – Adopt an **Open** posture to signify 'receive' mode. Crossed arms and legs may convey a closed stance towards the presenter. Such a posture may not

necessarily mean that you are closed towards the presenter, but it may convey it non-verbally to her. The key question to ask is: to what extent is my physical posture conveying an openness and availability to the presenter?

L – At times it is possible to **Lean** towards the presenter in a way that suggests engagement. We can see this when viewing people in pubs and restaurants by observing how people lean forward, lean back or lean away.

E – Maintain **Eye** contact with the presenter. This is a useful indicator of involvement with the presenter which does not have to be continual to be effective. It does not mean 'eyeball to eyeball' either!

R – Be relatively **Relaxed** in your behaviour. This means not being physically distracting or fidgety. It also means being comfortable with the presenter so that your body can convey non-verbal expression.

A commitment to listening to the speaker, utilizing SOLER, ensures authenticity. Artificially contriving a physical stance will convey messages that are counter-productive for the speaker. Negative or uncomfortable messages might include staring, getting too squared up where it becomes threatening, looking out of a window continuously or tapping a pencil on a table! Being aware of the effect of your physical and emotional presence is the key. SOLER is useful to convey the basic features of attending. To the reader unfamiliar with the approach it may appear that to adopt the features could suggest a lack of genuineness or manipulation. It is designed merely to highlight what we all do naturally when we are authentically attending.

Active listening

We have noted that the message is carried through both audio and visual channels. Effectively attending to the speaker means that set members are in a position to listen carefully to what the presenter is saying verbally and non-verbally. Egan (1990) includes in active or complete listening, the following components:

1. observing and reading the speaker's non-verbal behaviour; posture, facial expressions, movement, tone of voice, and the like;
2. listening to the whole person in the context of the social groupings of life;
3. tough-minded listening;
4. listening to and understanding the speaker's verbal messages.

1 Attention to non-verbal behaviour

This is an important factor in accurate listening, as up to 90 per cent of the message has been shown to be carried by the non-verbal or vocal channels. Over half of the message may be communicated by facial expression or body language, while over 30 per cent travels in the tone, pitch, volume, or paralanguage (ums, ahhs or grunts) of the voice (Mehrabian, 1971; Argyle, 1975). In relation to non-verbal behaviour, it is important to recognize that we seek to listen to the presenter in a way that deepens our understanding of what he or she is trying to convey in overall terms. It is inappropriate to fix on an expression of non-verbal behaviour and then to create a total impression from that single piece of information.

2 Listening to the whole person

At this point the listener does not form his responses to the presenter, but listens. An example would be when a presenter is telling what it is like for her, working in an office environment where a manager is continuously baiting her for not adopting the norms of the office which include late working in a predominately male workforce. While the presenter is telling the set what it is like for her as a working mother, coping with her job and her family commitments, the listener may have some views about how he would cope in such an environment. For example, he may reflect to himself: 'I could cope with that' or 'It would not be a problem for me.'

In this he is 'playing the doubting game' (Elbow, 1998) and falling into the trap of empathy, defined as 'the recognition of self in the other' (Kohut, 1978, cited by Jordan, 1991: 68). As he listens to his own thoughts on *his* way of coping he may detract from how she is thinking, feeling and being in *her* environment. The key is for our listener to 'put aside' his own responses to her situation, suspend judgement, and listen from the presenter's standpoint – where she is coming from. Such an approach has been named 'the believing game' (Elbow, 1998). To achieve acceptance without necessarily agreeing, the set member must contain his approval as well as his disapproval. As we shall see below, even when the set member responds, it is necessary to work with where the presenter is and not put his solutions to her predicament.

Our set member above, in listening to her story, will, if effective, place himself (as far as is possible), as a man, in her social context. He will endeavour to understand what it is like to be a woman in a family situation, to tackle a prevailing norm within which she feels oppressed. Rather than get trapped in his own contextual picture, what is it about *her* picture that he needs to understand to enable her to deal with it? In this way he will be endeavouring to get into her personal context – how life is for her, ie in Martin Buber's words, 'making the other present' or getting to 'imagine-other' (Buber, 1965, cited in Kohn, 1990: 133). We discuss this more fully under Empathy below.

Issues relating to the social grouping of a presenter's or set member's life may not be part of the verbal message. However, a set member who is a member of an ethnic minority may be visibly living with issues of exclusion and her message will convey something of her struggle, and may be very relevant to her learning and reflection. For example, black staff in an all-white office may be marginalized in group work and informal gatherings. Cultural factors may provide important cues for an active listener, who will need to be alert to the cultural context of the presenter, and provide what is known as transcultural caring in his responses (Leininger, 1987). Cultural-care has been defined as a listener using the speaker's notion of care, as defined by the speaker's culture, and accommodating to it, rather than depending on his or her own notion of care (Eleftheriadou, 1994).

3 Tough-minded listening

This requires that our listener places himself in the frame of the presenter so that he really understands where she is coming from. This means that he picks up what is perhaps being distorted or non-verbally leaked by the presenter. For example, our presenter may be talking about going for a promotion in the organization and expressing how she is well qualified for the promotion. However, she is also conveying less explicitly through her voice tone, demeanour and some of her words that she may feel that she is not confident to do the job if promoted. This in turn may affect her will to apply for the post. It is for the listener to pick up this inconsistency and hold it until it is appropriate to offer it as an observation.

4 Understanding the presenter's verbal message

This demands that set members engage in active listening as opposed to passive listening or just hearing, and we discuss these now.

Hearing, active and passive listening

Contrast the distinction between hearing, active listening and passive listening. If you close your eyes you can hear what is going on around you (unless you have a hearing impediment) as well as inner sounds inside you. As you hear, you are likely to be interpreting what you are hearing – we place meaning on the sounds we hear quite automatically. Alternatively, you may be passively not trying to grasp meaning from it or not really caring what you hear.

Now with eyes open, we listen to somebody such as our presenter.

Listening actively is not just hearing what she is saying but is a two-way process involving both sender and receiver skills. Active or effective listening can only be assessed by the presenter. So, in the example of our presenter conveying her message about her work and promotion prospects, I as listener need to convey to her that I have received what she has tried to communicate. It is possible at this point for active listening to seem passive and polite, whereas it is a procedure for connection. Anyone who has tried to learn to hear the other in the other's own terms knows how difficult it is to become 'an observer from within' (Schwaber, 1983: 274). This is why active listening is a tough-minded process. We have to really work at it and if we are really listening it shows! The presenter is aware of the listener really listening.

Active listening also involves listening to the whole person, not just the words they may be using at the level of intellect. Our culture emphasizes listening to what people *say*. We tend to listen at the level of words – the verbal channel. But active listening also includes listening to what a person's non-verbal messages are saying – *body* messages and, often forgotten, the messages in the vocal channel – the tone of voice used. As senders of messages we often convey our *feelings* through the vocal channel while denying them in the verbal channel, eg when we say in a wobbly voice, 'I'll be alright.' Underlying these channels is the spirit of the message, the presenter's will to act.

Let us take our example of the presenter talking about her potential promotion. She is saying that she is considering going for the promotion because she is well qualified for the post – the verbal channel. Her body is sending out messages that convey her lack of confidence about the post, as is her tone of voice. Underlying these messages is another that is transmitted about her will or spirit to go for the promotion. If as passive listeners we merely went by what she said, we would conclude that all she needs to do is to get on with the application form. However, by actively listening we are picking up the more complex messages from the other two channels.

Contrast passive listening and the signals that are conveyed between the presenter and set member. With passive listening the set member conveys, often non-verbally, that he is not really listening. Consider situations in which you have been on the receiving end of passive listening and identify the signals you picked up. Recall situations where you have given out the signals of passive listening to a person who wanted your attention!

Further aspects of effective listening

There are other ways in which we can impede the effectiveness of our listening. We can evaluate; filter; be distracted; be sympathetic; interrupt; or just be working out our own next response.

Evaluative listening

When we listen evaluatively, we may impose our own values upon the presenter's message. In our example where the presenter is considering promotion, we may do any of the following while apparently listening:

- think that she really hasn't a chance (or that it is a walkover);
- feel jealous (why am I not going for it?);
- who would want the job anyway?
- think that she should not go for it (women are not good managers).

The set member is judging what he is hearing while it is being transmitted instead of putting the thoughts to one side in order to hear what she is conveying. It is very difficult to put judgements aside entirely. It is important to recognize where they are coming from, however. Evaluations of the situation may be helpful at a later stage, provided they enable the presenter.

Filtered listening

Similar to the above, but more specifically, the listener is filtering out some of what the presenter is saying according to the set member's own view of the world, so may be missing important parts of the presenter's story.

Distracted listening

This occurs when, as listeners, we are distracted by tiredness, our own emotions, or our difficulty with differences of culture, gender, race, sexual orientation or disability differences which 'get in the way' of listening. Anyone can be distracted at any time and set members report that listening is an exhausting activity!

Listening with sympathy

A common and human response, but sympathy can get in the way for the presenter. For example, at a later meeting our presenter reports that she applied for the promotion but was 'pipped' to it by another candidate. As listeners we could offer our sympathy and replicate her feelings of sorrow and loss at not getting the promotion. By doing this, we could be disabling in our effect as she is unlikely to move on from there. Being with her empathically is different, as we shall see below.

Interrupting

Interrupting a person who is conveying her thoughts and feelings is a common trait in conversation, arising from enthusiasm, boredom, having something to say ourselves, not being able to wait, emotion, through to insensitivity towards the person speaking. In action learning sets, one of the earliest reflections given by set members is when they say: 'It is such a change being listened to without interruption.'

Given the time for each presenter is, say, one hour, she can use the early part of that time exclusively to talk. Her time is sacrosanct. It is for the other set members, as listeners, to take their cue from her. One of the few exceptions to this is where the presenter has the need to take time to talk a matter through using the majority of her allotted time without receiving responses. The presenter may indicate when she is ready to receive responses from the set.

Break a silence

At times the presenter may pause or not want to express words. There may be a tendency for a set member to fill the silence or space with a question or a response. There is, in fact, no silence – it is just that the presenter has stopped using words! That 'silence' can be precious for the presenter and for the set in being with the presenter without words. The time is the presenter's. It is space for her. If that space includes silence, it is to be respected.

How shall I respond?

A listener preoccupied with this question (and it is understandable when we first become conscious of our responses) may stop listening and therefore stop attending to the presenter. The key is to forget about our response and just 'be' with the presenter using the LAW rule, ie if in doubt – Listen And Wait.

Restatement of the presenter's story

Retaining the verbal content of a message can be modelled by the facilitator and learnt by set members. The technique of 'reflecting back' is one way of discovering what you do hear and improving your accuracy, as well as enabling the presenter to reflect on what *she* has said, and critique it herself: 'one of the most useful tasks we can perform as we seek to develop critical thinking in other people, is to reflect back to them their attitudes, rationalizations, and habitual ways of thinking and acting' (Brookfield, 1987: 75).

Once the presenter has conveyed her statement, any member of the set may respond to the presenter in order to clarify and confirm that what the set member has received is an accurate account of what the presenter conveyed. Dialogue is enabled when the presenter's contribution is affirmed and confirmed by set members. Indeed, when used effectively it can mean that the presenter benefits from having a number of people attending to her with what may be called a collective wisdom. One member of the set may attune to the presenter's story more closely than others and follow it through with reflecting back what has been conveyed followed by clarifications.

Given that the set member will wish to restate at least some of what he thinks he has heard, he may wish to start with phrases like: 'What I think you said was that you want to go for the promotion but you are unsure about how you would perform?' 'If I have understood you properly, you want to talk about how to prepare for the interview...'

This description may appear simple, obvious or even banal as set on this page. It is stated here because of our social tendency to assess and interpret and think what we are going to say even before the presenter has finished. It is an important process to disentangle so that we really are attending to the presenter and not imposing our own view of her reality. The set member, in responding, should aim to respond in a way that is not pedantic or interrogative. The tone of voice is important. A tone that suggests criticism or uncaring or agreeing is not helpful. The aim is to reflect back what is being said – her words and her meaning; her emotions – her feelings; her will or spirit.

The purpose here is *accurately* to reflect back to the presenter what the set member as listener thought she said. Using some of the presenter's exact words in 'reverse' may be helpful if it is unclear, ie changing 'I' to 'you' and changing 'my' to 'your' as above. An inappropriate response would be to give an interpretation of what was said rather than an accurate response, eg 'You're quite an insecure person, aren't you'; or to make and convey an assumption beyond what was said, eg 'You don't really want the job, do you?'

The restatement does not have to repeat the words our presenter used exactly, although use of the presenter's key words is useful for accuracy. It is useful to paraphrase, so that she can respond with, say, 'Yes, that's it' or 'Not quite, I would put it more like this' until there is assent between presenter and set members. Moreover, by paraphrasing, the set member is also going beyond simply saying 'I understand' when in fact he may not have understood completely. Because he has not demonstrated to the presenter that he has understood, she cannot be sure that he has understood. The use of the notorious phrase 'I hear what you say' may also convey the same lack of real understanding between set member and presenter!

For instance, when the presenter expresses concern about a job interview, with a sense of panic in her voice, an appropriate response might be: 'You are getting rather concerned about this interview – it's important to you', and an inappropriate one might be: 'Well, you'll just have to do your best' or, also inappropriate, 'Yes, these interviews are tough – you should be concerned.'

Many people find the prospect of 'reflecting back' embarrassing and are uncomfortable with it, possibly resorting to an inappropriate response because of that discomfort. The use of repetition is not a regular way of communicating in English. We mention the difference with other languages below. The presenter is unlikely even to notice that you are reflecting back – the luxury of being responded to is so rare and precious that the presenter is likely to move on enthusiastically. The discomfort is in the listener and, with practice, the awkwardness dissolves as the increased potential for understanding the message becomes obvious.

Summarizing

Restatement builds material for a competent summary, so often missing. A set which has reflected back key points will be able, with or without notes, to give a resumé of the presenter's issue for the benefit of the presenter. As part of the reflective dialogue, summarizing is a key skill for the process review session.

In particular, when set members are able to pick up some of the emotional content of the presenter's message and respond empathically as well as accurately, the set is really working for the presenter. We deal with empathy below.

One final point about set members who are inert and non-responsive, preferring to listen in silence: listening in silence has its place, especially where high levels of emotion are being expressed (eg weeping) However, in the initial stages of a set, the presenter will be seeking a response from set members and this is where the 'atmosphere' of the action learning set is established. If the first response is silence, which may be perceived as negative or critical, the presenter may withdraw. If, on the other hand, a listening response is given, eg a brief restatement, then the climate of support and safety is established from the start.

Empathy

The purpose of this section is to suggest that a set member can, with care and respect for the presenter, receive his or her story in a helpful way, using primary and, where necessary, advanced empathy, and we define these terms below. For a connected dialogue where the set member attempts to 'boldly swing into the life of the other' (Buber, 1965, cited in Kohn, 1990: 112), it is necessary to affirm the subjective reality of the presenter, particularly their emotional world.

If we wish to respond to another's feelings with understanding, we use the skill of empathy, the genuine response to an expressed feeling. The word *empathy* is of recent creation, being coined in 1904 by Vernon Lee from the German 'einfuhlung' or 'feeling-into'. The word has been variously defined as: 'Projection of the self into the feelings of others. It implies psychological involvement' (*Fontana Dictionary of Modern Thought*), or by the psychologist M F Basch as 'the ability of one person to come to know first-hand, so to speak, the experience of another', and 'inference, judgment, and other aspects of reasoning thought' are included as well as feelings (Basch, 1983: 110).

There has been a tendency to interpret empathy as 'feeling with' and this skates rather close to sympathy as well as excluding the reasoning and inference that is necessary to 'imagine the reality of the other' (Kohn, 1990: 131). For 'without imagining the reality of the other, empathic feeling is ultimately self-oriented and thus unworthy of the name' (Kohn, 1990: 131). Needless to say, an attempt to exclude the affective part of the presenter's message will not achieve the 'imagine-other' of empathy. For connected knowing/reflective dialogue, thinking cannot be divorced from feeling and for the set member to 'truly experience the other as subject... something more than an intellectual apprehension is required... the connection must be felt viscerally' (Kohn, 1990: 150). 'Viscerally' here means that there is a bodily response of some kind, a sense or feeling that connects to the presenter. The Western dualistic preoccupation with thinking as superior to feeling ensures that set members will often feel more comfortable with the cognitive aspects of a presenter's story, while the feeling content may be politely ignored (and therefore for the presenter, denied). Hence we deal at some length here with the emotive element in the presenter's world. We make the assumption that set members are already more than competent with the intellectual content of the presenter's message. To make a true connection in dialogue demands a marriage of both, and we offer a way of doing this below.

This particular skill requires careful handling as it *is* so rare in modern life. An empathic response from a set member may be the first such response ever received by the presenter, and the effect can be dramatic.

Primary empathy responds to feelings and experience which have been expressed explicitly, while advanced empathy endeavours to 'read between the lines' or respond to feelings which may have been expressed obliquely. However, because we inhabit an environment that largely devalues feeling and emotion, some advanced empathy skills may be called for where the presenter is suppressing or denying what she is clearly feeling. This is particularly important when the set is dealing with conflict, together with the ability to challenge or confront, and we discuss these in Chapter 11.

What exactly is empathy?

By empathy (either primary or advanced) we mean an ability to project oneself into another person's experience while remaining unconditionally oneself. Carl Rogers expresses it well as follows: 'Being empathic involves a choice on the part of the set member as to what she will pay attention to, namely the... world of the presenter as that individual perceives it... it assists the presenter in gaining a clearer understanding of, and hence a greater control over, her own world and her own behaviour' (adapted from Rogers, 1979:11).

Others have developed the meaning of empathy to be a 'bold swinging into the life of another' (Buber, 1965, cited by Kohn, 1990: 112) so as to 'make the other present' (Buber, 1965, cited by Friedman, 1985: 4). Some have warned that: 'Because empathy is by definition the imaginative projection of one's own consciousness into another being we will unavoidably find ourselves reflected within our gaze towards the other' (Margulies, 1989: 58). Noddings (1984: 30) suggests that if we endeavour to 'receive the other into the self' then we are more likely to succeed in 'excluding the intrusive self' from our empathic responses (Piaget, 1972, cited by Keller, 1983: 134).

Taking the above into consideration, we define empathy as 'an understanding of the world from the other's point of view, her feelings, experience and behaviour, and *the communication of that understanding in full*' (Brockbank and McGill, 1998: 195, original italics).

So *feeling* and understanding the presenter's story is fine, but this is not the skill of empathy-in-use. For true empathy there needs to be a communication of that understanding from the set member to the presenter. The tendency to believe that in order to communicate understanding the set member must also agree with the presenter's view of the world inhibits the use of empathy. To affirm does not mean to agree.

Egan (1976) built upon Rogers' ideas about empathy and developed a model of the skill which we adapt below. Primary empathy is based on two pieces of information (incorporating the affective and the cognitive domains): 1) what the presenter is feeling (expressed in words or non-verbal behaviour); 2) the experience and/or behaviour which is the source of that feeling (revealed by what the presenter has already said).

When these two pieces of information have been identified, the next step is communication of that awareness from the set member to the presenter. For example, the presenter might say: 'This job interview is too much with all the other work I've got to do.' The set member, if empathic, may respond with something like: 'You feel pressured about the interview, because of all your other work. It seems too much.'

In starting to use empathy, it may be helpful to use the form of words given in Box 10.1.

Box 10.1

'You feel..........because.........' or
'You feel.........when.........because.........'

Using this form of words can be a useful way to get into using the skill as it reminds us that there are two elements to attend to. First, the set member responds to the feeling and then communicates the reasoning element in what the presenter has said. If the feeling element is accurate (or near accurate), the presenter is enabled to work with the cognitive material in their story. Once familiar with the approach, using the skill will be less mechanical. We give an example below in our own words and recognize that set members will use their own words in their own way.

Egan (1976) describes a number of ways in which listeners have problems engaging in accurate empathy. We will refer to his headings and adapt them to the action learning set context. Let us take the following statement made by the presenter: 'I see myself as rather ordinary. I'm not sure I'm up to this senior management role. Perhaps I should just not bother and stay where I am. Ordinary.'

This statement can be followed by a number of less than appropriate responses, including:

- the cliché;
- questioning;
- interpretation;
- inaccurate;
- too soon/too late;
- parroting;
- incongruent;
- giving advice;
- giving an evaluation;
- making a judgement;
- challenging.

For instance, the set members may respond with clichés like 'I hear what you say' or 'I understand', which in themselves are of no help to the presenter. Such statements do not convey to the presenter that she is understood. They are more likely to convey to the presenter that she is *not* understood and that the set member is responding in an automatic and inauthentic manner.

A questioning response to our speaker's statement might be: 'In what ways are you ordinary?' The question does not take account of the fact that our presenter has taken a risk in disclosing how she feels. The question (which may be relevant elsewhere) does not convey empathic support about how and whether the set member is understanding her.

Interpreting the presenter's words occurs when set members respond by trying to guess what is implied in the presenter's disclosure. An example might be: 'This ordinary thing is the outward problem. I bet there's something else behind it that's upsetting you', eg 'You want to get to the top, don't you?'

The response may just be plainly inaccurate, such as: 'You're not very happy with the way your work is going.'

The presenter may be taken off-track or stop or hesitate because accurate empathy has not happened and she may be blocked by what has been said. The set members may be listening to their own agenda rather than attending to her. Giving the presenter a chance to express herself gives set members time to sort out feelings and content.

If set members merely repeat back to the presenter what has been said, they are parroting. The set needs to 'own' what has been said and then respond. This shows that the set has got 'inside' the speaker in a way that conveys accurate empathy.

Set members may use language that is incongruent with the presenter's. Using similar language in response to that used by the presenter encourages rapport, provided the language the responding set member uses is authentic to him. He then conveys that he is in tune with the presenter.

Giving advice, eg 'Oh dear, you mustn't worry about promotion – you're all right as you are'; judging what the speaker has said, eg 'Nonsense, you'll be fine'; or challenging the speaker, eg 'I bet you can do it if you try': when the presenter expresses a feeling in her story it is not necessary for set members to treat it as a problem, go into 'rescue' mode, or offer advice. Their solution may not be appropriate anyway. Understanding of the presenter's problem or issue is much more useful – provided set members communicate that understanding. We know from the work of Rogers (1992) and Egan (1990) that communication of understanding allows the presenter to move on to a discovery, in time, of her own solutions and to find ways of handling them, taking with her the knowledge of her own ability to learn and reflect.

We have listed above responses which are not empathic. Each of these responses has its place but none of them is empathic. This is not to say they are not appropriate responses, but we note that they are sometimes believed to be forms of empathy and we simply clarify that *they are not empathy*.

We offer now an example of an accurate empathic response (primary) to the presenter's statement on page 177 above about being ordinary. (We will use our choice of words here): 'You say you feel rather ordinary. You don't seem confident about taking on a senior management role and you are wondering whether to go for it after all' (we have assumed here some non-verbal evidence of anxiety).

Empathy commits the set member to the presenter and commits her to stay with the presenter. That is a sign the presenter is valuable and worthwhile, to be respected. The skill of empathy is rather rare in social interaction – few people experience it. When presenters experience empathy, they recognize the power of an understanding response that builds trust, establishing the basis for a relationship within which it is safe to engage in reflective dialogue, and thus enables the process of connection and reflective learning. We discuss advanced empathy under facilitation skills in Chapter 11.

Socratic questioning

The place for questioning comes after contributions have been received without judgement, so that some trust and confidence have been established, through the use of the skills and techniques described above. Questioning too early can be experienced as interrogation, and may halt the process of rapport-building. Why should this be?

Common uses of questioning carry connotations of status and control, and many situations involve questioning by persons with power in relation to the person being questioned, eg teachers, doctors, lawyers, police, job interviews etc. The person with 'authority' is asking the questions, usually with a view to making a judgement/diagnosis in relation to a diagnosis, arrest, selection, promotion etc. The style of questioning is interrogative rather than dialogical.

Enabling questions are different in kind from interrogative questions, but may be equally probing. The main purpose of enabling questioning is for the set members to enable a presenter to learn and develop, to reflect upon her actions, generate her own plans, and implement her own solutions. In other words, the questioning forms part of reflective dialogue as described in Chapter 5. Set members aim to unpack with the presenter aspects of her work of which she was unaware, either because they are tacit, what the presenter does without even thinking about it, ie reflection-in-action, or because the presenter has 'forgotten' and perhaps suppressed the memory. Where the questioning process uncovers reflection-in-action, the presenter gains insights into her professional but automatic practice, such as a manager's daily greeting to staff. Where the questioning process reveals forgotten material, the presenter may wish to consider why she has suppressed her memory of behaviour such as having a 'favourite' member of staff, without realizing it.

The questioner aims to enable the presenter to struggle with the issue under consideration, challenging embedded paradigms, encouraging consideration of possibilities, without restricting the range of possible solutions, and without providing a ready-made solution. This mirrors a style of questioning characterized by the Socrates character in one of Plato's dialogues, *The Meno Dialogue*, where Meno challenges Socrates to demonstrate his maxim that 'all inquiry and all learning is but recollection' (Jowett, 1953: 282).

Socrates engages a member of Meno's household, a slave boy, who is therefore guaranteed to have received no schooling, in a dialogue about a right-angled triangle, the famous Pythagoras theorem. Through repeated restatement and open questioning Socrates takes the boy through an elegant proof of the theorem, demonstrating that 'without anyone teaching him he will recover his knowledge for himself if he is merely asked questions' (Jowett, 1953: 284). The use of repetition and restatement is natural in Greek but less acceptable in modern English, so the process feels somewhat alien at first.

The use of open questions allows the presenter to develop their own agendas. Open questions begin with one of the following: what, how, why[1], who, where, when. On the other hand, closed questions may close down the presenter's willingness to speak or speculate, thus limiting opportunities for reflection. In addition, affect questions invite emotional expression, probing questions need to be open to be effective, and reflective questions are challenging to the presenter. Rhetorical or leading questions may divert the presenter from their own learning path, and multiple questions just confuse everybody. We give some examples below:

Open – What are the duties in the new post?
Closed – Have you done anything like this before?
Affect – How do you like the role?

Rhetorical – You know you can do it, don't you?
Probing – What exactly did you do last time you held the position?
Checking – You said you'd like to do x and y, is that right?
Multiple – Which manager did you have and how much of the job did you do, can you remember what you did?
Reflective – What would help you to feel confident about the job?

Of particular note here is the use of Socratic questioning in reflective dialogue, where learners may be developing preferred scenarios, a term borrowed from Egan (1990), to envisage the future as it would be if the possible visions were realized. For example, when the presenter says he 'wants to get the job', the questioning may go something like this:

What do you need to do to get the job?
How can you achieve that?
What might stop you?
What could help you?
Who could help you?
When will you be able to do this?

In addition, Socratic questioning has the potential to take the presenter into a place where previously-held assumptions are threatened. The taken-for-granteds (tfgs) are being questioned and reconsidered, and this is far from comfortable. In Plato's Meno dialogue described above, the boy who is learning a new theorem struggles with novel ideas, and Socrates' friend Meno observes that the process of learning is uncomfortable or difficult for the boy who is learning something completely new, compared to his previous comfortable state of ignorance: 'what advances he has made... he did not know at first, and he does not know now... but then he thought he knew... and felt no difficulty... now he feels a difficulty' (Jowett, 1953: 282).

The discomfort may lead to a complete reappraisal of previous tfgs, the crossover point in the double loop learning diagram in Chapter 7 on page 109, so that the presenter may feel some disturbance, which, in the Socrates story, Meno described as follows: 'We have made him doubt and given him the torpedo's shock' (Jowett, 1953: 282).

When set members question assumptions, eg 'Why do you want the job?', it can feel like an attack and the presenter may withdraw. Encouraging inspection of taken-for-granted assumptions needs questions that are encouraging rather than threatening, eg 'What is it about the job that attracts you?' Also, the follow-up must affirm the presenter, as there is no point in asking insightful questions and then destructively critiquing the answer. Non-verbal responses to answers are notorious here and set members may communicate negative views or even contempt through, for example, sighing, a tired smile, raised eyebrow, inflected voice or inappropriate laughter.

Feedback

Effective feedback does not only mean positive feedback. Negative feedback, given skilfully, is just as important. Destructive feedback is unskilled feedback that leaves the presenter simply feeling bad with little to build on. The most commonly voiced complaint is lack of feedback, or feedback that cannot be used by the presenter.

Feedback is of little value to the presenter unless:

a)   The presenter can accept it.
b)   The presenter can understand it.
c)   The presenter can use it.

To be helpful, feedback must be delivered by someone who is aware of the emotional charge that can accompany feedback and how this impacts on the receiver. Where the feedback-giver communicates emotion, usually via the vocal channel, ie tone of voice, this can have the effect of an emotional Exocet for the receiver. If the giver of feedback is angry, this should be owned and declared using congruent words, tone and non-verbal cues so that the presenter can separate the feelings from the feedback itself. For example, when a set member is feeling irritated by the presenter's avoidance, she should say so, and take responsibility for the feeling, which is hers, not the presenter's. She may say: 'Look, I'm sorry but I am feeling so annoyed with you.' Thereafter she can elaborate by describing what exactly is irritating her, eg 'it seems to me that you are avoiding the issue by saying it's not important', and this information, possibly from quadrant 2, may be valuable feedback for the presenter.

The prospect of receiving feedback often inspires fear as most people expect negative feedback and are not in a receptive listening mode. The set member giving feedback should take into account the presenter's emotional state and check out if the feedback has really been heard and received, possibly ensuring that it is recorded, especially if it is positive.

Should we always give feedback? The set member offering feedback must make a judgement about appropriateness. When – is this the right time? – and how can I do it most effectively? Where feedback is missing there is a tendency to 'fill in the gaps' ourselves, usually negatively, so presenters will normally appreciate feedback. However, presenters have the option to defer feedback if they would prefer to hear it at another set meeting.

Research suggests that helpful and effective feedback enables the receiver to self-assess more accurately and seek feedback again (London, 1997). It is possible to develop feedback skills, by practising, focusing on clarity and simplicity, and keeping in mind the dignity and self-esteem of the receiver.

What if the feedback is negative? How can I give positive feedback without sounding sloppy? We look at some of the difficulties below and identify the skills needed to give feedback properly.

Positive feedback

Often we may not give positive feedback, because we may be taking a person's qualities and skills for granted when something has been done well, and hence we may be more likely to draw attention to those aspects that have not gone well. Alternatively, we may be embarrassed to say something positive to others for fear that it may be misinterpreted or may not seem genuine or that the receiver may be embarrassed, as we may be brought up to think of self-effacement as better than too much self-confidence.

Some or all of these reasons may inhibit the giving of positive feedback, which is an important part of learning. Only set members can inform the presenter about what is not evident to him in quadrant 2 (see the Johari diagram in Chapter 9 on page 159).

Negative feedback

Set members may feel uncomfortable about giving negative feedback as they fear it may be distressing for the person receiving it. The fears associated with being the bearer of bad news, while archaic, are real. However, persistent failure to give negative feedback may result in either the tendency for negative feedback to be 'stored up' and, under pressure, explode in a destructive way, or to lead to no change in the presenter's practice because they are unaware that it is causing any difficulties, and hence a continuation of less effective practice.

(Note avoidance of the word 'but' when linking positive and negative feedback, as 'but' tends to devalue what has just been said.) The use of a feedback 'sandwich' has been recommended, where a negative piece of feedback is sandwiched in between two positives.

Giving feedback effectively

First of all, givers of feedback may need to check out who this feedback is for. Is it for the benefit of the giver or the receiver? Thereafter it is possible to give effective feedback by following some simple guidelines:

1. Clarity: Be clear about what you want to say in advance. In order to achieve clarity, first observe and listen carefully. Secondly, record observation in concrete and specific terms, ie what was seen and heard, eg details of behaviour and observed effects on others. Before delivering feedback verbally, it may help to practise mentally beforehand, and/or write down what it is you want to say.
2. Own the feedback: Effective feedback is 'owned', beginning with 'I' or 'in my view' rather than with 'you are...', which may suggest that a universally agreed opinion is being offered about that person. Starting with 'I' means that the person giving the feedback is also taking responsibility for what they are saying.

3. Start with the positive: Most people need encouragement, and the presenter needs to know when they are being effective. Do not take the positive aspects for granted. When offering feedback, it can really help the presenter to hear first what they have done well, for example: 'I liked the way you handled your manager. It sounds like you were able to be assertive without attacking him.'

4. Be specific, not general: General comments are not useful in feedback when commenting on a person's behaviour. For feedback to be useful (ie it can be used by the recipient) it needs to be specific. Statements like: 'That was brilliant' or 'You were awful' may be pleasant or dreadful to hear but they do not enable the person to learn what was brilliant or awful and act upon it. For example: 'I liked your approach to that difficult member of staff – you were clear about what was needed.'

5. One piece of feedback at a time: Try not to overwhelm the presenter with too much feedback at once. Highlight the most significant feedback, especially if you are giving negative feedback.

6. Focus on behaviour rather than the person: Reporting what was seen and heard ensures that the focus is on behaviour rather than the person. For example: 'I noticed that you didn't respond to A's question about delegation and I wondered why.'

7. Refer to behaviour that can be changed: It is not very helpful to give a person feedback about something they can do nothing about, eg a personal attribute, dialect or accent.

8. Descriptive rather than evaluative: Telling the person what has been seen or heard and the effect it had is more effective than saying something was merely 'good' or 'bad'. For example: 'When I asked that question, I noticed that you looked away without speaking.'

Set members may develop more advanced skills and, because these are facilitative skills, we discuss them under facilitation skills below. Over time, in an action learning set, the set members share the role of facilitating with the facilitator. The advanced skills we discuss in Chapter 11 include advanced empathy, immediacy, challenge and confrontation as well as processing and review skills.

NOTE

1. 'Why' questions are likely to be ineffective in facilitator situations, unless and until the relationships are resilient. They have been perceived as intrusive, like an interrogation, led by the questioner, for the questioner's benefit, and may cause the learner to lose their train of thought (Dainow and Bailey, 1988).

Chapter 11

Being a facilitator

In this chapter we discuss the facilitation of action learning. We start by assuming that an action learning facilitator is very different from a teacher or even a trainer. The first use of the term 'set adviser' for the person who facilitates a set implies a particular model of learning where a group of individuals seek the 'advice' of another individual who is perceived as 'expert' in some aspect of the set's activities. We depart from the term 'set adviser' and maintain that for action learning to promote the kind of learning needed for today's organizations, described in detail in Chapter 7, the term 'facilitator' is likely to be more appropriate.

The word 'facilitate', earliest use 1646, is defined (in the *Shorter Oxford Dictionary*) as meaning: 1) to render easier; to promote, help forward; or 2) to lessen the labour of, to assist, which begs the question 'to promote whom or what?', 'to render what easier?' In the context of action learning, who or what is the facilitator to assist? Our definition of action learning given in Chapter 1 may help us here, and while we recognize that some practitioners of action learning would not recognize this definition, we maintain it as our theory-in-use and, as far as we can, our theory-in-action. These terms were created by Argyris and Schön (1974) to describe the difference between what we say we believe in and what we actually do:

> Action learning is a continuous process of learning and reflection that happens with the support of a group or 'set' of colleagues, working on real issues, with the intention of getting things done. The voluntary participants in the group or 'set' learn with and from each other and take forward an important issue with the support of the other members of the set. The collaborative process, which recognizes set members' social context, helps people to take an active stance towards life, helps overcome the tendency to be passive towards the pressures of life and work, and aims to benefit both the organization and the individual.

We recommend primarily a person-centred approach to facilitation, described in Chapters 7 and 8, informed by psychodynamics, existential and behavioural concepts. We note that: 'It is easy to embrace the person-centred approach intellectually. However much personal work and practice is needed to eliminate old ingrained patterns – such as the need to be needed, to know best, to control, to solve the problem, to impress – before one can shift towards being truly person-centred' (Silverstone, 1993: viii).

In this chapter we discuss how the facilitator relates to set members, her stance in the set, and the extra skills which an action learning facilitator may be called upon to use in a set. This does not preclude them being used by set members. We are assuming that the facilitator routinely uses the presenter and set member skills already described in Chapter 10, such as listening, self-disclosure, empathy and summary. The more advanced skills we discuss here are managing emotion; advanced empathy; immediacy; challenge; and confrontation. In addition, we discuss the facilitation of a facilitator set, ie a set of individuals who are or are seeking to become action learning set facilitators and the appropriate training for such a group.

Facilitator presence

The first thing a facilitator brings to a set is her presence. When the set begins, she is likely to be in the room and is instantly present to set members by virtue of her posture, gesture, facial expression and her position in relation to them, even before she uses her voice or hearing to communicate. Her non-verbal messages are already in the room, such as body language, facial expression and voice, which are thought to deliver meaning quite independently of words (Argyle, 1975; Ekman and Freisen, 1975; Pease, 1981; Morris, 1977). In fact non-verbal and vocal channels often carry a bigger proportion of meaning than the verbal message. For instance, communication of approval has been explored and found to favour the non-verbal channel (90 per cent), leaving the spoken words with only 10 per cent of meaning (Mehrabian, 1971). Where the non-verbal or vocal channels are inconsistent with verbal messages, ie spoken words, receivers accept the meaning carried by the non-verbal channels. A clear example of this is sarcasm, where, whatever the verbal message, the voice tone is the message received. Clearly, cultural factors influence how far meanings carried by non-verbal channels are universal, and this point receives a thorough treatment, as do all non-verbal communication issues, in Bull (1983). Of particular interest are the findings on dominance and status and how they are communicated by interpersonal distance and posture (Bull, 1983). Suffice to say that a facilitator communicates, whether she knows it or not, a host of messages through non-verbal and vocal channels and, of course, set members will communicate through the same channels, eg yawning, sleeping, glazed eyes are all indications that set members have disconnected. Awareness of these non-verbal communication channels is likely to enable the facilitator to make sense of responses from set members. For instance, a set member who keeps his head down, avoiding eye contact, and fidgets while others talk is clearly preoccupied with his own concerns, which may relate to his work or personal life, and the facilitator may enable him to voice those concerns.

One key aspect of non-verbal behaviour that affects the facilitator is her physical stance. What physical pose is appropriate for facilitation? Heron (1993) suggests that a facilitator's personal presence enables her to be in 'conscious command of how she is appearing in space and time' (1993: 32). He suggests that many facilitators crouch in defensive positions, slumped in chairs with ankles crossed and head jutting forward. Heron suggests that in such a position the facilitator is 'about to talk too much, exhibits anxious control, and is missing a lot of what is going on in the group' (1993: 38).

When crouching in the way shown in Figure 11.1(a), awareness is reduced, and the facilitator is likely to be perceived as a talking head. A simple adjustment to posture with head, neck and spine rearranged with a sense of lift, lengthening and widening the back, pelvis, thighs and legs grounded through contact with the floor, as shown in Figure 11.1(b), is suggested by Heron. The facilitator moves from slouch and impotence into a commanding and potent posture. The body wakes up and is ready to receive energies in the field around it. Such a facilitator posture projects presence, and the posture *can be learnt*.

Facilitator speech time

The vocal channel is significantly influenced by the facilitator's pace of speaking, which we now consider. First, we look at the pace of delivery when the facilitator speaks. Again we draw on Heron (1993), who differentiates between rapid speech time and facilitation speech time. An awareness of the difference between the two and a sense of when and how to use them are an important facet of personal presence in facilitation.

Rapid speech time, used in most conversations and training/teaching, is often hurried, urgent, non-stop and over-tense. There are no gaps or silences, the speaker may say too much for too long, and continuous activity displaces anxiety about performance in the teacher. Skilled public speakers have improved their delivery by incorporating some of the characteristics of facilitator speech into their material.

Facilitator speech time is slower, with intentional pauses and silences, free of urgency or tension. It is likely to be warmer, deeper and rhythmic in delivery. It is appropriate for interventions which touch on matters of human significance, eg facilitator disclosure, responses to participants, matters of importance such as set ground rules. The test of competence in facilitator speech is toleration of silence, with the ability to remain fully present, without anxiety, during intentional (or indeed unintentional) silence. In silence the facilitator can tune in to her set and generate unstated meaning. Some facilitators learn a 'rhythm' of counting to six or ten before intervening into silences.

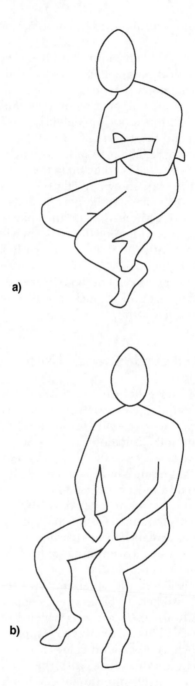

Figure 11.1   *a) Facilitator posture – crouched and defensive; b) Facilitator posture
– open and potent*
Source: Brockbank and McGill, 1998

We would say, however, that people tend to be used to rapid speech within traditional training situations where the tutor is the undisputed expert, so set members may expect the facilitator to use the rapid speech mode. The facilitator of a new set may need to convey to set members that she will be using a different approach, or possibly a mixture of approaches. The facilitator is responsible for informing the set about the quality of the relationship she will have with them, and, where the facilitator is moving between modes, she may need to alert set members to her intentions. We look now in more detail at the relationship the facilitator may have with set members.

The relationship of the facilitator to set members

The purpose of action learning is to enable the participants to take responsibility for their learning, their actions and to develop and/or enhance their autonomy. Inevitably, in the early stages of a set the facilitator is going to take a significant role in guiding and directing how the set works. The aim of the facilitator is ultimately to move away from this dependent relationship to one where the set members achieve greater autonomy.

John Heron's (1989) three modes of facilitation are useful to convey how the facilitator can move along a spectrum (Figure 11.2).

Hierarchical mode

Initially the facilitator is in *hierarchical* mode, directing the learning process, exercising power over it and doing things *for* the group. She leads the set, for it is usually a new way of working with which the set members are unfamiliar. We are continuously struck by how novel a way of working action learning is to set members, being totally unlike a seminar, training session or management briefing. This comes out at reviews when set members comment upon the effectiveness of the process and how unusual it has been in their lives up until that point to work in that way.

At this initial stage, adopting the hierarchical mode is entirely appropriate. To adopt another approach would be to abdicate the responsibility the facilitator has for the successful launch of the set. This mode of working means that the facilitator will clarify and interpret questions about procedures, the aims of set working, appropriate and inappropriate behaviours and interventions.

Hierarchical	Cooperative	Autonomous

Figure 11.2 *Mode of facilitation*
Source: Brockbank and McGill, 1998

However, she is also, even at this stage, modelling practice that will enable set members to take on a more participatory active role – ideally from the first set meeting. For example, she will encourage set members to support, clarify, question and challenge a set member. In this way participation is encouraged and set members learn not to let the facilitator alone interact with the set member, as presenter, whose time it is.

An important example is the tendency for a set member to give the facilitator eye contact to the exclusion of the other set members. The non-verbal and usually unwitting effect of this is to exclude the other set members from the dialogue and to focus the interaction on one set member and the facilitator. While the facilitator may try to cast her eyes around the group during the interaction in order to non-verbally encourage the set member to include the set in his interaction, she may consider it more effective to be explicit and say that we do tend to fix eye contact on the facilitator because of her initial influential and hierarchical role. In this example we have the facilitator being in hierarchical mode about a process and behavioural issue – eye contact – designed to lead to a less hierarchical outcome – shared eye contact – from that point onwards. We discuss the possible 'dependency' reasons for this eye-contact tendency in Chapter 8 on group dynamics.

Cooperative mode

As the set becomes more confident with the procedures, processes and norms of the set, our facilitator can move on to Heron's second mode – the *cooperative* mode. Here the facilitator shares her power over the learning process and different dynamics of the set *with* the set and the latter becomes more self-directing in the interactions within the set.

Set members no longer require only the facilitator's interventions to prevent unbalancing or disorientating the process. The set is more like a rowing boat where the crew (set members) are integrated and maintaining the system of an effective set. If there is a tendency to go off course, a set member will intervene to make the 'correction'. The facilitator is becoming one of the crew.

For example, in a set which had been in existence for six months, at one meeting, a set member picked up a point made by the presenter and began a monologue about the need for the law to be changed in the area of the presenter's issue. This was picked up and pursued by another set member. A previously silent colleague intervened to say that we were in danger of getting into a discussion that would be of no use to the presenter, detracted from the presenter's immediate concerns and was in danger also of using up the presenter's time – a brilliant intervention made without disabling anyone in the set and without any intervention by the facilitator. We discuss the possible 'flight' reason for the set's diversion in Chapter 8 under group dynamics.

The facilitator may still act as a prompt and support the set when set members are not going to pick up something that is happening that is militating against the progress of a presenter or the set. For example, a presenter may be saying he wants to do something but is conveying non-verbally that he wants to but there is no will apparent and the lack of will is not being noticed. Should the facilitator intervene? If other set members are not picking up the signals then it may be appropriate to intervene and ask the presenter what it is about undertaking any action that may inhibit or promote the action. We discuss this example under confronting interventions below.

A useful example of a facilitator moving towards the cooperative from the hierarchical mode is set out in Box 11.1 where the facilitator is able to 'let go' as the set grows more confident in action learning. The story also conveys another feature of action learning – the power of 'rehearsing' an issue before the real one happens.

Box 11.1   *The set taking responsibility; the power of rehearsal*

Deciding how far to keep people to the conventions and principles in action learning is a dilemma. I think I'm 'tougher' at the outset until the set gets into the process properly. In a mature set, as facilitator I can 'let go' and trust the set to work imaginatively and creatively. A good example of this was a set which had been working together for some time and which was growing more confident.

One of the members presenting was exploring his concerns and anxieties faced with a crucial and imminent work meeting. Another set member asked if the presenter could draw the room on the flip chart. The set then asked:

'Who would be sitting where? Please put names to them for us.'
'Now, what are you feeling like as you enter the room?'
'Where will you sit?'
'How will the meeting unfold...?'

It was quite an intense experience for us all as we 'entered' that room with him.

It was an inspired intervention. He thought through how he might handle it differently, how he would prepare, even where he would sit. Emerging was a lurking unnamed and unexpressed fear and anxiety that was more potent than the reality. Once identified, that fear and anxiety began to be dealt with.

They had also understood the power of 'rehearsal' that can take place in a set. Conducting a rehearsal is more than 'practising'. The value of 'rehearsing' is meant, not just in the sense of planning, but 'imagining', feeling yourself in the situation, understanding how you might react, what are the snake pits, practising avoiding them, 'facing the fear and anxiety' head-on and learning how to respond, understanding what 'makes us tick' in such a setting, feeling the dry mouth, the sticky palms. The reality may then be easier to work with. It does not take us by surprise.

I saw the value of a presenter being challenged to think this future scenario through in some detail. I hadn't, as a facilitator, seen this so clearly before. I learnt a lot that day and felt really pleased with how the set had developed.

As facilitator, I was pleased that the flip chart request had been suggested by them and not by me. It showed that the set had moved on, had developed a self-confidence. The set recognized the importance of using the flip chart as a tool to heighten concentration and focus for the presenter on the people, their names, their position in the room, etc. It allowed everyone's attention to be focused on the same thing at the same time.

Learning for the individual concerned was significant. He could take some control and have some influence on the situation if he could identify the source of his fears. He understood that he did have the skill and experience to deal with it if he stopped 'doing' and reflected and planned. He had not felt confident about his ability to deal with the situation at the start of his presentation but by the end of his time had identified some real strategies. As I recall, these included talking in advance to others who would be there; building alliances; obtaining more and better information in the process; being clear about the issues; and preparing his own document in advance with proposals that were well argued.

For me as facilitator, it was about trusting the set to have developed and to have ideas and suggestions and to 'let go' and not take sole responsibility for the process.

Autonomous mode

The next mode beyond the cooperative is the autonomous mode. Here the facilitator respects the total autonomy of the set members. They are now in their *own way* using the set to meet their needs as defined by them. Our facilitator may still be with the set but she is giving more space to the set members to determine their direction. Here the main responsibility is subtly to create and support the conditions within which the set members can self-determine their own learning. The fullest example of this is when the set becomes self-facilitating and our facilitator has withdrawn. We examine the working of self-facilitated sets in Chapter 3.

Summary

These three modes, in Heron's words, deal with the 'politics of learning'. We adapt this term to mean the management of the set, who makes the decisions and how the decisions are made about what is learnt and how learning takes place. We are also conscious that there will be swings back and forward along the continuum until the point where the set becomes totally autonomous. There may be external constraints. The set may be an integral part of an academic course which prevents the set moving beyond the hierarchical–cooperative modes. Similarly, with a set in an organizational context, management may require hierarchical–cooperative facilitation to be a condition of the set's existence.

Core qualities of the facilitator

Given the above modes of relating to set members, what core qualities do we as facilitators bring to the set? The purpose of being in a set for the participant is, through the task, issue, problem or opportunity he is addressing, to release and enhance the set member's capacity for understanding and managing his life, his development. The key question is, what climate can the facilitator model and encourage in the set that is conducive to that development?

Facilitator congruence

As noted in Chapter 9, the facilitator models self-disclosure for the set by being the first to do so. This is essential, as she will model the breadth and depth of appropriate self-disclosure for the set. For instance, she may begin by saying that this is a new set and although she is confident of the process as useful for learning, she is unsure about how the set will respond to her.

The facilitator also models congruence by demonstrating the crucial characteristic of 'owned' statements (which begin with 'I' or contain 'I' statements). Such statements are likely to be real disclosure, while use of the distancing 'you', 'they' or 'one' serves to mask disclosure. We discuss this in detail in Chapter 9.

When a set first forms and members are asked to speak, they often *don't know what to say*. They may be frightened of speaking in case they say the wrong thing and make a fool of themselves, and so they may remain silent, or gabble nervously. The facilitator can control the level of contributions by a very simple procedure, ie by starting off, that is, speaking first about herself, demonstrating the skill of self-disclosure. The act of self-disclosure is a direct example of trust behaviour, where the facilitator takes the risk of disclosing and thereby encourages others to do the same.

The facilitator may also model appropriate self-disclosure in the set even though she does not have set time for herself. Engaging in opening exercises, eg 'Trauma, trivia and joy' at the commencement of set meetings can help trust to develop (see Chapter 3).

Because self-disclosure is reciprocal in effect, this gives permission for everyone in the room to express some positive feeling about what they are doing and some negative feeling too. In particular, it allows set members to say 'I don't like the sound of this – I've never done it before', 'It feels like counselling'/'Alcoholics Anonymous'/'Evangelical meetings' or whatever it triggers for them. Note that the example given above, the facilitator's disclosure about method, includes some emotional material, namely her mixed feelings of confidence and unsureness. These feelings, expressed openly, although fairly superficial, are the hallmark of trust-building self-disclosure. We discuss the management of emotion as a facilitator below.

Where a set member refuses or is unwilling to present, the facilitator may judge that the set member has made a conscious choice and that choice should be respected (see guidelines in Chapter 4). We would urge facilitators to ensure that every member of a set is enabled to speak at least once, early in the set's life, thereby ensuring that members choose silence rather than being silenced. The learning group is embedded in a number of oppressive social systems, eg sexism, racism, ageism, etc. The silencing of minority groups becomes very clear in facilitation situations, and the facilitator may like to address the issue when agreeing guidelines at the very beginning.

Restatement and summary

We discuss restatement in Chapter 10 as a key skill for set members. For facilitators, the re-presentation to the presenter of her material is both affirming and incredibly useful, laying the basis for a complete summary later. Often as speakers we are not quite clear about what we want to say. When it is 'reflected back', we can adjust it or agree to it and move on. If responses are critical or questioning too early, a set's activity may be killed off before it starts, particularly if members' contributions are attacked or ignored. The skill of 'receiving' contributions from the presenter without evaluation is the basis of facilitation and probably the most valuable skill for aspiring facilitators to learn. Initially the facilitator may need to model restatement and summary until set members feel confident to receive the presenter in this way.

Socratic questioning

Where set members are new to action learning, the facilitator can enable them to formulate their responses in the form of Socratic questions, eg where the set member has offered advice to the presenter as 'What I think you should do is...'. The facilitator may gently suggest that the person concerned may like to rephrase their response to the presenter as a question, ie 'what can you do about this?' A detailed discussion of Socratic questioning can be found in Chapter 10.

Managing emotion in self and others

The facilitator will need to address emotion in the set, because of its key role in reflective dialogue, double loop learning and connected/constructivist learning. The expression of emotion is socialized on cultural and gender lines, eg privileging particular emotional expression to females but not to males, such as weeping. Some emotions are more acceptable than others, and this is inculcated very early in life and there is no further training in the handling of emotions (Skynner and Cleese, 1983), leading to the inadequacy of emotional matters in the wider (Western) society (Orbach, 1994).

Set members who declare that they feel no emotion are likely to reveal 'leakages' in some non-verbal way, often in their body language. When a set member's spoken expression matches their non-verbal messages, this is known as congruent behaviour. Non-verbal expression of emotion may include tone of voice, gesture and body language. Verbally, emotions may also be expressed inadvertently when the words belie the stated intention, as in Freudian slips! As living human beings for whom emotion is an integral part of ourselves, there is no such thing as a non-emotional person.

As discussed in Chapter 9, when we are 'known' by others, we are healthier, happier and less stressed (Jourard, 1971). Facilitators report that they have heard a presenter say that being able to give voice and express their emotions has been a major breakthrough in tackling a major task in work or in life. Facilitation offers set members the chance to express emotions safely.

Expression of emotion

We begin with emotions experienced by the self, ie the facilitator.

As part of our humanity, emotions in themselves are neither right nor wrong, and though we can suppress or even repress 'unacceptable' emotions, they are not so easily controlled and may be released verbally and/or nonverbally. Secondly, the motivating power of emotion provides the 'fuel' for the adventure of double loop learning (see Chapter 7). Emotion is an important source of energy to support and sustain the learner through the 'dip' of the learning curve. In addition, an ability to deal with emotional material is necessary for facilitators if we wish to 'unpack' the blocks to learning which emerge in reflective dialogue.

However, we recognize our heritage and in seeking to identify where our difficulties may lie we referred in Chapter 8 to the difficult/easy continuum, shown again in Figure 11.3, which is based on the work of Egan (1977) and indicates how awkward we find emotional expression, under a variety of circumstances.

The diagram suggests that we find it easier to express negative emotion and this is borne out by our lopsided emotional vocabularies which incorporate more negative feelings than positive ones, so facilitators will need to develop a positive emotional vocabulary. Also, the diagram shows that we

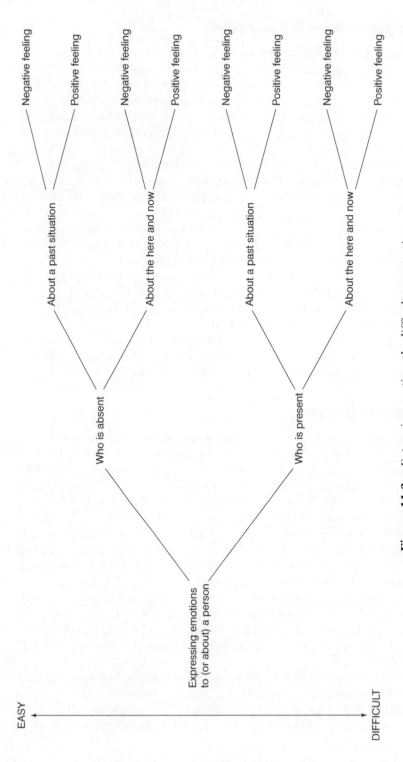

Figure 11.3 *Expressing emotion: the difficult–easy continuum*
Source: Adapted from Egan, 1977:81, in Brockbank and McGill, 1998

are able to express emotions about people in their absence more easily than to their face, and the set may avoid expressing feelings in the here and now. The facilitator, to enable reflective dialogue, is an important model of emotional expression in the here and now, so how might she express emotions appropriately?

Owning the feeling

Set activity will generate feelings in the facilitator and we discuss the psycho-dynamic reasons for this in Chapter 8. When, as facilitator, I feel impatient with a set member, what can I do with my impatience? I can express it like an accusation: 'You are really making me feel impatient' or, by owning the feeling, say: 'I feel impatient somehow – I think it's because I've lost the thread of what you're saying. Could we start again, please?'

With the latter, I am taking responsibility for dealing with my own feeling of impatience and trying to identify the cause. This is important. If I make the former statement, the person to whom I am making it may feel accused, threatened and defensive, while the latter statement relates only to me.

Storing or saving

Saving or storing up emotions is not helpful, for when they eventually erupt they may explode. The facilitator needs to make a judgement about whether the set can cope with hearing about her feelings and indeed whether they are relevant to the set. Although it is usually better to express feelings as they arise, even if they are negative, a skilled facilitator may decide to take her stored feelings to a colleague outside the set, to a mentor, or to her own facil-itator set. We describe such a set in Chapter 12.

Facilitator awareness of their own emotional state

Awareness of our own emotional states enables us to express clearly in words what it is we are feeling and why. Facilitators may have difficulty expressing some emotions, or express them indirectly. For example, the facilitator may feel frustrated or impatient, and if this is not expressed, it may be leaked in the tone of voice used by the facilitator. Facilitators can be daunted by the seniority and power of the set members, and expressing this is preferable to leakage.

As noted above, feelings and emotions as basic human characteristics are neither good nor bad, right nor wrong. As a learnt style of behaviour, we show some of our emotions and not others, eg hurt or anger. As a consequence, we may not be able to handle it in others, and this has implications for the facilita-tor when set members express their feelings. For instance, if a set member becomes tearful, the facilitator might feel embarrassed and deal with the situ-ation by pretending it isn't happening or being overly sympathetic. A skilled facilitator will allow the expression to occur without intervening.

Whatever the emotional expression in an action learning set, how should the facilitator respond?

Responding to emotion

We turn now to John Heron's work on facilitation (Heron, 1999). Where the facilitator is responding to expression of emotion in a set, Heron defines the activity within the Feeling Dimension (Heron, 1999: 195), and defines feeling as 'the capacity of the person to participate in what is here and now' (1999: 199). He offers a series of responses to expressed or 'leaked' emotion of which the presenter/set member may be unaware and identifies them as one of the three modes of facilitation described above, ie hierarchical (H), cooperative(C) or autonomous (A).

Firstly, he recommends that the facilitator either 'attributes' the feeling directly to the presenter/set member in hierarchical mode (H) by offering direct empathy (basic as in Chapter 10 or advanced, discussed below), saying something like 'You seem frustrated by...'. Alternatively, if the set is in cooperative mode (C), either the facilitator or set member may invite the presenter/set member to 'own' the feeling as yet unnoticed by him, in cooperative mode (C), by saying something like 'I wonder if you feel strongly about...'.

Secondly, Heron promotes the principle of emotional expression as healthy, human and healing, and advises facilitators to discuss openly the set's prevailing emotional dynamic and to give permission directly, in hierarchical mode, to presenter/set members to express emotion, eg weeping or swearing – a permission he describes as 'directed at the hurt child within' (1999: 200). He further recommends that the set is invited to take responsibility for its own emotional dynamic, which he calls 'an ocean of shared feeling' (1999: 200), by negotiating with members how to proceed (C). In this case the facilitator invites the set to consider the feeling in the set-as-a-whole. The action learning principle of individual time for the presenter's issue follows Heron's recommendation that individuals be encouraged to use their time for emotional work (C).

Thirdly, the facilitator clarifies with the set, again in hierarchical mode, the distinction between content issues, ie 'what the presenter/set member is saying', and process issues. ie 'how the presenter/set member is saying it', which is more likely to include emotional material.

In responding to expressed or leaked emotion in a set, the facilitator may use empathy, as described in Chapter 10, or advanced empathy, which we discuss now.

Advanced empathy

As mentioned in Chapter 10, advanced empathy differs from primary empathy in that the feelings to which we respond are not necessarily expressed explicitly. They may be revealed obliquely, through verbal or non-verbal codes. For instance, a presenter/set member may be talking about his work issue in a puzzled tone of voice. The facilitator may 'sense' that the speaker is actually rather worried about the work, and not clear about what is needed for the job. We reiterate our understanding, given in detail in Chapter 10, of empathy as having both a cognitive and affective component. Our rationale for concentrating on the emotional component here is that set members are very likely, if Western educated, to be more than competent in the cognitive field and less so in the affective. The definition given below includes both.

The process of advanced empathy is the same as for primary, only in this case, because the feeling is not clearly displayed by our presenter and, more important, *he may be unaware of the feeling himself*, care is needed in communicating what we think we understand about his world. A tentative approach using qualifiers such as 'perhaps', 'it seems', 'I wonder if' and ' it sounds like' means that the speaker may dissent if he so wishes. Offering advanced empathy needs care so that the presenter/set member doesn't feel trampled on.

So for advanced empathy, the definition as given in Chapter 10 for primary empathy is valid, with the addition of some hesitancy and caution, as the facilitator may be mistaken in her 'sensing' and her response may be based on a 'hunch'. So for advanced empathy, the facilitator will, *in a tentative and careful manner*, offer 'an understanding of the world from the other's point of view, her feelings, experience and behaviour, and *the communication of that understanding in full* (Brockbank and McGill, 1998: 195).

For instance, in response to our presenter above, the facilitator might say: 'You have some concerns about your work, John. I am also wondering about how you see the job. It seems to me that you might be feeling a little confused about what is required of you exactly.'

An experienced action learning facilitator is well placed to 'guess' a lot of what is going on for set members. What is unusual is for set members to be offered empathy before, and possibly instead of, judgement. Presenters are often their own harshest judges and offering empathic understanding may provide them with a basis for tangling with their problems.

Facilitators may also 'hunch' about their presenter/set member's feelings, being prepared to be mistaken. In this case, a tentative response may have 'hunched' as follows: 'You seem very angry, John, perhaps you are angry about being overlooked at the last promotion round. I know you were shocked when you got your manager's feedback.'

The presenter/set member concerned may not agree with your hunch, and, whatever the facilitator thinks is really going on, she may prefer to return to the 'safe' primary version of empathy, based on expressed feelings, giving the following response: 'You were talking about your work, John, and to me you sounded puzzled about it.'

The facilitator's skill in summarizing also offers an opportunity for advanced empathy, as the sum of a person's statements may reveal a consistent feeling, such as resentment or lack of confidence, and, in summary, the facilitator may be able to draw the threads together and, tentatively, comment on the overall feeling being communicated, albeit obliquely or in code.

Conflict, challenge and confrontation

Conflict is inevitable in human interaction. We experience conflict as causing pain and loss of trust. We usually receive no training in dealing with conflict in our lives, so we are left with whatever we learn at home. Many people tolerate conflict and can use it productively, but there are those of us who dread it and avoid it at all costs because our early experiences of conflict were frightening and painful. So we can fear conflict, but we may also use its benefits to build trust, create intimacy and derive creative solutions. When we deal destructively with conflict we feel controlled by others, we seem to have no choice, we blame and compete with others, and we hark back to the past rather than grappling with the future.

So to deal with conflict productively we need the courage and the skill to confront. We draw on Egan (1976) to place confrontation into the context of challenging skills, an absolute requirement for reflective dialogue. These skills 'lay the ghost' of so-called 'niceness' in facilitation. Egan puts three challenging skills together: advanced empathy, confrontation and immediacy. The use of advanced empathy is 'strong medicine' and we discussed its use above.

The manner of using advanced empathy as defined above, ie tentatively and with care, is also the manner needed for confrontation. In addition, Egan stressed the importance of a strong relationship in which to challenge, an established right to challenge (by being prepared to be challenged yourself) and appropriate motivation, ie whom am I challenging for? Is this for me or them? The state of the receiver should also be considered; is it the right time? What else may have happened to the speaker today – does he look able to receive challenge today? And one challenge at a time, please!

Confrontation

The word denotes 'put-in-front-of', so that when I confront I take someone by surprise, hence again I need to do it with care and tentatively, as I might be mistaken. The word confrontation inspires fear owing to the common experience of destructive confrontation, known as the MUM effect (from keeping *Mum* about *Undesirable Messages*), the primal memory of what fate awaits the bearer of bad news (Rosen and Tesser, 1970). Experience suggests that a great deal of time is spent on unresolved conflict owing to people being unable to confront and deal with it productively (Thomas,

1976; Magnuson, 1986). Because it is a fearful behaviour, for both confronter and confrontee, we sometimes avoid it and then do it clumsily. For effective confrontation we need to speak directly, assertively and then listen with empathy to the response we get. Note here that confrontation is in the 'eye of the beholder'. Anything can seem confrontational if I'm in that mood, and what may appear low key can seem outrageous to others.

Confronting is the process whereby the facilitator or set member seeks to raise consciousness in the presenter/set member about some restriction or avoidance which blocks, distorts or restricts learning. Heron describes the process as: 'To tell the truth with love, without being the least judgmental, moralistic, oppressive or nagging' (Heron, 1999: 182) and for the confronter the test is: 'you are not attached to what you say, you can let it go as well as hold firmly and uncompromisingly to it' (Heron, 1999: 182).

Note: Confronting here has nothing to do with the aggressive combative account of confrontation that is sometimes applied to legal, political and industrial disputes in our society. However, the confronting effect of identifying taken-for-granted assumptions can be perceived as threatening, and may be threatening in reality. The revolutionary nature of breaking paradigms implies a threat to existing models and this can have real negative repercussions.

Effective confrontation is non-aggressive, non-combative and deeply supportive of the confrontee, with the intended outcome of *enabling learning* in the confrontee. In particular, the power of confrontation for learning lies in its 'surprise' element – the fact that what was previously unknown is now known to the learner (quadrant 2 in the Johari window; see Chapter 9 page 159). If the learner can be 'held' and supported in her 'surprise' then she is free to consider how she might use the information. Facilitators may like to point out or suggest in ground rules (see Chapter 4) that the presenter/set member has a choice, ie to act differently or seek further information from other sources – as we noted under the Zucchini connection in Chapter 9, page 160.

Impending confrontation generates anxiety in the confronter (Rosen and Tesser, 1970). Because confrontation is necessarily revealing that which was previously unknown, the receiver will experience shock, even if they are prepared. A simple preamble is a good way of warning the confrontee that a surprise is coming up! Confronting takes nerve to cope with the natural anxiety of causing shock, and this natural existent anxiety may be confounded by archaic anxiety from past distressing experiences of confrontation.

There are two options traditionally available to the facilitator/confronter: *pussyfooting*, being so 'nice' that the issue is avoided, or *clobbering*, being so punitive that the response is aggressive and wounding. We are proposing the third option, of skilled, supportive and enabling confrontation. 'The challenge is to get it right. Too much love and you collude. Too much power

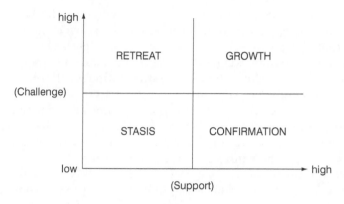

Figure 11.4   *Mutual dependence of challenge and support*
Source: B Reid in Palmer et al, 1994: 38

and you oppress. When you get it right, you are on the razor's edge between the two' (Heron, 1999: 183). This is not an easy task, and we illustrate this in Figure 11.4 and, as previously mentioned, in Chapter 8.

Our earlier comments about challenging pertain here. Who confronts and why? Confronters may like to consider whether they have earned the right to challenge by being open to challenge themselves. Self-disclosure offers the invitation to challenge by others. What motivates my confronta-tion? Sometimes there are murkier motives than the benefits to the learner operating, and we need to be aware of possible contamination along the lines of 'it's for his own good' (Miller, 1983), where discipline is enacted for the benefit of the parent or teacher, masquerading as a concern 'for the good of' the child or learner.

Has there been sufficient listening and understanding to justify the confrontation? Will the relationship support a confrontation at this point in time? Does the confronter have a history of accepting confrontation herself? Is this the right time/place? Is the confrontee in a good state to receive a confrontation? These are just some of the points to consider before launch-ing into confrontation.

So how is this difficult operation to be done, particularly in the context of an action learning set? We offer some types of confrontation, based on Egan (1976), which might occur in an action learning set, with some examples:

Checking previous information, eg 'Correct me if I'm wrong, but didn't you say you wanted to go for promotion?

Observing discrepancies, eg 'You seem anxious about your interview and you have said you're not good enough; having listened to you talk about your work and appreciated the quality of it, I'm wondering why you are worried.'

Observing distortion in what X says, eg 'X, you say that you want to go for promotion but you haven't applied.'

Articulating games (perhaps being played unconsciously by Y), eg 'Y, I'm realizing that we've been here before – at our last set meeting you were talking about another job, weren't you?'

Observing strength, eg 'I got a sense of your ability last time you presented and I suppose I wonder why it's not in evidence today. I saw that you were clear about your plans for the job and how you would implement them.'

Observing weakness, eg 'I know you believe in the right to silence, but I feel a bit deprived of your contribution here, especially when I know you could offer a lot.'

Encouragement to act, eg 'Is there any reason why you can't go for it?

Heron (1986) has offered some ideas on the 'how to' of confronting and we offer some examples below:

Interrupt and identify the agenda, eg 'Can I just check if you realized, John, that you've cut across Jane while she was speaking just then?' Explain relevance and give space, eg 'Jane was talking about how difficult it is for her to speak at all-male management briefings and I suppose I saw Jane being silenced in a similar way'.

Open questions and silence, eg 'When can you do this, Karen?'

Information to the presenter of which she may be unaware, eg 'I am getting the impression, Jen, that maybe you don't know about the policy documents which came out this year?'

Correcting the presenter if mistaken about a matter of fact, eg 'I heard what you said, Peter, about a written warning. Is that correct, Peter, perhaps you could check?'

Disagree, eg 'I recognize your view here, Mark, and I am aware of finding it difficult to agree with you.'

Moving the discourse from 'what and why' to 'how and when' and from 'then and there' to the 'here and now', eg 'James, you are saying what you want to achieve in terms of making a new start and you've told us why. I'd like to hear today how you intend to do this and when you think that might happen.'

Mirroring, eg 'You say you want to get promoted within six months.'

Attend, eg silent attention after someone has spoken can effect a confrontation as the speaker considers her own words in silence.

Moral, eg 'You said you had mixed feelings about using an idea from one of your staff – perhaps you felt concerned about being totally professional?'

Immediacy

Immediacy is an operational form of congruence, one of the presenter skills described in Chapter 9. Egan (1976) identifies this as 'you–me' talk, reminiscent of the process of constructing our humanity through interactions of the

'I–Thou' kind (Buber, 1994) where realities are forged in relationship and the interplay between you and me.

Immediacy is defined as: 'the ability to discuss with another person what is happening between the two of you in the here and now of an interpersonal transaction' (Egan, 1976: 201).

We remind readers of the difficult/easy continuum in expression of emotion given in Figure 11.3 above and note that saying a feeling to a person who is present about the here and now is the most difficult and challenging way of expressing emotion. For example: 'I sense you're feeling resistant to the action learning process, Eddie, I can feel you withdrawing from the set and I feel disappointed.'

Immediacy is a complex skill, and in terms of reflective learning it is 'strong medicine' and may have powerful effects. The facilitator needs to be aware of what is happening internally and externally, and make a judgement about what is appropriate to express and what is appropriate to 'park'. The skill of immediacy takes courage; there is no knowing how the receiver will react – for many it's a shock, but our experience is that when the receiver recovers from the shock, immediacy is incredibly appreciated and the relationship moves into a new plane. However, it is daunting and the facilitator may wait too long.

Another example: 'I'm aware that you feel strongly, Peter, although you haven't said so. I see by your look and your tone of voice that you are angry. I feel confused and I would prefer you to say how you feel out loud.'

Really, immediacy is high-level self-disclosure and feedback wrapped together – what-is-happening-to-me-right-now disclosure which relates to the relationship and the purpose of the action learning set.

Processing skills

The facilitator should take responsibility for conducting a review of each action learning set, making sure that sufficient time is left after presenters' time for a process review of the whole day or half-day. This means that the set members revisit the processes of the set and identify their impact in terms of learning and development. Some sets like to review each presenter's time individually as it occurs, and this should be in addition to, not instead of, the global process review at the end of the day (see Chapter 13).

Facilitating the process review

The process review offers set members the opportunity to reflect on the whole action learning set. This has been identified as the set members' reflection-on-reflection or the process of learning about their learning. The process review is itself another instance of reflective dialogue, so all the skills described in Chapters 9 and 10 are appropriate. The facilitator in the process review will additionally need to become a chairperson, ensuring that contributions are heard and that the group does not get drawn into detail, or revisiting the content of an earlier presentation.

The material for the process review relates to *the learning process*, as it has been discovered in the set dialogue, not the details of any one person's presentation. For example, a set member may have identified, in dialogue with colleagues, that she does not in fact wish to apply for promotion and would rather wait for a more challenging opportunity. When reflecting on the learning process in plenary, this may be reported as a realization which came from the dialogue process itself, and questioning, empathy and confrontation enabled her to get there.

The facilitator's clarification and summary of what has been said is an opportunity for the whole group to take part in reflection-on-reflection. The facilitator's role includes ensuring that a record is kept (not necessarily by him) of the process review, as contributions represent evidence of critically reflective learning and the set may wish to record such evidence for CPD purposes and the like.

Towards the end of the process review the facilitator ensures the psychological safety of the group by conducting a wind-up session, basically a closing down of the group, where set members may express any feelings that remain and that they wish to voice. Such a wind-up session, which may take no more than a few minutes, is likely to be important as a time for 'healing' the group. Through reflective dialogue, set members may discover inadequacies in themselves or others and may be hurt/angry etc. These feelings may be expressed obliquely, so the facilitator will need to have advanced empathy skills at the ready as unfinished business can block the future learning process. The facilitator should allow all the fears and worries *relating to the session or the set* to be expressed and received, but stop discussion about other issues or other people.

In this chapter we have described the further skills needed for facilitators of action learning sets as a requirement for engaging in reflective dialogue and leading to critically reflective transformatory learning. We have explained how managing emotion, offering empathy, questioning and challenging, as well as giving and receiving feedback, can contribute to reflective dialogue in an action learning set and we have offered examples of the skills in practice.

Training facilitators and running a facilitator set

Many facilitators take on the role serendipitously in that they are asked to start action learning in their organization and find themselves acting as set facilitator. Where the action learning programme is planned and structured in advance, there may be the possibility of training facilitators for the programme, and we recommend this. The offer of training is almost always taken up by aspiring facilitators and the support included in the training, ie being a member of a facilitator set, is an opportunity to be a set member, for some people for the first time. We discuss how the training programme can be tailored to organizational requirements and linked to accreditation in Chapter 12.

Chapter 12

Development and accreditation of facilitators of action learning

Context

Accreditation is a part of the growing trend of work-based learning and represents a means for acknowledging a standard of learning acquired by an individual in and from their work. Work-based learning:

> is the term used to describe a class of university programmes that bring universities and work organizations together to create new learning opportunities in workplaces. Such programmes meet the needs of learners, contribute to the longer term development of the organization and are formally accredited as university courses. (Boud and Solomon, 2001).

The characteristics of work-based learning are: partnerships formed between an organization and an educational institution; the learners usually have a contractual relationship with the organization; the work is the curriculum rather than being formed as part of a discipline or professional curriculum for which there would be a clear structure of knowledge; the programme starting point will recognize the experience of the individual learner; the learning activities and outcomes will be significantly drawn from the workplace; the educational institution assess the learning outcomes according to a framework of standards and levels (Boud and Solomon, 2001).

The above is significantly different from conventional programmes in higher education. With work-based learning there is no fixed core content on which to draw. Learners may draw upon disciplines where relevant. Assessment may also take novel forms such as completion of a project (often in-house) or a portfolio representing the learning outcomes of the work-based learning.

Action learning has traditionally avoided the academic world, the emphasis being on learning directly in and from work, with applications within and across organizations. While developing action learning in academic environments in his early years, Revans, when applying action learning in the British National Coal Board and in Belgium, eschewed the traditional academic environment for most of his life. His interpretation of MBA being 'Moral Bankruptcy Assured' was perhaps his most trenchant remark about some aspects of higher education where there has been an assumption of relevant management training combined with academic rigour. Since the late 1980s there has, however, been a growing field of practice that links work with academic achievement in higher education.[1]

As will be recognized by readers, we have been fortunate to bridge what is no longer a yawning gulf between higher education and the world of work via action learning. It is in the context of our work with public sector organizations recently that we have once again found a valuable link between the two worlds (which increasingly intermesh).

Organizations may seek to train and develop facilitators of action learning, so that the organization can resource its own action learning by having in-house facilitators and thereby reduce the need for external consultants. At a less expedient level is the desire by emerging facilitators and their organizations for them to have recognition of the skills and attributes attained by becoming effective facilitators of action learning. Below we elaborate a typical programme for developing facilitators, as well as explaining how we progressed to accreditation for those facilitators who were undergoing an in-house facilitator development programme.

Ealing

The first formal programme for facilitators was developed in a large London (England) local authority. Introducing action learning into the London Borough of Ealing in 1995 was a way of bringing reflective learning into the organization as part of a new management development programme. The aim of the programme, promoted and supported by the chief executive, was to support managers in the face of extensive organizational and cultural changes affecting the Council, like other local authorities in the 1990s. Action learning could provide managers with the opportunity to take time out, reflect on their practice and explore new ways of managing: to 'see the wood for the trees'. It would help them get the most from the management development programme by supporting, reinforcing and developing their learning. And because it was much more than problem solving, it would give them transferable skills and make them better managers.

Management staff experienced action learning over a six-month cycle of six meetings as part of a wider in-house management development programme. If the set wished to continue beyond the first cycle, it could do so but would have to be self-facilitating. This approach was dependent upon the enthusiasm of the set without the continuing support and guidance of an external experienced facilitator. Inevitably, some of these sets fell by the wayside. We found that within the original sets and in some of the self-facilitated sets there were some staff who wished to develop their facilitation skills in a more formal way. A specific programme was developed in association with senior management staff, lasting over one year, using the action learning format as the basis for developing and enhancing the facilitation skills of the aspiring facilitators. Participants commenced the programme with a two-day workshop followed by membership of a facilitator set run by one of the authors.

Thus the initial two-day workshop was followed up with day meetings of the group (numbering eight in addition to the facilitator) which took place over one year, meeting at 4–6-week intervals. Aspiring facilitators brought live issues from their work and took turns in leading the facilitation, with the facilitator sitting outside the set circle to observe the process. Over the year, each set member gained experience of facilitation as well as enhancing their skills and becoming effective in reviewing process. As more six-monthly cycle sets were created for managers, the group decided they would initially prefer to co-facilitate, that is, two facilitators to a set, perhaps with someone who had more experience of action learning. The programme proved popular, with a second group of aspiring facilitators requesting a repeat programme.

One of us, in association with Ealing's programme director, approached Dr Yvonne Hillier of the Department of Continuing Education at City University (London, UK) about accreditation at Master's level (Hillier and McGill, 2001). The aim was to have the programme accredited so that participants could have their work recognized and be able to transfer their accredited skills elsewhere as appropriate. The result was a fusing of the two groups into one for the purposes of accreditation with City University. Participants who opted to engage in the accreditation programme would gain a City University Postgraduate Certificate in Independent Learning. Readers may also refer to Binns and McGill (2002) for detail about particular outcomes for some of the participants on the programme.

The university offered a customized residential programme followed by tutorial support and continuing support within two facilitator groups. We show in Figure 12.1 the range of activities to support the programme.

In order to meet the requirements for academic validation, the course director at City, with the programme director at Ealing and Ian McGill, prepared the following accreditation documents for participants (Figure 12.2). We relate these in some detail below, except for the reading and resource list which is incorporated in our references.

Context and purpose

The basis for the accreditation of facilitators of action learning through the auspices of City University was laid out for participants. The Department of Continuing Education, offered accreditation through the Independent

City University
Facilitating Action Learning: The Independent Study Module
MSc in Continuing Education and Training

Accreditation Programme

Two-day management development centre workshop
One-day professional tutorial
Two group sessions (3 hours each) per group
+ 3 hours' personal tutorial
Facilitated set meetings
Portfolio presentation
Submission of portfolio

Figure 12.1   *The programme*

Context and purpose
Underpinning principles
Requirements for entry and accreditation
The core training programme
Criteria and evidence for assessment
Reading and resource list

Figure 12.2   *Accreditation documents*

Learning module, representing 30 M-level credits. (This approximated to 1/5 of an MSc programme leading to a Master's in Continuing Education and Training.) Participants were invited to compile an individual learning plan or contract which would enable them to meet their personal and professional aims for becoming accredited facilitators of action learning.

Underpinning principles

The accreditation programme was guided by the following principles:

- It was developmental for participants. The process of reflecting on and demonstrating that the criteria and values were met was designed to model the intentions of the programme and enhance effectiveness.
- It was transparent. Through the regulations and procedures, the programme espoused, modelled and conveyed visibly the values and criteria.
- It was rigorous. Accreditation involved demonstrating a valid, criterion-based and widely accepted standard through rigorous assessment.

Requirements for entry and accreditation

The participants were required, after participation in a two-day management development centre workshop, to be actively facilitating or co-facilitating an action learning set for a minimum of 30 hours. Alongside this, aspiring facilitators engaged in parallel participation in group and individual tutorials to work on issues deriving from facilitating their sets, and their emerging learning contract. These arrangements therefore provided opportunities for supervision.

As a Master's-level programme, participants were required to complete a programme of reading which provided a knowledge-based understanding of learning approaches, and applications of models of reflective practice. Tutorials included an interim portfolio presentation of an aspect of their learning that was of significance.

Facilitators, once accredited, were expected to contribute their experience of facilitating action learning by adding to the body of understanding within the action learning community as well as within their organizations.

The learning outcomes were those laid down by City University's MSc programme and stated that by the end of the programme the learner will have:

- distinguished critical differences between major types of learning and reflective practice;
- understood and worked with action learning formats and processes in a range of professional and managerial contexts;
- acquired the skills necessary to undertake the facilitation of action learning;
- recognized and worked with the emotional, organizational and social contexts;
- facilitated the development of participants in the action learning process through the use of a developmental model which enables the participant to explore and identify their needs and articulate how they will be met;
- undertaken a portfolio which demonstrates their understanding of the theory and practice relating to the facilitation of action learning.

The core programme

The content of the programme included, in summary:

- Context and conceptual framework: Nature of learning and development. Dimensions of reflection and reflective practice. The use and development of reflective dialogue. Critically reflective learning and its applications to knowledge, self and the social context.

- Learning: theories and applications: Critical analysis of theories of learning, action learning and reflective practice. Critical evaluation of the work of Schön, Revans, Brockbank and McGill, Marsick and O'Neil, Pedlar, Eraut.
- Skills development in facilitating action learning: Developing and enhancing the skills applicable to action learning: listening and attending; reflecting back and questioning; disclosure and assertion; management of emotion and conflict; rapport; empathy; language and discourse; summarizing and immediacy.

The teaching and learning methods used on the programme were prescribed by the independent study module as participants were concurrently engaged in action learning as set members and or facilitators.

A key feature of the programme was the use of 'learning partners'. Participants were asked, at the workshop, to select a colleague with whom they would meet after the workshop and over the remainder of the programme, in order to work on issues arising from the creation of their portfolios and related matters. The review pairs were created during the workshop and as a group they created their own guidelines for working in review pairs together.

The programme launch took the form of a management development centre workshop, the first core activity undertaken by participants who wished to be accredited as facilitators. The objectives of the workshop, which were deepened and extended through the remainder of the programme, developed and enhanced participants' ability to facilitate action learning sets with attention to key values and ideas; their confidence and theoretical competence; attending to their skills development; applications of action learning.

The two-day residential programme sought to model, and be, an exemplar of the action learning methods, processes and values. This included the use of the facilitator set, triads, and similar activities that created the conditions for individual and shared development.

The residential programme was followed by completion of the learning contract, and support with one-to-one tutorials with university staff, group sessions and an interim presentation day. At this event, all the participants presented their portfolios at the point of near completion, with other participants and university staff and facilitators giving feedback on their work to date. Participants then had one month to complete their portfolios in the light of their reflections of the day.

Assessment and criteria

In order to complete the module and qualify for accreditation, participants presented a portfolio which provided evidence of the learning outcomes/criteria. The portfolio was designed and assembled by the candidate to give evidence of his or her skills, competence and growth as a facilitator. The portfolio formed the basis for accreditation. If the criteria were not met, the candidate was referred for resubmission within one month. Evidence for the criteria showed a variety and depth of examples of each of the criteria to demonstrate a theoretical understanding, use of the skills necessary for effective facilitation of action learning sets and the contribution that the programme had made to their own personal and professional development.

Finally, participants were assessed by academic staff at City University led by Yvonne Hillier. The portfolio was assessed on the basis of evidence of:

- the learning contract;
- material that may be drawn from a learning log/journal;
- a narrative account of learning gains (4,000 words max);
- a learning contract review.

The portfolio was defined as a vehicle for the recording of, and reflecting on, individual learning, as a source of evidence for assessment. Specific examples were self and other reports of facilitator behaviour which demonstrate skill, knowledge and understanding in each criterion. The relationship to underlying theory and related reading was also an expectation in the submitted portfolio. Participants, as candidates for accreditation, were given further detail on the compilation of the documentation.

In order to qualify for their Postgraduate Certificate, candidates were required to show evidence as set out in Box 12.1.

Box 12.1

- Gained a conceptual understanding of what action learning is in the context of learning theory, its potential aims, and how the process can contribute and influence development and change in individuals, groups and organizations that is potentially transformational as well as instrumental.
- Facilitated the development of participants in the action learning process through use of a developmental model which enables the participant to explore and identify their needs; and articulate how they have been met.
- Facilitated an action learning set over a total of 30 hours in order to convey evidence of how, as facilitator, the roles and responsibilities have been fulfilled, as well as what contribution he or she made to support the effective creation and maintenance of the set.
- Demonstrated the application and use of the following key skills and attributes as a facilitator:

- facilitator presence;
- listening and attending;
- assertion;
- reflecting back;
- summarizing;
- management of emotion;
- empathy;
- questioning;
- conflict, challenge and confrontation;
- giving and receiving feedback;
- group process;
- contracting and setting boundaries.
- An understanding of the nature and models of reflective learning and how, as facilitator, reflective dialogue has created the potential for reflective learning on the part of a participant.
- Reflected on their own personal and professional practice and development in relation to becoming and being a facilitator, such that they are able to demonstrate how they have met their own developmental objectives in the context of the accreditation programme.

The programme lasted approximately 9 months from the initial residential workshop through to submission of the portfolio. Of the eight candidates, seven graduated successfully, and the experience was summed up as follows:

> By the end of 2000 a group of experienced and skilled facilitators had emerged – we were the engine driving action learning forward – and it now has a life of its own outside of the management programme. Inside the space provided for facilitator development we discovered a wealth of creativity, which has benefited us individually and can have an impact on the organization. (Binns and McGill, 2002: 139)

City of Birmingham

The programme was followed with a similar one for the City of Birmingham Social Services Department. The Department had made extensive use of action learning as part of a significant change management programme and some of the staff chose specifically to become facilitators of action learning and were offered the opportunity for accreditation through City University.

We again approached Dr Yvonne Hillier of the Department of Continuing Education at City University (London, UK) about accreditation (Hillier and McGill, 2001). The aim was to have the facilitator programme more formally accredited so that participants could have their work recognized and be able to transfer their accredited skills elsewhere as appropriate. Participants who opted to engage in the accreditation programme would gain the City University Postgraduate Certificate in Independent Learning.

A similar programme was therefore offered to the Birmingham group of facilitators, with an introductory workshop where participants decided whether they wanted to take on the accreditation programme. The same content was offered, with learning partnerships as before, and a similar set of learning outcomes were required for completion. Seven candidates began the programme and six graduated successfully. Portfolios covered the candidates' experience as action learning facilitators, their development in the role, and how this process impacted on the organization. Individual participants reported that the programme had enabled them to develop skills and confidence as facilitators through the reflective process within it. The reflective dialogue element of the programme was identified as transferable to supervision, management teams, and the journey from trainer to facilitator. In addition, graduates of the programme identified action learning as a powerful tool for management development and change management in the organization.

'External' observation of process

As stated earlier, the accreditation work with Ealing Council and with Birmingham City Council Social Services Department was programmed alongside continuing support by Ian McGill, as set facilitator with meetings of the group becoming facilitators. The support took the form of a facilitator set where participants brought issues relating to their own practice in facilitation of sets as well as work issues. The sets used the usual procedures for set meetings, which were full-day meetings. An important feature that emerged as the sets became more skilled was the option for at least one set member to sit outside the set during a presentation and observe the process.

There were initial reservations about one of the set sitting outside the circle, namely that the set would find it obtrusive and distracting as it is not a normal feature of action learning. However, once the observer was settled outside the circle and in a place where he or she could see most set members, the set soon became fully involved in the presentation and dialogue.

It is appropriate here to include another example of a skilled facilitator on a programme distinct from those in this chapter but where the set members were also honing their skills as facilitators while engaging in action learning. The story also conveys the potential value of the skilled facilitator being able to offer support perhaps based on greater experience:

Box 12.2   *Observing the process: support and challenge*

This case is interesting in that it gives us an example of the facilitator sitting outside the set to observe process, yet intervening when the set reached a critical moment that might have inhibited the maintenance of the set. Note the questions posed by the facilitator during the intervention.

This incident occurred during an action learning set with a group of senior nurses who had been in action learning for over 18 months. The focus of the learning set was on the development of leadership potential and practitioners' expertise in practice development. It is a large set with a membership of 11 people. This large membership is facilitated by the use of different roles in the set (observers, facilitators and process reviewers). On this occasion, I was acting as an 'observer' and sitting outside the group, while a member of the set was 'practising' being a facilitator.

During a presentation by a set member, it became increasingly obvious to me, as observer, that one or two set members were overly challenging the presenter. It was also clear to me that the facilitator was aware of the situation and did not know how to handle it as she had a 'look of panic'. Other set members were not managing to create a more even balance of challenge and support through their questioning.

I decided to intervene and re-enter the set. I stated that I wanted a 'process check' and asked the presenter if that would be helpful to her. She agreed that it would be and became tearful. I posed the following question to the group: 'What is going on in the group at this time?' This question appeared to act as a release from the situation for set members and the facilitator, and they each replied with varying levels of awareness and understanding about what was happening.

I then returned to the presenter and asked her: 'What would be most helpful to you at this moment?' Her reply was that she would like to hear views from set members about the issue she was struggling to make sense of. Her view was that they were challenging her in order to make sense of the issue, but that she was unable to be clear, as she couldn't make sense of it herself. It was my view that this was an accurate reflection of the process I observed, ie the lack of clarity of the presenter resulted in increasing levels of challenge by the enablers as they struggled to make sense of the issue. In addition, the facilitator had not helped the presenter to focus the issue at the outset and thus the presentation was very confused. I asked the presenter if 'doing a round' would be helpful (we had used this process before) and she agreed. I asked each set member to finish the statement 'The important thing I am hearing in this presentation is...'. Each set member finished the statement and I then asked the presenter if 'there was anything in these responses that was helpful to her'. She identified three issues that resonated with her. I asked her if there was one in particular that she would like to focus on and she identified one. She briefly presented on that issue and the set began questioning again with a much greater balance of challenge and support. I removed myself from the set and took the role of the observer again, and the set worked well together for the remainder of the session. During the process review that followed, all the set members identified what had been important about the session and the significant learning that had occurred. This included:

- increased awareness of the need for all set members to take responsibility for maintaining a balance of challenge and support;
- the importance of spending time on getting a focus if the presenter is not clear about the 'key issue' or what helps meet her needs from the group;
- greater clarity about what the 'helping relationship' means in action learning;
- the importance of responding to non-verbal communication in a set and the responsibility of set members to clarify their interpretations of body language/non-verbal communication;
- the role of the observer in action learning and how this role can help set members develop their facilitation skills.

In this example we have the facilitator sitting outside the set observing the process. It is valuable for all set members to experience observation. For the observer, one of the key skills is being able to record the process issues as they unfold. This can be overwhelming given the sheer amount of information that becomes available. However, it is worth persevering as the set member acting as observer soon develops a means to record process issues alongside the continuing dialogue. One way of doing this is to divide the recording sheet in half vertically, making a note on the right-hand side of what is being said, while recording on the left-hand side the behaviours which are observed or heard occurring in the set. For instance, when a presenter is talking about being bullied at work, he may grimace or look pained, or fidget. Eye contact and body orientation may indicate active listening and attending. Restatement and empathy can be identified, and Socratic questioning noted. Questions should be categorized as open, closed, probing, rhetorical or multiple so that members become aware of the difference. Tone of voice, speed and volume of speech are material for the observer to record, as well as silence, of course. The observer's role is to record, give specific feedback, conveying what she has seen and heard, but not to interpret. We identify the characteristics of effective feedback in Chapter 10.

At the end of the presentation the observer would return to the circle and give her feedback on what had been significant in observational terms for the set. Occasionally the observation would be undertaken by the facilitator, with a set member acting as facilitator. The benefits for set members in being able to concentrate mainly on observing process is invaluable in heightening their awareness of process issues as well as improving their skill in giving constructive feedback.

Conclusion

We had found that a significant proportion of aspiring facilitators wanted some kind of accreditation, so that their emerging skill and competence as facilitators were recognized through certification. Most candidates were already experienced and skilled in facilitation, so that the academic programme enabled them to identify, name and categorize the operational skills they were using as well as being more adept at relating practice into theory and evolving back into practice reflexively. Their accreditation and graduation from City University gave them confidence in their respective organizations, and enabled them to move on to the challenges presented in their work context.

NOTE

1. The Revans Institute for Action Learning and Research at the University of Salford is a testament to this change in attitude towards action learning in higher education. There is a lengthy story to be written about the mutual hostility in Britain of much of academia and the world of work over many years, with action learning long remaining outside the purview of the higher educational world. Revans did give his endorsement to the Salford Centre.

PART IV

Evaluating action learning

Chapter 13

The process review

Many of the earlier chapters assume that the processes of an action learning set are effective in order to realize the benefits for set members when addressing their issues, projects and opportunities. The issues, projects and opportunities may be referred to as the tasks of the set, whereas *how* the set enables set members to achieve their tasks is referred to as the process. Detailed consideration of process has tended to be understated in the literature, and possibly the practice, partly because of the attention given to project and task orientations. We endorse Mumford (1991): 'The task is a constantly seductive feature of the total process. Learning about the process by which the task is achieved has been given a derisory amount of emphasis.'

Hence our giving attention to ground rules (Chapters 1 and 4), and skills that enhance the process used by set members and facilitators (Chapters 8, 9, 10 and 11). The use of skills, their enhancement and reflection upon their use in the set provide an opportunity for set members to utilize them with more 'intention' in the set. Processing these skills in the set process deepens set members' use of these skills. The result is, ideally, to enhance their process skills and problem-solving effectiveness outside the set. As Morgan (1988: 194) suggests: 'The special character of this approach [action learning] is that it generates knowledge *(and skills)* through the design of a learning process that itself proves to be a means for approaching and "solving" problems being addressed. In other words, the medium, the research *(the action learning process)* is part of its message' [italics – our addition]. The medium of the action learning process is part of the message for learning and tackling problems elsewhere.

The process review offers set members the opportunity to stand back from the work they have been doing and 'process' it. The meaning of 'process' has been explored by John McLeod (1998) in a counselling setting, but the generic elements of process can be applied in any learning situation. McLeod defines process as: 'the flow of what happens in a... session. Most of this flow is probably beyond any conscious control... either because it occurs so quickly or because it is so multi-dimensional and complex' (adapted from McLeod, 1998: 234).

A process review, whereby the set takes time to look at *how* it is working, can be novel for set members new to action learning. Because it is an intentional act, set members are asked to stand outside what they have been engaged with in order to describe and reflect upon how they have worked.

Take a simple example. One of the typical ground rules is that set members do not give advice. Yet, when immersed in an issue with a presenter, the tendency to give advice is often seductive and unconscious in that the set member may be unaware of engaging in advice giving. Taking time at the end of a presenter's time can give the set the opportunity to unravel the nature of the dialogue and bring the advice giving to the surface. Indeed, facilitators may intervene, without expressly saying it is a process issue, by asking the set member to endeavour to turn their statement into a question. This draws attention to the nature of the 'advice' statement as well as enabling the set member to struggle with expressing the 'advice' in the form of a question to the presenter. The implicit articulation of the process moment may have a valuable impact in the approach taken by all the set thereon.

The value of understanding process is that it can sensitize set members to what is happening in the set, while it is happening. We have said earlier that the only person who need not be concerned with process is the presenter, who can be immersed in their content. Simultaneous reflection on the process by set members and facilitator enhances the quality of the process. Reflection on the process by the set after a presentation and at other apposite occasions is also designed to enhance the effectiveness of, and the learning by, the set.

Process review can also aid the set to 'see' and understand all five reflective dimensions they will be endeavouring to utilize (Chapter 6). Processing being an intentional activity is also a means of slowing down the flow of the session in order to gain an appreciation of what is really going on.

If we refer back to Chapter 6 where we described the five dimensions of reflection, we can recall them as follows:

1.   the event itself;
2.   reflection-in-action;
3.   description of the event (and) any connected reflection-in-action (1+2);
4.   reflection on the description;
5.   reflection on the reflective process.

When presenting, the set member engages in dimension 3 by describing the relevant event of the recent past. Clearly, to enable an accurate description by a presenter of a given event we usually rely on the presenter's memory of what has been said during her initial description. Following the presenter's initial statement, set members will clarify that their understanding of the statement is as accurate as possible before moving on to enable the presenter to reach level 4, reflection on the description.

An example may be useful here. A set member, a chief executive new to a large health organization, is concerned about creating a strategic plan for the future. She describes the organization to the set (who are not part of the organization but are all chief executives of other organizations). Her 'story' includes the recent history of the organization, structures and relationships, its overall purpose, her senior colleagues and other stakeholders. At the end of the initial presentation she appears uncertain and tentative about her description. One of the set says that he is not entirely clear and she is asked if she would like to describe the organization in any other way. She opts for the flip chart. Her description becomes more confident as she displays the picture in this different format. Her voice becomes stronger and a clarity of description emerges. Set members seek some minor clarifications and also ask pertinent questions about some of the other actors in the organization.

The description of her situation has revealed an important kernel of reflection upon the description. Clarifying the issues has enabled her to learn about the organization and its potential strategic future through the description of it. Not only has she learnt more about her organization but she is also beginning to see the means to determining the strategy.

The set, during this stage, did not realize the full significance of this until after her session ended and the set examined process – dimension 5, what she may have learnt from the work she had done. There were a number of process reflections, the most significant for her being that simply conveying the multifaceted picture of the organization and its relationships and responding to specific questions from the set had enabled her to 'see' with clarity. She knew much about her organization. Standing 'outside' had enabled her to draw upon that which was tacit and implicit. She also realized that she had become emotionally trapped by the apparent complexity and detail, from which she emerged when she enunciated her picture of the organizational relationships.

Thus we have significant learning about learning that emerged, *after* the presenter's time, in the period provided for a review of the process which the presenter had experienced. The process review or analysis contributed to the overall learning of the presenter as well as to that of the other set members.

A structured process analysis is likely to direct set members to events or incidents which were 'most helpful' or 'most hindering' as well as those where new insights emerged as a consequence (McLeod,1998: 233). Set members may then be invited to explore the chosen events using methods developed to uncover processes which occur 'behind the scenes' in any interpersonal encounter. Such methods are designed to reveal the covert processes within the set's activities. An example is IPR – Interpersonal Process Recall (Kagan and Kagan, 1990) – where individuals or sets consider an account of events or incidents in detail, analysing their particular significance for learning. Where the process analysis occurs within 24 hours, ie within the time allocated for the set meeting, a good deal of direct recall is possible (McLeod, 1998). We look at this process in more detail below.

The set may choose to consider its process at any stage, even in the middle of a presentation, if members so wish. In general, however, process review would normally occur as follows:

- a process intervention by the facilitator or any set member;
- individual process review by/for the presenter;
- set process review;
- set process intervention;
- periodic review after several meetings;
- reviewing the norms of a set;
- individual review of entire action learning cycle;
- set review of entire action learning cycle.

We will examine these in turn.

Process intervention by the facilitator or set member

An intervention can occur at any time in the presenter's time. Initially, in the early meetings of a set, interventions are usually undertaken by the facilitator. When set members become more familiar with the operation of the set they will also intervene. Interventions can occur when the ground rules are breached. Examples include:

- giving advice (see example above);
- more than one person talking at a time;
- rapid questioning of the presenter without giving time to respond;
- pace of the dialogue being determined by the set members rather than the presenter's needs;
- set member 'taking over' from the presenter with a prolonged personal example;
- use of 'you' rather than 'I';
- presenter not 'owning' the issue;
- assumptions being made by and/or about the presenter;
- set avoidance of underlying feelings being exhibited by the presenter – staying with surface meanings.

Intervention by the facilitator does not have to take place. Examples like the above will happen. It is sometimes useful not to intervene at the time in order to enable the set to realize the impact that the breach of the ground rules may have. The effect of a later review of the breach may be more valuable. Too frequent intervention by the facilitator may inhibit set members from taking the initiative themselves and inhibit expression of process issues. In contrast, a timid facilitator who lets process issues continuously pass will find that the set may decline in its effectiveness to the detriment of all the set. Some questions that may be asked by the facilitator (or set members) are:

- What's going on now in the set?
- For whose benefit is your question?
- Could you turn your statement into a question? (when advice is being given)
- I feel we are getting stuck – can anyone say what this may be about?
- How do you feel right now? (to the presenter)
- Could you pose just one of those questions to the presenter? (with multiple questions)

Box 13.1   A facilitator's story:

This story is included here as it clearly has significance in terms of process intervention, in this instance mainly by the facilitator. The story conveys the thoughts and feelings of the facilitator while maintaining the set in its work. At the end of the set member's presentation there was also a set process review which we consider later in the chapter.

Maintaining the process

The action learning set from which this story is drawn is a development group sponsored by an agency within a government department. The context is that the participants are all 'leads' for a series of pilots setting up new geographically based virtual organizations, which provide services for area-based organizations and across existing boundaries for their service.

The group are all men, who are working at a similar level in different parts of the country and are expected to collaborate. There are high expectations for their pilots to deliver new ways of working and effectiveness for the sponsoring body. Five out of the six are carrying out their existing roles based in one of the local organizations while leading for the pilot.

This group had not had experience of management development, have come up through a technical route and are also not used to working with a woman who has had senior management experience. They have found the processes of the set challenging, as this is so different from their current experience, which reflects the difficulties they are all finding in their new leadership roles, which they have to exercise with little authority. They met on their own the night before. On this occasion the director of the national sponsoring body joined their evening meeting and meal.

The group felt uncomfortable at the start. They updated on some issues but they were not very forthcoming. It became clear that they had not achieved everything that they had hoped for in the meeting with the director. One of them then said: 'We have issues from last night that we'd like to cover and discuss, as they are general for everyone, although we don't want to dominate the agenda!' This went against what they had previously agreed about not discussing the agenda of the learning set in their own meeting, as well as being a clear attempt to have a discussion group, rather than a learning set!

I was really quite shocked. I thought rapidly on my feet and remembered about the importance of them working collaboratively, so I said: 'We can perhaps do a mix?' I defended the 'process', saying we had to avoid it becoming a discussion group like any other, and one of them said: 'Absolutely right.' I said we could use a person presenting to cover/get at the issues that they had selected. I asked them what their issues were and whether the two issues they had selected would be covered. Then there was a little struggle between them as it became clear that one had a personal issue, and then another one said he had an issue that might not be covered in a general discussion. Then a third said that he had a small issue. The outcome was agreement that there should be three presentations and that those would probably cover the general issues. So they both did and did not want to stick to the process.

The first presentation was then taken by Neil. His issue was about how to obtain support from stakeholders for an expansion in the budget, which he thought was necessary to achieve the management targets. He started by putting a lot of figures on the board from the detailed case he and his team have developed which shows the gains that they can make with additional resources. He would have happily spent weeks telling us the detail. The group asked good questions but there were some really difficult patches for the group, and for me. They were cutting me out and not hearing and cutting each other out. There was a patch with cutting across, and Harry was clearly making Neil feel defensive and not asking questions but telling, and I was trying to move it away back to questions. Harry interrupted me at least twice, possibly three times, so on the third I felt it shouldn't go on and it was not sticking with the presenter's issue. So I said: 'Did you realize that you had interrupted me twice and Neil's flow?' He did say 'Oh yes, OK' and apologised to both of us.

The group felt easier after that. Were they waiting for me to intervene? Neil also appeared cross with me but I wasn't sure why. Perhaps it was because I had got the set to use the process or because I kept pushing him to think about the broader picture? It was only much later that he was able to do that. He kept his back turned to me while using the flip chart, and addressed the others rather than me!

There was a good exploration of who the decision makers were. With a question from me as facilitator, Neil had a sudden realization of the importance of some key stakeholders, which he had overlooked. It was after this 'aha' point about stakeholders that he came and sat next to me and related to me for the first time in the set.

It was fascinating watching him follow through on a question and then chunk through until he got an answer that he would articulate and put on the flip chart. The group got good at waiting for it. And towards the end he was asking them to tell him what he should do on a specific point, which would have taken too long, so I got him to say it and actually the group were hanging on waiting for him to 'get it' and he did, and said thank you. But he would not have heard the solution if it had been said too early.

As he worked through issues it became clear that there were options he had not thought of, issues he could now take action on, and by taking other actions he could reduce significantly the resources he was asking for.

Early on Neil said that if he did not get more resources he would be so frustrated he would have to leave. So I asked later, was he still frustrated? No, he now had some ideas about what to do. He had made a very big shift from being immersed in the detail to seeing the larger picture and to seeing that he might need to let someone else front the presentation. This arose from useful feedback from Martin. 'Your passion could get in the way. I am like you, have you thought of having someone else to introduce the case?'

The process review started by someone saying 'Did it feel as if you were in the hot seat like it did at the first meeting' 'No,' said Neil, 'very helpful.' Fred said 'It felt more like we were working together than at the first meeting, although it was difficult. People were challenging, speaking their minds, but without giving offence.' I fed back that the word collaborative had been used. Other comments were that it was focused, constructively challenging, that it was dealing with something for the whole group.

Neil took away a series of action points on his flip charts and there was a decision for collaboration with another set member to turn this case into one that could be used by the whole set. This was a significant step forward. Also, the group had worked with the process, and worked through some difficult dynamics.

Individual process review by/for the presenter

This is always conducted with the assent of the presenter in question. The facilitator is likely to offer the presenter the opportunity, either immediately after her 'time' or towards the end of the meeting. Memories will be at their clearest at this point and process issues most apparent. The presenter should be given space to recount her session as she experienced it, and set members consider the presenter's account, commenting on what they were observing, thinking and feeling at the time, as well as questioning the presenter. Before set members offer their observations, it is useful here to designate clearly what is observation and what is interpretation by set members. The facilitator's role is to identify which is which, and to allow the presenter to respond as she prefers to either. For instance, the presenter may confide that she had 'never seen her management style in that way before' and set members may observe that the presenter looked 'stunned'. Interpretations that the presenter was stunned may or may not be accurate. The presenter may be simply overcome by a new and exciting possibility in her managerial style and it is the facilitator's role to call attention to inter-pretations by set members. The presenter should never be pressed to respond to interpretations by set members.

The purpose of the process review is to unpack the 'how' of the presen-ter's session. The presenter should have control of the review and be able to stop it at any time. The set members can operate in questioning mode and in observation mode, using the language of reviewing, and we give some examples in Table 13.1 which include language for the presenter/learner in a process review. The facilitator may have to intervene if there is a tendency to revert to the content of the presenter's time when the set inadvertently returns to the dialogue as if it had not been closed.

A process review usually relies on set members' memory and the facilita-tor's recall. Some sets choose to designate a note-taker during the presen-ter's time and these notes become an important resource for the process review, as well as providing records for individual presenters.

Before moving on to set process review it is important to add a further means by which a presenter may engage in a process review. This involves the use of recording methods using audiotape. Audiotape recording of sessions may not be acceptable to some sets and the set must choose this option for themselves.

The set usually holds a dialogue about the use of tape recorders before embarking upon their use. In sets where tape recorders have been used by the authors, the taped material is owned (and remains in their ownership)

Table 13.1

Presenter/Learner mode	Observer mode	Questioner mode
I think...	I noticed...	What did you know...?
I want...	It sounds as though...	How did you feel...?
I realised...	You seem to be saying...	What were you aware of...?
I know...	You seem to be feeling....	What could you do...?
I found out...	You look...	How would you know...?
I thought I knew...	I saw that...	How does that make you feel...?
I was unaware...	I heard you say...	What would make a difference...?
I knew...	You said...	What do you think is important here...?
I felt...	You didn't answer...	What do you want...?
I was overwhelmed by...	You were hesitant...	What helped you...?
I went blank...	You seemed doubtful...	What got in your way...?
I wanted...	I felt...	Tell me what you have learnt...
I am feeling...	I imagined that...	How did you learn...?
I am wondering about...	I believe that...	What else...
I will...	I had the feeling...	
I was surprised...		
I am surprised...		
This feels difficult because...		

by the set member who is presenting. Set members then take 'their' tape away to listen to and possibly transcribe in private.

In a recent set, one of the authors invited the set to consider the questions that set members may use in conducting their own review of material taped when they were presenting. The following questions emerged:

1. What was the key focus of my presentation?
2. What significant questions did group members ask?
3. What 'novel' issues did these questions raise for me?
4. What do I know now that I didn't know before?
5. What existing knowledge was reinforced?
6. What action[s] do I want or need to take now (if any)?
7. Process comments if any[1]

The questions provided an appropriate context for presenters to conduct a further review following the set meeting while listening to the tape. This is valuable for the presenters for it enables them to go over significant moments in the dialogue that may have been missed by them and the set. Importantly, it also enables presenters to hear their part in the dialogue and may well convey information they were not aware of in the set. The presenters may then make notes from the tape/transcript which they can then bring to the set for a further process review. In one set where this became a familiar part of the process review, set members e-mailed their reflections to all other members of the set. When the set next met, time was allocated to take in a further review and reflection from a process perspective. Set members may well wish to use the absorbed reflections in subsequent presentations.

The set therefore has another resource which can benefit from greater recall and add to the depth of process analysis. Where set members are relying on their memories, a filtering process is probably already operating so that only notable events or incidents are remembered. The disadvantage of taped material is that if used at subsequent sets it will require time to be used to work with the material. The purpose of the set can then be important in determining whether tapes are used or not. The sets referred to above consisted of set members who were action learning facilitators in other contexts and who had a particular professional interest in process issues. The more focused time on process was an intrinsic part of the set members' purpose in being in the sets.

Set process review

Review by the set of its process is negotiated by the set and usually takes place prior to the end of the meeting, after all presentations. Time should be allocated for this as here the reflective learning is most likely to occur. When the set is processing itself, set members question themselves, as a set, and here an understanding of group dynamics (Chapter 8) will assist set members to realize where some of their behaviours originate.

A structured process involves addressing questions as follows:

- What actually happened in the set during the session?
- What was the sequence of interactions in the set?
- What were the underlying thoughts and feelings in the set?
- What was left unsaid in the set?
- What were the consequences in the set?

Set members should consider their thoughts, feelings and observations about themselves and others during the set meeting. The facilitator's role here is significant, as much of the set's dynamic is invisible to members, but may have been noted by the facilitator. For example, the set may have pursued a topic with a presenter which took the set away from the presenter's issue, both presenter and set members being unaware of it.

Another approach is to enable the set to consider the following:

- what I have gained from being in the set today;
- what I have learnt/gained about the way the set works;
- what I would like the set to consider that I am not sure about;
- something I want to share that I have difficulty with when I am presenting or when I am a set member supporting a presenter;
- something I want to share about the set, myself, the facilitator, other set member(s).

The facilitator, who should be included, should choose one or two from the above. To work on all of them would be overwhelming and not containable in the space allocated near the end of the meeting. Again, facilitators will exercise caution in the early meetings about the extent of reflection, as it is worth while building up the resource from set members' experience of action learning.

Set process intervention

Distinct from a set process review is an intervention about the overall set process. Such an intervention can be raised by a set member or the facilitator. An intervention of this nature raises issues fundamental to the whole group and its maintenance. This type of intervention is also distinguished from the first type above which is usually about maintaining the ground rules, eg use of multiple questions to a presenter. *An example of a set process intervention fundamental to the life of the set is appropriate here from the experience of one of the authors.*

Box 13.2   Trust in the set

The set membership was drawn from the private sector and higher education. All were particularly interested in process issues and facilitation of action learning. Some members of the set had been in a set with the facilitator in an earlier cycle. Two new members had joined the new set with three members from a previous set. One member from the previous set knew one of the new members of the set.

Trust had been developed afresh when the new set started, at its first meeting. What had not had sufficient regard were norms that had developed and carried over from the previous set which were implicit and not realized until the process intervention had commenced.

Trust building is a key role of the facilitator – lack of trust within the group severely limits the work of a set and can be threatening for the facilitator, who has a primary responsibility to maintain the set and its effectiveness. This raises the matter of how a process issue about the way a set is working can be raised without blame being attributed.

At the third meeting, a set member was asked if she wanted to present at that meeting. She declined because she felt she had not come to really know the group and did not feel safe in the group.

As facilitator, I (Ian) felt that the statement the presenter had made was a challenge to how the set was being facilitated. I did not feel personally threatened, though I feared the set was potentially at risk. I knew that we were at a very critical moment in the life of the set (it was the third meeting of eight full-day meetings and midway through the morning). My response was partly based upon my experience of action learning and facilitation but was mainly intuitive. I recognized that I was 'in the moment' – I could not call upon routine responses to this situation beyond my first response. My first response to her comments was to ask the other set members how they felt about the set. This evoked responses ranging from feeling very comfortable in the set to one person feeling angry (one of the members who had not been in the first cycle). Each person was also asked to explain why they felt the way they did. It was near lunchtime and I suggested we break for lunch. We did not discuss the process issue at lunch and I did not know precisely how I would carry the set forward following lunch.

We returned to the set. Inwardly I had been mulling over how we would engender trust in a group that appeared to be in freefall. What emerged for me was a question to all in the group – what would a safe group look like? I asked everybody to consider this question on their own and to record whatever came up for them. I had not used this device before and it just emerged as appropriate at that moment. With hindsight it was a type of reflection-in-action (see Chapter 6; Schön, 1983, 1987; Brockbank and McGill, 1998), with the action being the set in a process crisis from mid-morning to that point and the subsequent time that followed.

In asking what a safe group would look like, we came up with the following:

- not cautious;
- being able to articulate feelings;
- feeling people are pleased to see you;
- not feeling judged;
- feeling there is high challenge and high support;
- being able to take risks;
- people wanting to present most of the time;
- feeling safe only when I know everybody else feels safe;
- feeling issues stay with the group;
- well-being of the group is cared for;
- honesty;
- feeling able to say 'I don't know';
- being in control of risk taking;
- being able to see the real me with all its wobbly bits;
- feeling comfortable around process at the end of the day.

The set relayed the above, each member offering one example (including myself) until we had all described the examples we had individually recorded. At the end of this, I still thought and felt that the set was not yet ready to resume. Another idea emerged from an internal question to myself – what question might flow from what we had just undertaken? The question that came to me emerged from the responses above: 'What would I be willing to say about myself that I had not previously shared with the set that would also be taking a risk to say to the set?'

I invited the set to respond to this question (including myself) when they each felt ready to do so. What followed were very personal and 'risky' examples from set members about their recent lives that were surprising, authentic and honest. The examples were a living embodiment of what a safe set would be like! The short stories that the set members relayed had a cathartic effect on the group as a whole.

Following this further reflection-in-action, I asked the set if they were ready to resume set work. All the set were positive about moving on.

My reflections on the action (after the event) were relief that we had moved with the crisis and not avoided dealing with it; surprise that I had not become defensive but remained grounded at the same time as having a deep concern about the future of the set; I noted that set members did not engage in blame or attack and took responsibility for their feelings. The effect on the set was very positive and deepened the quality of the set's work subsequently.

Process interventions which challenge how the set is working will be a major responsibility for the facilitator. If sets are self-facilitated the responsibility is shared across the set. Another example where the facilitator intervened when a set appeared to be going into a process crisis can be found in Chapter 13.

Periodic review after several meetings

When this takes place is determined by the set. A typical range of questions may include the following:

- What am I gaining or learning from the set or doing differently as a result of the set, for myself, for my personal work and my relationships with colleagues?
- What am I gaining or learning in terms of my understanding of the *process* of the set that I have applied in my work?
- What are we gaining as a group?
- How can I/we improve the operation of the set to make it more effective?
- How do I wish to utilize the set for the remainder of the cycle?
- Any other issues I may wish to raise.

These questions are designed to enable set members to reflect upon the value of the set for themselves, their work, and the set itself so far. If the set is in-house it may be useful to invite line managers and sponsors.

Reviewing the norms of a set

When starting the set, the facilitator guides the set and establishes, with set members, the basic ground rules upon which the set will be organized and run (see Chapter 4). Setting the ground rules means that the set has created explicit ways about how it wishes to work. For example, a basic ground rule will be that one person speaks at a time – simple, yet crucial for effective set working.

As the set progresses over a few meetings, other ways of working begin to emerge that may be obvious to everybody and articulated, for example: 'Have you noticed that we are tending to slip over the time allocated for each set member with the effect of diminishing the time available for whoever takes the last slot?' This can then be considered and the tendency modified.

However, not all ways of working are articulated or conscious to the set. The facilitator has a responsibility, because of her greater experience, to focus on what is happening, what is not being said, but she may also not be conscious of all that is happening.

Examples of ways or patterns of working that can emerge without the set realizing consciously that the patterns are happening include:

- One set member tends to ask few questions of a presenter compared to the others.

- A set member tends to come in first and quickly after the presenter has made his initial commentary.
- The facilitator gets into 'rescuing' a particular set member when she is struggling to find her own solution.
- A set member regularly avoids making specific the actions that he will take on between set meetings and makes generalities instead.

What is happening within the set, which these examples convey, is that the set is not noticing that some patterns of working are implicitly emerging that may limit the effectiveness of the set or the work of a set member. Sets can, like any group, begin unconsciously to develop implicit patterns or norms, some of which can limit the effectiveness of the set. The set can begin to collude and become not just a safe place, but too safe a place. The set may get into a position where it never challenges a set member who is perhaps unconsciously seeking collusion in his way of seeing the world.

These patterns or norms of behaviour need not be limiting. For example, a norm may emerge that set members start to bring a 'present' to the set, such as biscuits. Such norms can 'oil' the set and help to make the interactions more effective and relaxed.

How can the set uncover these implicit norms and review them to assess their value to the set? The set can agree to put aside time in a meeting or outside set members' time to consider the norms and dynamics of the group. Box 13.3 provides a few open-ended questions for set members (and the facilitator) to consider individually and then to discuss them in the set.

Box 13.3   Exploring the norms and dynamics of the group

1. The unwritten rules of this set are...
2. What I find it hard to talk about in this set is...
3. What I think we avoid talking about in the set is...
4. What I hold back on saying about other people here is...

The activity, adapted from Hawkins and Shohet (1989), is one where safety and trust need to be present.

Individual review of entire action learning cycle

When the action learning cycle is nearing completion, set members are asked to engage in a review of the entire cycle. A typical content of this review is given in Figure 13.1 and includes the possibility of set members being part of an organizational in-house programme. Typical responses within such a review are given below.

Question 1 gives the set member the opportunity to reflect upon the impact of the set for the set member personally, in relation to her personal working practice and in her interpersonal relations. Typical responses under this heading have been the following:

- 'I have found a place that I can unload my burdens.'
- 'I feel that I matter.'
- 'I now plan my work in a much more effective way.'
- 'I am now more confident in managing my staff, delegate more effectively and have learnt how to challenge staff who were previously not pulling their weight.'

Question 2 is about making the processes inherent in action learning sets explicit. Managers rarely get the opportunity to get feedback and to reflect on their capacity, for example, to listen effectively. Action learning provides a living laboratory to get that feedback, reflection and practice. For many of our sets, participants commented:

- 'I never realized how important it was just to listen.'
- 'I now give my staff the time to really listen to them.'

---

1. What have I gained/learnt from the set or done differently as a result of the set:
   a) for myself?
   b) for my work in relation to:
      i) my personal work practice?
      ii) my colleagues and staff?

2. What have I gained/learnt in terms of my understanding of the *process* of the set that I have applied in my work?

3. What have we gained as a group?

4. How can I/we improve the operation of the set to make it more effective?

5. How do I wish to utilize the set in the next year?
   and/or
   Where do I go from here?
   and/or
   What issues do I wish to bring to the set that are important to me and my work?

6. How might we link up, and to what purpose, with the other staff in the department who have experienced/are experiencing action learning?

7. Are there any implications for the department as a result of the operation of the set/s?

8. Any other issues you may wish to raise.

Figure 13.1 *Typical content of cycle review*

- 'I now enable staff to work through problems rather than providing solutions.'

Question 3 moves from the individual to the group. While this is a personal reflection on the set member's view, she can incorporate her view in a collective reflection at the review meeting. Examples include:

- 'Trust grew in the group. This helped me and others open up and deal with things I felt vulnerable about.'
- 'As a group we have become more powerful. Powerful in the sense that we are better equipped to provide solutions to problems rather than just moaning. It has also been useful for individuals to tackle problems after sharing them in the group'. (This was a set where the set members all had the same job – but worked separately and in isolation.)

Question 4 is designed to bring out set members' ideas on how they think the set could be improved. It places them in constructive critical mode. The question is designed to elicit positive suggestions.

Question 5 invites a set member to ask how she wishes to use the set in the period following the review.

Question 6 is appropriate to organizations using action learning sets as a vehicle for management development where sets have been created. The question is designed to supplement any intentions senior management or those responsible for the creation of sets may have. Question 7 is linked. Action learning may have implications for the organization in terms of its capacity to collectively learn and bring about change.

Question 8 is a self-explanatory sweep-up question for set members.

The review process can be undertaken by the set members and the facilitator alone. However, in an organizational setting where set members are sponsored by their line managers, it may be appropriate to have the review with the line manager(s).

The review may also include additional reflection and review where the set member has completed a project for a client in the set member's organization and/or a project that has been completed as part of a course leading to a qualification. The project may have been documented. However, it is valuable to ask a set member to compile a reflective document (Brockbank and McGill, 1998: 100–4) which highlights what she has learnt from undertaking the project and what she has learnt about learning in the process.

Set review of the entire action learning cycle

This review is not about individual achievement, more what the set has achieved as a set and what contributed to the set's development. This can be addressed by verbal or written feedback sheets or alternatively as we suggest below in order to assist creatively the set's recognition and identification of its history and growth.

Draw what you have learnt

The set members are asked, as a group, to draw what they have learnt during the cycle, on a large sheet of paper. No words are permitted so set members need to find symbols for what they want to communicate. The restriction to right brain imagery influences what is put on paper, often accessing learning which has remained unrecognized or unconscious before.

The essential review for reflective learning is the individual review and the set meeting review, as here the presenter is enabled to reflect on improvement or transformation, while the set meeting review, by reflecting on the reflective learning process itself, achieves meta-reflection. Further reviews will provide personal records of learning for set members, and, where acceptable to set members, some of the material needed to evaluate the set's life. Beyond this point we move from forms of process review to evaluation, where the set member and sponsoring organizations (where appropriate) ask the question: What value has the action learning been to the development of the individual(s) and to the organization(s)? We discuss programme evaluation in Chapter 14.

NOTE

1. Thanks to Brendan McCormack for developing these questions on behalf of the set.

Chapter 14

Evaluating action learning

For organizations that wish to use the action learning approach for development of staff, evaluating action learning is an important issue. Sponsors of a programme and staff developers will want to assess its effectiveness or value for the organization and for the staff who take part. This chapter sets out a process for evaluating action learning and here we draw on the work of Simons & McCormack (2002). In addition, we will convey some of the methods used, and the outcomes of specific evaluations undertaken for the benefit of the organizations sponsoring action learning, where we have been involved.

An early commonsense approach to evaluation suggests that it is a means of determining the degree to which a planned programme achieves the stated objectives. Modern approaches to evaluation enhance this idea and maintain that the aim of evaluation is 'to determine the value (or worth) of a programme, including the achievement of intended or unintended outcomes' (Weiss, 1996); intended and unintended consequences (Owen and Rogers, 1999); and benefits to individuals and communities (Owen and Rogers, 1999; Guba and Lincoln, 1989; Kushner, 2000).

Evaluation methods have inherited a tendency to positivism in the search for objective truth, which means that they often fail to appreciate the range of perspectives as well as the range of implicit and explicit stakeholder values that a broader approach is likely to capture. Our chosen evaluation method echoes what is known as fourth-generation evaluation (Guba and Lincoln, 1989), a process where 'the effort to devise joint, collaborative, or shared constructions solicits and honors the inputs from many stakeholders and affords them a measure of control over the nature of the evaluation activity. It is therefore both educative and empowering, while also fulfilling all the usual expectations for doing an evaluation, primarily value judgements' (Guba and Lincoln, 1989: 184).

Three earlier approaches focused on measurement, description and judgement, and these have been criticized as: tending to managerialism; failing to accommodate value pluralism; and being ontologically driven. Hence the revised approach is the 'fourth generation', as described by McCormack and Marley (2002). Our approach encapsulates elements of these earlier practices in that the method provides for recognition of initial objectives, but includes the possibility of unintended outcomes/consequences.

Who or what are stakeholders here? Stakeholders are defined as 'groups who have something at stake in the evaluand (ie the entity being evaluated)' (Guba and Lincoln, 1989: 81). In our case, described in this chapter, the stakeholders were:

- action learning set participants;
- action learning sets;
- facilitators;
- the client organizations.

Involving stakeholders harmonizes with the cooperative approach to learning described in Chapter 11 (Heron, 1999) so that the evaluation works *with* people rather than *on* them. The value system of action learning made the stakeholder approach a natural choice for the evaluation. Hence the evaluation design included feedback from stakeholders about the proposed evaluation material.

This chapter does not seek to evaluate action learning against other forms of personal or management development. We set out to enable participants in action learning sets and facilitators working with sets to conduct evaluations to determine the following:

- outcomes for organizations deriving from participation in sets as a development tool;
- learning by participants in sets in respect of changes in behaviour and recognition of the action learning process in other contexts;
- effectiveness of facilitators in relation to their work in sets.

In order to ground this chapter, we give a specific example of an evaluation undertaken by one of the authors of a significant development initiated by the British National Health Service (NHS). To date, there have been three intakes of action learning sets taking about one year, with up to eight sets in each intake. We will examine the second intake. We draw on the final report to the NHS Leadership Programme entitled: *Evaluation of Action Learning for Chief Executives and Directors in the NHS and Local Government in England.*[1]

The NHS Leadership Centre[2] (on behalf of the NHS Executive) invited NHS chief executives to join with local authority chief executives and directors of social services in sets based on the action learning approach, each set to be facilitated by a facilitator familiar with action learning and experience of working with this level of staff. For the purposes of the programme the action learning sets were referred to as development sets. Six development sets were to be created, each to consist of eight participants drawn from across both sectors, with the intention of an equal mix from each sector.

Each development set was to meet for a total of six day meetings with a commitment given by each participant at the end of the initial meeting after which the participant could decide if this form of development and the set was appropriate for them. The sets would meet over nine months to one year.

The aims of the programme were: 1) to facilitate cross-boundary working, improving mutual insight into carrying out responsibilities at a senior level in the fields of social and health services; and 2) to provide personal development in a challenging and supportive environment.

The invitation letter defined action learning as 'a method of learning that focuses on actual managerial issues raised in a learning group by the individual group members and therefore has immediate and practical applicability. There is learning about each other's world and context, about the issues and how they have been handled or are handled in someone else's environment.' This definition enabled participants to adhere to the action learning approach while ensuring that the sets were relevant to the needs of senior staff from these services.

The development set design

The NHS Leadership Programme employed a senior member of the staff with administrative support and together this formed the crucial base for ensuring structural support to launch the programme, recruiting participants from amongst NHS health authorities and local government agencies with responsibility for social services.

Launching the programme required diligent work in creating up to six sets with a maximum of eight participants and a balance of NHS and local government senior staff in each set, as well as securing facilitators with significant action learning experience. Because of the nature of their work, some of the participants had to withdraw as a result of other pressures on their time. Their places were to be filled with reserve participants wherever possible and still maintain the balance between the distinct sectors in each set.

The participants

The participants in the second intake consisted mainly of chief executives of health authorities and directors of social services in local government. The total number of participants, before any withdrawals, was 44. After withdrawals, the total was 37 distributed across six sets. Seventeen questionnaires were returned (46 per cent), a respectable figure for a questionnaire survey. The questionnaires were sent directly to the evaluator (one of the authors of this book, who was also one of the facilitators).

Evaluation method

The evaluation was designed to assess the extent to which the aims were fulfilled and in particular to seek participants' responses to:

- the facilitation process – what worked well and what was less successful;
- general themes addressed in the development sets;
- the skills and knowledge gained by individual participants.

There were three strands to the design which was developed in consultation with the client organization (one of the stakeholder groups). Evaluation was to be undertaken by the participants, the development sets and the facilitators (the other three stakeholder groups) and the process began prior to the start of the programme, being completed at the end of the programme.

I The participants

All participants received an evaluation package prior to the programme to familiarize them with the evaluation process as well as to promote reflection on their potential outcomes as they emerged. The package included:

- a statement setting out the evaluation process for the whole programme;
- an evaluation questionnaire to complete from the perspective of each participant at the end of the programme (Figure 14.2);
- a format for maintaining a learning log/journal to be used at the discretion of the participant.

The aim of the package was to provide an overview of the evaluation process as well as enabling consideration of the themes/questions that may underpin the evaluation. Although stakeholders (other than the client organization) did not contribute to the design, facilitators were consulted about the package and asked to comment on it. At the first meeting of the development sets, each facilitator invited some discussion about the evaluation, so that the participants could voice any concerns they had about it. As each set completed, participants were reissued with the material for completion and invited to forward it direct to the evaluator.

II Each development set

Each set was asked to conduct its own evaluation with their facilitator. The sets collectively shared and reviewed the experience of their set, including the facilitation process, as a normal part of their work.

III   *The facilitator set*

The facilitators formed their own additional self-facilitated set to take an overview of their experience as facilitators throughout the programme. Their shared learning in this set was another contribution to the evaluation. Facilitators did not disclose individual identities of participants in their sets to other facilitators, and all participants in the programme knew of the existence of this set in advance.

I The questionnaire for participants' evaluation

Part A of the questionnaire invited participants to list their expectations at the start of the programme and we present these here in Figure 14.1.

Part B was divided into four parts and is set out in full in Figure 14.2:

1.   the participant's development;
2.   the operation and effect of the development set;
3.   cross-boundary working;
4.   other issues.

II Development set evaluation

The second part of the evaluation was for each set to conduct its own evaluation with their facilitator. The sets collectively shared and reviewed the experience of their set, including the facilitation process, as a normal part of their work. This process was supported by a short list of questions prepared by the evaluator in conjunction with the other facilitators to provided focus for their evaluation. Thus the collective development set review fed into the facilitator evaluation for submission to the evaluator. We report development set responses about attendance on page 247.

III Facilitator evaluation

The facilitators contributed by assessing their own role in their sets by using the following questions as triggers:

Facilitator contribution
● What is your perception of your part in the set process?
● Is there anything you would now do differently?
● Are there any other comments you would wish to make to contribute to the evaluation?

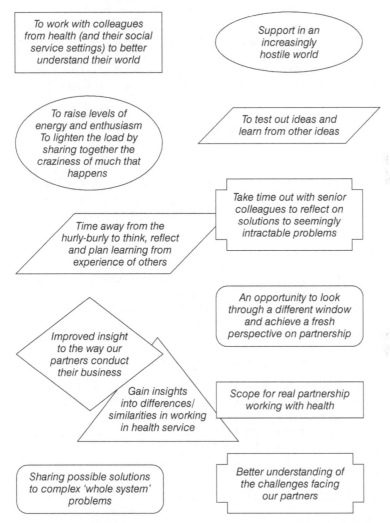

Figure 14.1   *Participants' responses to Part A: on starting the programme*

The facilitators also formed their own set to take an overview of their experience as facilitators throughout the programme, and their shared learning in this set was another contribution to the evaluation.

Evaluation results

After data analysis the evaluator was able to present a report to the NHS Leadership Centre entitled *Joint NHS/Local Government Development Sets: Programme Evaluation: Executive Summary*. We now draw upon the executive summary and parts of the main report below.

You are asked to complete the questionnaire at the end of the programme. Please forward as soon as possible with the enclosed stamped addressed envelope.

Self

1) What have I done/am I doing differently as a result of my work with the set and what have I achieved/gained/learnt from the work in the development set:
   -- for myself
   -- for my work in relation to:
         my personal work practice
         my colleagues
         my organisation

It would be very helpful for the evaluation if you could specify a very tangible and specific outcome in terms of a task or change in behaviour that you set yourself and have achieved. Please convey the difference between the past, implementation and after if possible

The development set

2) What have I gained/learnt in terms of my understanding of the process of the set that I have applied in my work/outside work?
3) What do I consider we have gained/learnt as a group?
4) What went well in the set in terms of the process?
5) How could I/we have improved the operation of the set to make it more effective?

Cross-boundary working or Wider aims of the programme

6) Please describe the insights; benefits; limitations; outcomes, there have been for you as a result of cross-boundary learning between health and local government.
7) Please describe any other themes/outcomes that have emerged as a result of the work with the development set.

Other issues

8) Other issues not covered in the questionnaire you may wish to raise.

Confidentiality

The information provided will be confidential. Any data collected from the questionnaires will be anonymous and if presented in any report or publication so as not to be attributable to a particular person or geographical patch. It would be helpful if you could put your name to the questionnaire in order that I can draw together shared insights expressed by participants who may have a common experience/background. I would like to be able to approach participants should we wish to seek attribution, with your permission, for a particular comment.

Thank you.

Figure 14.2   *Participant evaluation questionnaire: Part B*

General points

Participants to the programme were invited to contribute to the evaluation of the programme by responding to a questionnaire. Seventeen participants responded, representing a 46 per cent return of those continuing on the programme. The responses were overwhelmingly positive about the programme as a whole and the approach taken in using action learning as the means of enabling the aims to be realized. Only one questionnaire was totally negative about the programme. Four questionnaires, while positive, considered that for them the programme was marred by the collapse of their set owing to lack of attendance. Because of the choice of anonymity by some respondents, it was not possible to ascertain the complete match between attendance and responses to the questionnaire. However, it is broadly clear that those who completed the programme were those who mainly responded and these represented the overwhelming positive response.

I   The questionnaire responses

Part A was designed to identify their expectations at the beginning of the programme and these were described above.

Part B set out the questions to be completed at the end of the programme and responses are given below.

Responses to Question 1 are given in Table 14.1: 'What have I done/am I doing differently as a result of my work with the set and what have I achieved/gained/learnt from the work in the development set; for myself, in my personal work practice, with my colleagues and for the organization?'

In addition, participants were asked the following question in order to draw out *specific outcomes*: 'It would be very helpful for the evaluation if you could specify a very tangible and specific outcome in terms of a task or change in behaviour that you set yourself and have achieved. Please convey the difference between the past, implementation and after if possible.'

This proved to be a difficult question to respond to typified by:

- This is difficult to specify. I would describe the usefulness of the learning set in terms of increased understanding and improved morale. I am sure that the former has influenced my approach to regional office, and the latter has helped to revive me from time to time.
- The change to 'my organization' above, in relation to corporate working, is the closest I came to a specific outcome I can have. Very difficult to distinguish cause and effect.

Some outcomes derived from changes wanted in *career*:

- I asked for help on how to create partnerships in order to set up X (a new health organization) for which I was project manager and how to involve partners in appointing a director. This worked. X is now set up and working well.

Table 14.1

For myself	My personal work practice	Colleagues	The organization
I have understood somewhat better strengths and weaknesses and I have gained in confidence from talking to others	A greater willingness to *share experiences*	Sharpening my responsibilities to colleagues, providing them with a safe place to talk about uncertainty	Leading from Social Services Directorate on interface issues such as Intermediate Care with confidence
For myself and colleagues, greater transparency pays off	That it is not necessary to have all the answers	Listening allows better solutions to emerge than talking too much	Painting the big picture
The set enabled me to have one or two huge leaps in understanding	I am better at working my relationship with local authorities into discussions about the future of public health locally (A senior health manager)	Helped me support colleagues through major organizational change	Being honest with all staff about the uncertainty we all face. Providing as clear a picture as possible for the organization + its staff as to next steps
Understanding more about what I need/want to do next	More open to health colleagues' possible dilemmas and more able to ask 'What do you mean by that?' (A senior local authority manager)		
I am being more confident in my working life	Strengthening belief in what one is doing as well as *endeavouring to be 'good enough'*		
It has helped to give me some space as I have attended regularly, not allowing it to be squeezed out – an improvement (this may not seem significant but it is!)	Being more questioning as well as recognizing that *being different is OK*		

- I sought advice about a career move. I applied for a job.
- I felt more empowered to reclaim my own destiny and re-engage with particular 'local' problems.
- Main (memorable) outcome was in helping me to decide to apply for a particular CE role in local reorganization. Unfortunately, I was unsuccessful.

Others were able to take a *different perspective* on a task or in relation to work

- I have taken on the lead on Intermediate Care for the Authority regionally and locally with the Health Service.
- I have been able to reposition my relationship as Taskforce Director of the Xs I am working with. I am able to strike a balance between 'empathy' and results.
- Set aside previous serious political difficulty, put it in its proper place and moved forward.
- Better understanding of how government performance manages whole of public sector.
- My unresolved conflict is about to be resolved.
- My 'concern' is less of a concern – I've come to terms with it and am actively addressing it and my cup is still overflowing!
- In the past I have tended not to be frank enough about my intentions, aspirations and fears around organizational change. Frank discussions in the set enabled me to be more able to live at work and have seen it achieve more.

Responses to Question 2 and 3: 'What have I gained/learnt in terms of my understanding of the *process* of the set, and the set itself, that I have applied in my work/outside work?' are shown in Table 14.2.

Responses to Question 4: Comments on facilitation are shown in Table 14.2. Responses to Questions 6 and 7: Cross-boundary learning and any other issues are shown in Table 14.2.

II Development Set Responses

Responses addressed *attendance* both negatively (poor attendance) and positively and we discuss the attendance issue below.

Attendance

Attendance for the sets for this second intake averaged 71 per cent, with a set range from 60 through to 83 per cent attendance. Attendance was affected by travel problems (strikes, floods), illness and leaving the set at a point in the set's life. While attendance could have been higher in some sets, this did not necessarily detract from the capacity of a set to bond and work effectively.

Table 14.2

Process	The set	Facilitation	Cross-boundary learning	Any other issues
The value of listening and not being judgemental! – quite a challenge	Respect for each other and our relief and an even greater acknowledgement of the value of partnership working	Facilitator took risks to enable the set to work by not being rigid in the application of the 'rules'. People were very open	As usual in such a useful group – the appropriateness and the sameness of the experience for us all. A feeling that nevertheless there are very real cultural differences which are not necessarily bad. Diversity in the set and in our organizations is healthy	A personal sense of strength. Confidence in the people running this world; sense of common values
Listening and not asking leading questions or giving advice until/unless requested to	The value of the time spent with each other. Also, as the team was mostly men, we have got underneath the football talk to the real people	The set was skilfully facilitated	Able now to understand the differences and therefore the real routes to change	Camaraderie – even within health – people you know 'of' but not about – become friends and allies. Respect for each other and increased self-respect
The importance of the concentration on the personal.	Shared sense of the wider public sector agenda and that we are more in control than we might think	I found the model worked well and found it intellectually challenging. The facilitator was particularly skilful and sympathetic	Able to appreciate different governance issues	Need to improve my listening skills

Table 14.2 continued

Process	The set	Facilitation	Cross-boundary learning	Any other issues
The extraordinary and sometimes very upsetting individual journeys that colleagues in the set have gone through is a testament to the turmoil in public organizations over the past year	Having the opportunity to reflect while talking about work issues	Opening up, honesty, time to think	Less than I had hoped, but a clearer picture of the complexity of the health arena	Need for more transformational/less transactional leadership
High respect for confidentiality – some very complex issues explored. Group challenging but supportive	The power of articulating issues and the support that can be engendered	All had a chance to air one or more 'wicked' issues	Better understanding and appreciation of local government working and the role of members	The importance of sorting out the personal in order to free us up to do the job. Sometimes the impact of the job on personal life is so overwhelming that people's effectiveness is severely undermined
The listening, sharing and confidentiality. We listened well	All who wanted time got it. No pressure to take time if you did not want it. Mutual support	People engaged; everyone contributed; lively discussion		Fundamental shift in determination to achieve better outcomes for users and stronger delivery – structures don't do it – relationships do

Attendance at set meetings has proved to be an important factor contributing to the maintenance and effectiveness of sets. The two examples below represent the range across one of the programmes. Set members in Set X had difficulty attending and this impaired the working of the set. Set Y had good attendance, which from the beginning worked toward the set's maintenance.

Set attendance for Set X

Set X is representative of a set where attendance impaired the maintenance and effectiveness of the set.

Set member	Meeting 1	Meeting 2	Meeting 3	Meeting 4	Meeting 5	Meeting 6
A						
B	✓	✓		✓		
C	✓	✓				
D		✓	✓	✓		
E		✓		✓	✓	
F	✓	✓				
G	✓					✓
H	✓		✓	✓		

The set has been fraught throughout with difficulties of attendance even though all maintained their commitment. Only one person officially withdrew from the programme because of conflicting demands on the last two sessions.

Attendance for Set Y

Set Y is representative of a set where attendance contributed to the maintenance and effectiveness of the set.

Set member	Meeting 1	Meeting 2	Meeting 3	Meeting 4	Meeting 5	Meeting 6
A (1)		✓				
B (6)	✓	✓	✓	✓	✓	✓
C (5)	✓	✓	✓		✓	✓
D (4)	✓		✓	✓	✓	
E (5)	✓	✓	✓	✓		✓
F (4)		✓	✓	✓		✓
G (5)	✓	✓	✓	✓	✓	
H (5)	✓	✓	✓	✓	✓	

It is clear from the data that there were sufficient participants at the initial meeting to begin the momentum for maintaining the set. The individual responses to the questionnaire did suggest that this was for them an effective set and this set commenced a further cycle of meetings.

Conclusions from the examples of attendance at sets X and Y:

- Attendance is a necessary but not a sufficient condition for the maintenance of and effectiveness of a set.
- It is ideal and certainly desirable that *all* set members attend the first meeting.
- Attendance by all or most at the first set meeting helps to underpin commitment for the remainder of the set programme.
- Too long a gap between meetings may undermine the momentum of the set.
- As absence in a set becomes recurrent, the priority given to set meetings may be diminished in favour of other commitments.
- All were chief executives of health or local authorities or directors of social services. These roles require a long timescale to achieve agreement on dates for meetings. Attendance by all or most ensures that everybody can agree the subsequent dates for the programme. Contact can be made with an absent set member's PA by mobile to ensure agreed dates.

Despite the above salutary data, a number of the development sets continued into a second year, often with a slight change in membership but usually with a core membership from the first year. Indeed, some sets have continued into a third and fourth year (sponsorship from the NHS Leadership Centre ceasing after the second year).

III Facilitators' evaluation

Issues brought to sets as identified by the facilitators were:

- 'moving on' in career and life;
- relationships between Social Services and Health;
- relationships with others within the participant's organization;
- future-issues re Health;
- impending disciplinary/tribunal issues;
- recognizing and utilizing influence and power;
- sustaining self through tough times, eg with the Social Services Inspectorate;
- restructuring;
- cross-boundary and partnership

Issues which emerged for facilitators included:

- Listening effectively.
- Endeavouring not to give advice.
- The value, but difficulty, of moving out of our 'comfort zone'.
- Handling emotion.
- Importance of sensitive questioning and challenging.
- Attendance was a critical issue in the maintenance of sets.
- Feeling OK after having 'bared soul' and used the set as a 'confessional', and wondering about the judgements that others might be making.

In the facilitator set, facilitators considered the overall benefit of the sets for participants. The most significant conclusion was the view that sets provided an oasis for senior staff in these services. Being a chief executive (in the NHS or local government) or a director of social services can be a very isolated role where the capacity to share thoughts and vulnerabilities is rare. The development sets significantly provided that opportunity because the sets had the time and will to build trust amongst set members. The format that facilitators used, much reflected in this handbook, ensured that sets, from the first meeting, created the basis for trust.

Reflections on the development sets: aims and outcomes

The development sets were formed in a period of significant change and transition for the NHS. Ninety Health Authorities were abolished and replaced with 28 Strategic Health Authorities. Primary Care Trusts were formed to grasp emerging policy, giving new priority to primary health care. New partnerships were being forged to overcome the institutional boundaries between health and social care. Senior staff in health and local government were in the front line of these changes. Frequently sets were working with potential or actual redundancy, applications for new posts with different status and new careers. The opportunity to have a resource to unravel the complexities of these changes was a key element for many participants.

Set members stressed how much they valued the oasis effect of being able to bring private and tacit thinking to the set which could not be shared elsewhere. Participants were often not able to talk elsewhere – it was not politically possible. The reasons are that in their roles the pace of work inhibits time for adequate reflection and they are often in contexts requiring highly sensitive negotiation where candour may mean 'burial'. In a set with peers (and not in competition with each other) they have the opportunity and trust to do so.

Another reservation that may be addressed is the limited degree of specific outcomes mentioned in the questionnaire responses. Two issues emerge here, one in respect of evaluations by questionnaire and one where the opportunity has been taken to go beyond the limitations of questionnaires.

Firstly, when faced with a request for a specific outcome in a questionnaire, are we looking for a measurable outcome, eg specific patient benefits?

The development sets were not created to initiate and implement projects with precise terms of reference seeking specific outcomes. The aims of the sets were: 1) to facilitate cross-boundary working, improving mutual insight into carrying out responsibilities at a senior level in the fields of social and health services; and 2) to provide personal development in a challenging and supportive environment. Given these aims, the responses to the question on specific outcomes were reflected in statements about organizational opportunities and difficulties addressed and overcome, and critical dilemmas around careers in these services.

Secondly, in subsequent dialogue with participants who have continued into further cycles of set meetings, the following has emerged. I have occasionally remarked to set members that there appears to be no 'follow through' to specific action after a set meeting. However, the robust response to this comment by set members is that set members internalize the learning from the set and it lives with them in their work and feeds their approach when in harness. One person's experience in a presentation enables not only 'resolution' and catharsis for the presenter. It greatly deepens other set members' learning by listening to that experience with 'follow through' questioning. Often a presenter is addressing an issue that is personal to them while also being very relevant to other set members' work. Thus a set is considering an issue at three levels – the grounded level of the presenter's presentation with its frequent dilemmas and complexities, another level of potential application to other set members (while not detracting from the presenter's context) and a third level of policy emergence and implementation. The next time the set returns to the theme underlying that presentation it does so through another set member and at a deeper level of understanding, appreciation and application.

The evaluation process revealed that for these NHS/local government sets for senior staff the aims declared were achieved. The NHS Leadership Centre can be confident that their investment in the programme provided good value in terms of individual growth, healthy sector relationships, and the potential for innovation and development in the NHS and local government.

Reflections on the evaluation design

The evaluation design was undertaken at the outset of the programme before the first tranche of participants. The design was created by the evaluator in consultation with the client representing the NHS Leadership Centre. Facilitators on the programme were consulted about the design and invited to comment and offer amendments. Thus three of the four major stakeholders were involved in the creation of the evaluation design. The questionnaire was slightly modified for later tranches to simplify the questionnaire.

Learning on the part of the evaluator has been significant. Firstly, that the work of collecting, collating and analysing questionnaires is a very time-consuming task. Secondly, while the responses were good compared to standard questionnaire responses, they could have been better. Underlying this is the issue of ownership of evaluation design. The design had been essentially a top-down process by the evaluator and client, with lesser involvement on the part of facilitators and none by participants. The assumption was made that participants would not have time to engage in the process. This approach is now questioned. Any future evaluation design should involve all major stakeholders as described in the fourth-generation model (Guba and Lincoln, 1989). Such an approach would bed down more ownership in participants in the evaluation process early on, as well as having a beneficial outcome on their development.

NOTES

1. The innovative feature of this programme, initially undertaken in 1999–2000, was the creation of sets with membership crossing the institutional boundaries of two significant public sector organizations, the NHS and local government. They each have radically different forms of administration. The background to this was the recognition and requirement by these governmental agencies to engage in a partnership of functions, which overlap from the users' perspective. An example is care of the elderly during the transfer from hospital to residential care, currently divided between the respective agencies.
2. Now the NHS Modernization Agency Leadership Centre.

Chapter 15

Endings

Action learning sets have a life which comes to an end with the conclusion of the cycle of meetings agreed at the outset. Action learning sets have a pre-determined length of life and their ending date is likely to be fixed from the start. Even when the set is reconvening for a further series of sessions, these will effectively be a new set. The set members will need to finish off their engagement in the first set before moving on to the new set, where new conditions and ground rules may emerge with different patterns of working, timings etc.

In addition, each meeting of the set comes to an end. It is important for these events to have recognition. Without recognition set members will leave with what is known as 'unfinished business' in the psychodynamic tradition. We discuss this in more detail below. We will now distinguish ending a set meeting from ending a set cycle.

Ending a set meeting

The set will have conducted a process review for the day prior to departure. If the set is ending its first meeting, it is important that the facilitator acknowledges the significance of the day as a beginning of a cycle that may continue.

What suitable endings to the day can be introduced? Below are alternative endings that can be used before departure. It is important that the facilitator undertakes this task as well as set members:

- How do set members feel about the set?
- What has been my significant learning for me today?
- What would I have liked more of?
- What would I have liked less of?

or:

- What did I want?
- What did I get?
- How do I feel?

The above is useful particularly where the set is new and somewhat tentative about its formation.

Some sets are created with a commitment subject to experiencing the first meeting. Therefore the facilitator will need to attend to this before departure, checking out how participants are feeling about the process and enabling them to opt out if that is their decision. The voluntary nature of action learning requires that set members are willing participants, rather than conscripts, so there is no advantage to having unwilling participants.

Ending a set meeting should enable set members to realize their learning and development from the process as well as the action to which they have committed themselves. The recording process is important here, as is who will hold the action points for the next set meeting. Some sets choose to circulate action points by e-mail and others prefer not to, but, whatever is decided, the facilitator should encourage the set to take responsibility for recording.

The tangible outcome of a set meeting is the intention to act by set members. Action points emerge from each presenter's time, decided by the presenter themselves, after the set dialogue. Action points should be specific, measurable, achievable, realistic and time bounded. Examples are given below:

Good action points	**Not so good action points**
I will meet with my manager on Tuesday to discuss my salary	I will talk to my manager soon about things
I will require reports from all my staff by the end of the week	I will start asking my staff to do reports
I will meet with my direct reports once a month	I can see my direct reports anytime
I will ask for a 50% increase	I can insist on a rise of x%
I will meet with him at 2 pm on Tuesday	I will see him soon

Ending a cycle of set meetings

We recommend that the set conducts a thorough process review of the complete programme of sessions, ie the set's life from beginning to end, as part of their ending. We describe process review in Chapter 13. This ensures that set members have the opportunity to engage in reflection at all five levels as described in Chapter 6. The process review should ensure that the learning and change achieved by set members can be sustained beyond the life of the set (see Ross, 1991).

In addition to the process review, set members may like to offer each other feedback about how they found their colleagues as fellow set members. This should be carefully structured and the set may like to revisit the characteristics of effective feedback given in Chapter10.

Every group has a life, and, just as it was brought into being, so it must have an end. The process of ending a set should be planned as effectively as the process of bringing it into being and the transition effected with care (see Douglas, 1984). The ending task in helping the set to disengage is almost the complete opposite of the process of building trust and rapport at the beginning of the set. Set members may need help to disengage emotionally and this activity has been called the termination phase of a group or set.

The psychology of endings

Experts in group work recommend that the process of ending a group (or set) should be planned and arranged as carefully as the process of beginning it (Ross, 1991) The process of ending is believed to be a reversal of formation so that the issues which concerned us in chapter 4, ie comfort, inclusion, safety, disclosure and trust, are attended to in reverse order (Schutz, 1979). This process is sometimes called 're-entry', as the group or set member is re-entering normal life after the ending of the meeting cycle. The above suggests that the facilitator presides over a reduction in cohesion in the set, just as he or she presided over its creation at the start.

Endings (Ross, 1991) can bring out feelings associated with earlier losses and other endings for set members. It is important to acknowledge that these echoes are real and present and part of the process of ending the set. Some groups find it difficult to disband themselves, and members seek to forestall the ending with suggestions of reunions and/or social meetings, and this can affect action learning sets too. Hence it is important to anticipate potential feelings attached to endings, such as loss and sadness. The set should devote time to sharing their feelings about the ending. This enables set members to accept the ending and come to terms with it.

The ending of a set cycle is the time to assess each member's achievements in the cycle and part of the ending process is giving members the space to articulate their achievements. In addition, the ending process highlights for set members the quality of the relationships they have formed within the set. Their development in relationships is what they are taking away with them to apply to future work or personal relationships.

One aspect of group or set endings which has been noted is a recurrence of earlier, less empowered behaviour, as set members tend to revert to their dependence on the facilitator, as this after all is a new situation for the set. The feelings of loss experienced by members of a group or set at the end of its cycle have been well documented in the literature (Fox *et al*, 1969) and action learning sets are likely to display loss-avoidance behaviours at their ending, by promising to 'meet up' with each other and have a reunion.

How can the facilitator ensure that set members assess their achievements and recognize their growth? If we consider how we deal with loss outside the set, the importance of ritual emerges as a key factor. Different cultures have different ways of dealing with loss, eg the Jewish *shivah,* the Irish *wake,* and the Hindu Samskara. It is believed that the lack of such ritual can make bereavement more difficult to deal with.

Clearly, the set is not dealing with death or loss at such a level, but responses to the set cycle ending may mirror how we have learnt to deal with other losses in our lives. The stages of bereavement come to mind, as the set members may go through at least one of the 'grieving' stages in the form of denial, as when the set members promise to 'meet up' and have a reunion, mentioned above.

What procedures can be used for ending a set?

In order to prepare for feelings of loss, and enable the feelings to be accepted and shared, the set may adopt a termination ritual. A termination ritual is a group experience which provides set members with opportunities to practise leaving the set, saying goodbye and letting go, and helps to validate their feelings of loss, sadness, anger or despair.

We offer here a selection of 'termination rituals' often used for group endings which can be used for ending a set.

The ending game (Ross, 1991)

In this, one person says 'goodbye' to the set and to the set members that she wishes to address. She then leaves the room and waits outside for a few moments. While the person is gone, the set members are instructed to think of anything they, as individuals, have not said or would want to say again to that person as a goodbye. The person outside the room is instructed to consider the same issues and what feelings arise for her when she leaves the set. Then she returns to the set and shares with set members what she has decided to say, as well as receiving from set members what *they* have decided to say. The process is repeated for everyone in the set.

The long goodbye

A light-hearted end game, using a large ball of string. The set sits in a circle and someone (usually the facilitator) starts the game by holding one end of the string and throwing the ball of string to someone in the set, while saying goodbye to that person, saying why she will particularly miss him. It is important that the statement is specific, not a generalized comment, eg 'Goodbye, Martin – I'll miss your probing questions.' The receiver then holds onto the string and repeats the process by throwing the ball of string to someone else and saying goodbye with his why. The whole process is continued until everyone in the set is holding a webbing of the string, which is a physical representation of some of the networks of affection within the set. When the goodbyes are finished the starter takes a pair of scissors and cuts herself out of the network by snipping the string in front of her. The scissors are passed round so that set members can do the same, cutting themselves away from the set, in a symbolic action.

Present giving

This does not mean exchanging material gifts, but offering fellow set members some positive opinion about them, which is given freely and is therefore a 'present' or 'gift' in that sense. Present giving is often done in writing using a series of billets-doux, so that set members leave with a bundle of 'presents' from the set. Each set member completes a slip of paper for each of his or her fellow set members, marking each 'note' with their name. The slips are placed in a basket or box in the middle of the set. When all are complete, the slips are given to the named set members to read for themselves. The facilitator may suggest that this is done in silence.

Resent and appreciate (see Brandes and Phillips, 1978)

Here set members in turn say what they resent about themselves and what they resent about other set members. This is followed by a round of what set members appreciate about each other. This is strong medicine and depends on a strong sense of trust in the set.

What I want to tell you before you go

A similar idea but less structured – again the facilitator may need to hold painful feelings in the set.

What am I taking away?

This has a link to evaluation, but may be a chosen way of ending, particularly where the set has struggled for relevance.

Evaluation

If set members are included in the evaluation process, the evaluation is more likely to be useful. It has been said that evaluation is not likely to be successful where feelings associated with the set ending remain unexpressed. So the process of ending the set needs to be in hand before the evaluation is attempted (Ross, 1991).

We discuss evaluation in Chapter 14.

Draw what you have learnt

The set members are asked, individually or in pairs, to draw what they have learnt during the cycle, on a large sheet of paper. No words are permitted so set members need to find symbols for what they want to communicate. The restriction to right-brain imagery influences what is put on paper, often accessing learning which has remained unrecognized or unconscious before. We offer here an instance of using such an exercise at the final session of a series of action learning set meetings, told by the facilitator.

I was working with a group of executives and it was their last session. Each member created a collage, working with the idea of creating a vision for their future. One woman was reviewing her vision and I asked her the question: 'What is not in your collage?' She became tearful and said, 'My husband, he is older than I am and this picture is about the next 10 years. I am sure I will be without him before that time and I need to plan for the long term without him.' This opportunity allowed the set member to begin thinking that she must plan for her future as it will be – at some level. Had she been talking and not done a picture she might not have begun the process of planning for her long-term future alone.

What I like about you is...

Completed by each set member for every other set member. The reverse of the sheet is a series of 'What you like about me is...'. Recorded as each set member is given their feedback.

More of; less of; recommend:

This is similar in form, with a list of set members and headings as above in matrix form.

One more thing...

This really is the last activity and may be a round to end the day.
   Thus the set ends its life.

Conclusion

Given our desire for users of this handbook to undertake action learning effectively, a number of conclusions emerge that we would like to emphasize to make that happen.

Getting started

Action learning requires a clear initiative on the part of the person(s) starting a set or sets. If organizationally based and supported, this person may be termed a 'champion', who can enable the time and, if necessary, financial resources to be allocated to the work required for sets to happen. Secondly, there must be a clear management and/or organizational developmental purpose to justify the creation of the sets. Action learning sets created in organizations simply because they are considered desirable in themselves will, generally, not last. This applies to sets created across organizational boundaries as well. Moreover, benefits must accrue to both the organization and the individual participants, otherwise withdrawal of support is likely on both sides

Similarly, sets created by individuals require an overall sense of purpose for their effective creation and operation. More onus is placed upon the set members to be clear about the purposes for which they wish to use the set.

We have endeavoured to demystify action learning in order to enable those new to the approach to enhance their skills as they begin to work in this way. Chapters 1 and 4 provide the essential means of starting action learning. Provided set members, with or without a facilitator, adhere to the basic structural form, they will by 'doing' it be learning as they proceed. So what are the essential minimum features for a set to be accurately termed an action learning set?

The number of members in the set is an important prerequisite. For those new to action learning, a minimum of five and a maximum of eight is an important benchmark. Below five the set may not be viable and, to allow for occasional absence, six is safer. Beyond eight, the numbers begin to become too large to allow sufficient time per set member during the meetings. Attention to ground rules is critical. These should be agreed by all the set and adhered to and be reviewable over the life of the set. The ground rules are designed to maintain the set as a group and to enable each set member to be effective as a set member and presenter by ensuring that all have a voice, which in turn promotes equality and collaboration across the set. The existence of a skilled facilitator in the set does not detract from these prerequisites. The skilled facilitator has the responsibility to create these conditions from the outset, even though he or she may initially play a leading modelling role.

The set does not have to strive to be perfect! Mistakes can be and will be made. The significance of mistakes is that they are a vehicle for learning for the whole set. Through making mistakes the set learns how to modify its approach and behaviour in order to keep the set in balance to achieve the aims of each member as well as maintaining the set. Asking what has happened in the set as it proceeds and learning from what has happened is the first step to reflecting on the set's process – how it is working – that is key to learning by the set.

Thus it is feasible for sets to be formed of members with a wide range of skills and abilities provided they adhere to the above: intended purposes; attention to size of the set; and basic ground rules that need to be observed. Even where the set consists of members entirely new to action learning and without recognized interpersonal skills, set members as adults will be bringing a wealth of life and work experience from which they will draw. An explicit part of the set's work includes reflecting consciously and together on the process of how the set is working. This will begin to promote the skills used by set members that enhance the work of the set. Careful attention to how the set is working will help to ensure that the set is not sloppy in its work.

Knowledge

The contrast can be made between the knowledge gained in adult life, for example in universities or through professional training, as against knowledge acquired later in application at work or in practice from which the action learning set draws its *raison d'être*. Gibbons *et al* (1994) provide a valuable distinction which describes two different, distinct ways in which knowledge is produced, naming them Mode 1 and Mode 2:

> in Mode 1 problems are set and solved in a context governed by the, largely academic, interests of a specific community. By contrast, Mode 2 knowledge is carried out in a context of application. Mode 1 is disciplinary while Mode 2 is transdisciplinary. Mode 1 is characterized by homogeneity, Mode 2 by heterogeneity. Organizationally, Mode 1 is hierarchical and tends to preserve its form, while Mode 2 is more heterarchical and transient. Each employs a different type of quality control. In comparison with Mode 1, Mode 2 is more socially accountable and reflexive. It includes a wider, more temporary and

heterogeneous set of practitioners, collaborating on a problem defined in a specific and localized context. (Gibbons *et al*, 1994: 3)

Action learning can be identified as a closer fit to Mode 2 in comparison to the propositional knowledge acquired in university or early professional context. Action learning is an applied transdisciplinary activity, operating without hierarchy and including a wide range of participants. In addition, action learning, through its values and reflective process, is more socially accountable and reflexive than traditional learning methods.

Code of ethics?

The history of action learning has not allowed for the development of so-called experts. However, a body of facilitator expertise exists without a required professional qualification. A key question for the present and the future is: how can practitioners observe standards appropriate to quality action learning while not creating a boundaried professional association?

We have referred to accreditation of facilitators in Chapter 12 where the process, which included values and ethics, provided certification. The launch of a new academic journal, *Action Learning: Research and Practice*, from 2004, supporting the development of practice as well as advancing knowledge, is a new initiative for practitioners. In addition, the International Foundation for Action Learning (IFAL), based in the UK, with international chapters in USA, Canada and Sweden, exists to: 'identify and encourage a network of enthusiasts who will support and develop the work of action learning worldwide' (Mahoney, 2003: 18).

Membership is open to all those 'who believe in the value of action learning' (Mahoney, 2003: 18). IFAL thus has open unboundaried membership, but it does not have a code of ethics to which members subscribe. We consider that IFAL should promote a dialogue as to whether the membership has a code of ethics, while maintaining an unboundaried membership. If there is a positive outcome to this, the next stage of drawing up a code of ethics could follow. We recommend that dialogue without pre-empting its substance.

Action learning is again becoming well established in the United Kingdom, as well as internationally, after a period in the 1980s when it appeared to be in the doldrums. This is in part the result of a number of enthusiasts who picked up the staff of Revans and pursued action learning in novel ways, while still maintaining the underlying principles embodied in this particular approach to the development of individuals within and beyond organizations.

Appendix

Group action learning

This handbook is primarily about projects and issues undertaken by individuals progressed with a set. A variant is a group project where the members of the set are undertaking a group project for the organization. In this form the set divides the project work between members of the set. It is important to recognize and distinguish two features here which, if a facilitator is present, will need to be highlighted for the set. There will be team issues which the set members will wish to resolve and work on. There will also be individual issues that each set member may wish to bring to the set to reflect upon and progress. It is appropriate for the set to work on the latter. Where the issues are team ones, it is better to go into team mode. For example, there may be conflicts in the group over the progress of work. The facilitator and members can aim to keep the distinction clear so that the action learning set method is used for progressing individual parts of the project.

We have found that some trainers and managers confuse action learning with team improvement and team building. We stress that the two issues be kept distinct for the reasons outlined above. In the next section we show how one of us developed a method for progressing a group project or an issue common to the whole group by adapting the action learning format. Readers new to action learning may wish to defer this section pending more familiarity with action learning for individual applications.

Group action in dialogue[1]

One of the main features of action learning is the potential ability of a set, with or without a facilitator, to enable each set member to progress a task or explore an intractable issue to a satisfactory outcome or resolution. That has been the primary design purpose for action learning. As outlined above, action learning is less successful for progressing issues where the group as a whole wishes to achieve an outcome or progress an issue towards resolution.

The usual format for a group to progress an issue is one where the group is ostensibly operating as a team with or without a team leader or line manager. Difficulties sometimes arise here. Firstly, the creativity of the group may remain leashed because the group is inhibited by the line authority of the team leader or manager who is exercising their authority to the detriment of the group for fear of losing authority. Secondly, the group may be unclear in respect of distinctions about task and process, with the latter being subordinated to the disadvantage of the task. For example, a group may pitch into solutions and actions before rehearsing earlier processes. Thirdly, where there is no line authority, or authority for facilitating the group is unclear, then there may be no means of holding the process while the group is struggling with the task – even if the group is clear what the task is! There may also be conflicts and competition within the group that militates against optimum outcomes.

How then can action learning be utilized for group action? The key is in using a format like action learning but in adapting it to fit the group needs, thereby retaining some of the creative advantages of action learning for group purposes.

In Chapter 4 we explore how triads (groups of three people) can be used to introduce action learning to new users. The effect of triads is to create an action learning set writ small so that task and process and the key role of facilitating process can be clearly identified. The triad method also highlights the attention on the presenter. Group action in dialogue is another such method.

Group action in dialogue – the method

Group action in dialogue develops a group's capacity to produce helpful outputs relatively quickly and cooperatively as well as paying attention to a wider range of ideas and possibilities.

The method enables collaborative working on a problem or issue which otherwise can often seem enormously complex and potentially contentious, as well as preventing the tendency for groups to pitch in to priorities for action. In the example below, drawn from experience with senior staff of a large university department, 18 staff were divided into two groups, each working with the same common strategic issue about the future direction of the department. Within each group of 9, staff volunteered to undertake the roles specified in the example in Box A.1.

Box A.1   Group action in dialogue

Groups of 5–10 work with individuals taking one of the following three roles.

Presenter: the person 'holding' the issue

Prepare to present to the enabler(s) on the following:

1. Select a significant issue relating to the key question being addressed by your group.
2. Identify what you consider is important and yet problematic about the issue.

Work in the mode that you own the issue and want to 'move it forward'. Take a few minutes to relate your thoughts to the enabler(s).

Enabler(s): the person who responds to the presenter's thoughts with a view to enabling the presenter to move forward

You are to work with the presenter to think through how she will tackle the problems and issues that are raised. The purpose of enabling is to help the presenter to:

- focus on the issue(s);
- take and maintain responsibility for moving forward the issue(s);
- move to some specific action(s) that can be undertaken.

Ask open questions. The object is to enable the presenter to define or redefine the issues as they arise and their relationship (and potentially that of others) to the 'resolution' of the issue. The aim is to help the presenter to take some steps towards action that will be specific, tangible and realisable.

Try to focus on what can be done by the presenter – not what she ought to do or what you would do. Some helpful questions may include:

- How do you propose to meet your needs?
- What can you do to make this... easier?
- How do you feel about that...?
- What do you think really goes on...?
- What do you think would happen if...?
- Do you think that...?
- How would you know if...?
- What could you do...?
- How can you...?

The questions are suggestions. Actual questions should derive from the presenter's thoughts and ideas. Questions are not mechanically delivered but to create and respond to the rapport being developed in the dialogue.

The enabler(s) will also distinguish questions and statements that clarify (context, purpose) from those that resolve choices for action, influencing others and/or further investigation. This is in addition to the value of support and challenge for the presenter.

Reporter(s): the person(s) observing the above event

The reporter listens to what is being said, observes the interaction and considers what questions/responses are more/less helpful to enabling the presenter to move forward her needs, competencies and related issues. The reporter also listens to/senses what the feelings of the presenter are in relation to the issues.

Finally, the reporter also listens to/senses what the presenter has 'invested' (or not) in the issue. What is the presenter's 'will', 'commitment' or motivation towards the issue and its possible resolution?

Listening in the above ways means gathering insights through verbal and non-verbal behaviour as well as attending to the 'content' of what is said by the presenter and enabler.

Further points the reporter may wish to consider include:

- Is the enabler providing solutions for the presenter?
- Is the presenter focusing on what she can do?
- Is the presenter avoiding resolving some of the problems?
- Is the presenter's proposed action specific enough?

Timing

In preparing for the dialogue the presenter will have had some individual time. The presenter and enabler(s) take about 20–25 minutes for the briefing session, at the end of which the presenter specifies potential actions or resolutions for the group at this stage in the dialogue. After the briefing and a pause, the presenter and enabler convey what they have learnt from the dialogue that may also be added to the conclusions to date. The reporter(s) then gives feedback for 10 minutes to the enabler(s) and presenter as well as initiating reflection on the process by the whole group. The timing can be amended depending upon requirements of the group.

Continuing the dialogue

The group can continue consideration of the issue by changing roles. The group can agree where they have got to and what is still outstanding. A presenter can emerge who is willing to 'pick up' the issue and who has some energy to pursue it from that point.

The group then continues as before, taking time for reflection on the process following the next round.

At the end of the discourse with, say, two or three rounds of 'presenter–enabler' dialogue followed by reporter feedback on the process, the group can reflect on the whole process as well as having recorded their outputs for carrying forward and implementing.

The method makes apparent three distinct roles of presenter, enabler and reporter. The identification of these roles also helps to make very explicit the way in which the group is working: the process.

The reporter has a key role. The reporter/observer is there to look, listen and feel the process – the group is working on its task. The group can agree that the reporter may intervene during the dialogue as well as at the end of the cycle to convey his or her observations. The aim is to enable the group to reflect on its process so that when the group recommences it works having had the benefit of that reflection. The group has incorporated its reflection-on-action into reflection-in-action! Thus the group works towards achievable, tangible outcomes as well as reflecting upon the processes that enable the outcomes to happen most effectively.

Process issues that can emerge that can be addressed to promote effective group action are:

- Are colleagues adopting 'positions' or their own 'agendas' rather than sharing their perceptions?
- Is the group working interdependently or combatively?
- Are colleagues aware of their own process – how am I working right now within this group?

The enabler is there to guide the presenter towards a point of action.

The reporter can ask themselves (as the group should do collectively and individually):

- Is the group:
  - clarifying purpose?
  - trusting each other?
  - leading to achievable action (via the presenter)?
  - sharing responsibility in the here and now?
  - challenging rhetoric?
  - checking that the action proposed is specific enough to ensure it can happen?
- Are identifiable measures/criteria for success being adduced?
- Is there energy right now in the group? If not, why not? What is happening?

All group members, in reflection on the process, may also find useful the following framework for working through issues which will contribute to the effectiveness of outcomes:

- the situational: joining together – participating – leaving the meeting of the group;
- the rational: presenting – analysing – synthesizing/proposing;
- the emotional: engaging – commitment – sharing – achieving – letting go.

Finally, the group will, following the dialogue process, determine collectively what should be done next. In our example of the university department, the two main groups outlined their conclusions and recommendations to each group and created a synthesis which was then left to the head of department and two deputies to put into a format that acknowledged their line authority. We consider that this group approach to pursuing a common goal requires further experimentation.

NOTE

1. Group action in dialogue was originally developed in collaboration with Bob Sang.

References

Alvesson, M and Willmott, H (1992) On the idea of emancipation in management and organisation studies, *Academy of Management Review*, **17** (3), pp 432–64

Antonacopolou, E (1999) Developing learning managers within learning organisations: the case of three major retail banks, in *Organisational Learning and the Learning Organisation*, ed M Easterby-Smith, J Burgoyne and L Araujo, Sage, London

Argyle, M (1975) *Bodily Communication*, Methuen, London

Argyris, C (1991) Teaching smart people to learn, *Harvard Business Review*, May–June, pp 99–109

Argyris, C and Schön, D (1974) *Theory in Practice: Increasing Professional Effectiveness*, Jossey-Bass, London

Asch, S E (1974) Group effects, in *Obedience to Authority*, ch 9, Tavistock, London

Ashby, W R (1952) *Design for a Brain*, Wiley, New York

Bandura, A (1978) The self-esteem in reciprocal determination, *American Psychologist*, 33, 344–58

Bandura, A and Walters R H (1963) *Social Learning and Personality Development*, Holt, Rinehart & Winston, New York

Barnes, B, Ernst, S, and Hyde, K (1999) *An Introduction to Groups*, Macmillan, London

Barnett, R (1992a) *Improving Higher Education*, SRHE/Open University Press, Buckingham

Barnett, R (1997) *Higher Education: A Critical Business*, SRHE/Open University Press, Buckingham

Basch, M F (1983) The concept of self: An operational definition, in *Developmental Approaches to the Self*, ed B Lee and G Noam, Plenum Press, New York

Bateson, G (1973) *Steps Towards an Ecology of Mind*, Paladin, London

Belenky, M F, Clinchy, B M, Goldberger, N R and Tarule, J M (1986) *Women's Ways of Knowing: The Development of Self, Voice and Mind*, Basic Books, New York

Binns, S and McGill, I (2002) Action learning at the London Borough of Ealing, in *Reflective Learning in Practice*, ed A Brockbank, I McGill and N Beech, Gower, Aldershot

Bion, W R (1961) *Experiences in Groups*, 2nd edn, Basic Books, New York

Bloom, B S (ed) (1964) *Taxonomy of Educational Objectives, vol II, Affective Domain*, McKay, New York

Bohm, D (1996) *On Dialogue*, ed L Nichol, Routledge, London

Boud, D and Solomon, N (2001) (eds) *Work-based Learning: A New Higher Education?* SRHE and Open University Press, Buckingham

Bourner, T (2003) The Broadening of the Higher Education Curriculum, 1970–2000: A Teacher's Perspective, Unpublished paper

Bourner, T, O'Hara, S and Webber, T (2002) *Learning to Manage Change in the Health Service*, in *Reflective Learning in Practice*, ed A Brockbank, I McGill and N Beech, pp 59–68, Gower, Aldershot

Bowlby, J (1969) *Attachment*, Hogarth Press, London

Bowlby, J (1979) *The Making and Breaking of Affectional Bonds*, Tavistock, London

Brandes, D and Phillips, H (1978) *The Gamester's Handbook*, Hutchinson, London

Brockbank, A and McGill, I (1998) *Facilitating Reflective Learning in Higher Education*, Open University Press/Society for Research in Higher Education, Buckingham

Brockbank, A, McGill, I and Beech N (eds) (2002) *Reflective Learning in Practice*, Gower, Aldershot

Brookfield, S D (1987) *Developing Critical Thinkers*, Open University Press, Buckingham

Browning, G (1998) Office politics, *Guardian*, 24 October

Brundage, D H and Mackeracher, D (1980) *Adult Learning Principles and their Application to Program Planning*, Ministry of Education, Toronto, Ontario

Buber, M (1957) Elements of the inter-human contact, *Psychiatry*, **20**, pp 95–139

Buber, M (1965) *Between Man and Man*, Macmillan, New York

Buber, M (1994) *I and Thou*, T&T Clark, Edinburgh

Bull, P (1983) *Body Movement and Interpersonal Communication*, John Wiley, Chichester

Burley-Allen, M (1995) *Listening: The Forgotten Skill*, John Wiley, New York

Burr, V (1995) *An Introduction to Social Constructivism*, Routledge, London

Casey, D and Pearce, D (1977) *More than Management Development*, Gower, Farnborough

Chickering, A and Gamson, Z (1989) *7 Principles for Good Practice in Undergraduate Education*, Johnson Foundation, Racine, WI

Clinchy, B M (1996) Connected and separated knowing: towards a marriage of two minds, in *Knowledge, Difference and Power*, ed N Goldberger, J Tarule, B Clinchy and M Belenky, Basic Books, New York

Cooper C L (1983) *Stress Research: Issues for the 80s*, John Wiley and Sons, London and New York

Coopey, J (1995) The learning organisation: power politics and ideology, *Management Learning*, **26** (2), pp 193–213

Cox, R W (1981) Social forces, states and world orders: beyond international relations theory, *Millennium*, **12** (2), 129–30

Cozby, P C (1973) Self-disclosure: a literature review, *Psychological Bulletin*, **79**, pp 73–91

Cunningham, I (1994) *The Wisdom of Strategic Learning*, McGraw-Hill, Maidenhead, Berkshire

Dainow, S and Bailey, C (1988) *Developing Skills with People*, John Wiley, Chichester

De Board, R (1978) *The Psychoanalysis of Organisations*, Routledge, London

Douglas, T (1984) *Group Processes in Social Work*, Wiley, London

Egan, G (1973) *Face to Face: The Small Group Experience and Interpersonal Growth*, Brooks/Cole, Monterey, CA

Egan, G (1976) *Interpersonal Living: A Skills/Contract Approach to Human Relations Training in Groups*, Brooks/Cole, Monterey, CA

Egan, G (1977) *You and Me: The Skills of Being an Effective Group Communicator*, Brooks/Cole, Monterey, CA

Egan, G (1990) *The Skilled Helper: A Systematic Approach To Effective Helping*, 4th edn, Brooks/Cole, Pacific Grove, CA

Ekman, P and Freisen, W (1975) *Unmasking the Face*, Prentice Hall, Englewood Cliffs, NJ

Elbow, P (1998) *Writing Without Teachers*, 2nd edn, Oxford University Press, London

Eleftheriadou, Z (1994) *Transcultural Counselling*, Central Book Publishing, London

Eraut, M (1994) *Developing Professional Knowledge and Competence*, Falmer Press, London

Ferenczi, S (1916) *Contributions to Psychoanalysis*, Richard Badger, Boston

Fetherston, B (2002) Double bind: an essay on counselling training, *Counselling and Psychotherapy Research*, **2** (2), pp 108–25

Fordham, F (1982) *An Introduction to Jung's Psychology*, Penguin, Harmondsworth

Foucault, M (1976), *The History of Sexuality*, vol 1, Penguin Books, London

Foulkes, S H (1975) *Group Analytic Psychotherapy: Methods and Principles*, Gordon and Breach, London

Fox, E F, Nelson, M A and Bolman, G M D (1969) The Termination Phase: A neglected dimension in social work. *Social Work* October 1969.

French, R and Vince, R (eds) (1999) *Group Relations, Management and Organisation*, Oxford University Press, Oxford

Friedman, M (1985) *The Healing Dialogue in Psychotherapy*, Jason Aronson, New York

Gaunt, R (1991) *Personal and Group Development for Managers: An Integrated Approach through Action Learning*, Longman, London

Geertz, C (1986) The uses of diversity, *Michigan Quarterly Review*, Winter, pp 105–23

Geuss, R (1981) *The Idea of a Critical Theory*, Cambridge University Press, Cambridge

Gibbons, M, Limoges, C, Nowotny, H *et al* (1994) *The New Production of Knowledge: The Dynamics of Science and Research in Contemporary Societies*, Sage, London

Giddens, A (1992) *The Transformation of Intimacy*, Polity, Cambridge

Goffman, E (1969) *Strategic Interaction*, University of Pennsylvania Press, Philadelphia, PA

Goldberger, N, Tarule, J, Clinchy, B and Belenky, M (1996) *Knowledge, Difference and Power*, Basic Books, New York

Guba, E G and Lincoln, Y S (1989) *Fourth Generation Evaluation*, Sage, Newbury Park, CA

Habermas, J (1972) *Knowledge and Human Interests*, Heinemann, London

Hartley, P (1997) *Group Communication*, Routledge, London

Hawkins, P (1994) The changing view of learning, in *Towards the Learning Company*, ed M Pedler, J Burgoyne and T Boydell, McGraw-Hill, London

Hawkins, P and Shohet, R (1989) *Supervision in the Helping Professions*, Open University Press, Buckingham

Heron, J (1977) *Catharsis in Human Development*, Human Potential Research Group, University of Surrey, Guildford, UK

Heron, J (1986) *Six Category Intervention Analysis*, Human Potential Research Project, Guildford

Heron, J (1989) *The Facilitator's Handbook*, Kogan Page, London

Heron, J (1993) *Group Facilitation*, Kogan Page, London

Heron, J (1999) *The Complete Facilitator's Handbook*, Kogan Page, London

Hillier, Y G and McGill, I J (2001) Lifelong learning in the workplace: learning through facilitating the learning of colleagues, in *Travellers' Tales: From Adult Education to Lifelong Learning... and Beyond*, the proceedings of the 31st annual conference of Scutrea, 2001, pp 186–89

Hindmarsh, J H (1993) Tensions and dichotomies between theory and practice: a study of alternative formulations, *International Journal of Lifelong Education*, **12** (2), pp 101–15

Jacoby, M (1984) *The Analytic Encounter*, Inner City Books, Toronto

James, K and Baddeley, J (1991) The power of innocence: from politeness to politics, *Management Learning*, **22** (2), 106–18

Janis, I (1982) *Victims of Groupthink: A Psychological Study of Foreign Policy Decisions and Fiascos*, 2nd edn, Houghton Mifflin, Boston

Jordan, J (1991) Empathy and self boundaries, in *Women's Growth in Connection: Writings from the Stone Center*, ed J V Jordan, A G Kaplan, J B Miller, I P Stiver and J L Surrey, pp 67–80, Guilford Press, New York

Jourard, S M (1971) *The Transparent Self*, Van Nostrand Reinhold, New York

Jowett, B (1953) *The Dialogues of Plato, vol I, book XVII, Meno*, Oxford University Press, London

Kagan, N and Kagan, H (1990) IPR – A validated model for the 1990s and beyond, *Counselling Psychologist*, **18**, pp 436–40

Keller, E F (1983) Women, science and popular mythology, in *Machine ex dea*, ed J Rothschild, pp 131–5, Pergamon Press, New York

Kemmis, S (1985) Action research and the politics of reflection, in *Reflection: Turning Experience into Learning*, ed D Boud, R Keogh, and D Walker, pp 139–163, Kogan Page, London

Kets de Vries, M F R (1991) Whatever happened to the philosopher king? The leader's addiction to power, *Journal of Management Studies*, **28** (4), pp 339–51

King, Martin Luther (1963) Address given at Birmingham, Alabama, December 1963.

Kohn, A (1990) *The Brighter Side of Human Nature: Altruism and Empathy in Everyday Life*, Basic Books, New York

Kohut, H (1978) The psychoanalyst in the community of scholars, in *The Search for the Self: Selected Writings of Heinz Kohut*, vol 2 , ed P Ornstein, pp 685–724, International Universities Press, New York

Kolb, D (1984), *Experiential Learning*, Prentice-Hall, Englewood Cliffs, NJ

Kushner, S (2000) *Personalising Evaluation*, Sage, London

Laing, R D, Phillipson, H and Lee, A R(1966) *Interpersonal Perception*, Springer, New York

Leininger, M M (1987) Transcultural caring: a different way to help people, in *Handbook of Cross-Cultural Counselling and Therapy*, ed P Pederson, Praeger, London

Lewin, K (1951) *Field Theory in Social Science*, Harper and Row, New York

Lieberman, M A, Yalom, I D and Miles, M B (1973) *Encounter Groups: First Facts*, Basic Books, New York

London, M (1997) *Job Feedback*, Laurence Erlbaum, Mahwah, NJ

Luft, J (1984) *Group Processes: An Introduction to Group Dynamics*, 3rd edn, Mayfield, Palo Alto, CA

Magnuson, E (1986) A serious deficiency: the Rogers Commission faults NASA's flawed decision-making process, *TIME*, March

Mahoney, R (ed) (2003) IFAL: the work of the charity and the benefits of membership, *Action Learning News*, **22** (2), May

Margulies, A (1989) *The Empathic Imagination*, W W Norton, New York

Marsick, V J and O'Neil, J (1999) The many faces of action learning, *Management Learning*, **30** (2), pp 159–76

Maslow, A (1969) *The Psychology of Science: A Reconnaissance*, Henry Regnery, New York

McCormack, B & Manley, K (2002) Evaluating Practice Developments. Unpublished paper

McGill, I and Beaty, L (1992) *Action Learning: A Practitioners Guide*, 1st edn, Kogan Page, London

McGill, I and Beaty, L (1995) *Action Learning: A Guide for Professional, Managerial and Educational Development*, 2nd edn, Kogan Page, London

McGill, I and Beaty, L (2001) *Action Learning: A Guide for Professional, Managerial and Educational Development*, rev 2nd edn, Kogan Page, London

McGill, I, Segal-Horn, S, Bourner, T and Frost, P (1990), Action learning: a vehicle for personal and group experiential learning, in *Making Sense of Experiential Learning*, ed S W Weil and I J McGill, Open University Press/SRHE, Milton Keynes

McLeod, J (1998) *An Introduction to Counselling*, Open University Press, Buckingham

Mearns, D and Thorne, B (1988) *Person Centred Counselling in Action*, Sage, London

Mehrabian, A (1971) *Silent Messages*, Wadsworth, Belmont, CA

Mezirow, J (1990) *Fostering Critical Reflection in Adulthood*, Jossey-Bass, San Francisco

Michelson, E (1996) The usual suspects: experience, reflection and the (en)gendering of knowledge, *International Journal of Lifelong Education*, **15** (6), Nov–Dec, pp 438–54

Miller, A (1983) *For Your Own Good: Hidden Cruelty in Child-rearing and the Roots of Violence*, trans Hildegarde and Hunter Haanum, New American Library, New York

Miller, A (1990) *Banished Knowledge*, Virago, London

Morgan, G (1988) *Riding the Waves of Change*, Jossey-Bass, San Francisco

Morris, D (1977) *Manwatching*, Cape, London

Mumford, A (1991) Learning in action, *Personnel Management*, July, pp 34–7

Nelson-Jones, R (1986) *Relationship Skills*, Holt Rinehart & Winston, London

Neumann, J (1998) *Women's Work: Workshop Notes*, Tavistock Institute, Devon

Nitsun, M (1989) Early development linking the individual and the group, *Group Analysis*, 22 (3), 249–61

Noddings, N (1984) *Caring*, University of California Press, Berkeley, CA

Orbach, S (1994) *What's Really Going On Here?*, Virago, London

Owen, J M and Rogers, PJ (1999) *Programme Evaluation – Forms and Approaches*, Sage, London

Palmer, A, Burns, S and Bulman, C (eds) (1994) *Reflective Practice in Nursing: The Growth of the Professional Practitioner*, Blackwell Science, Oxford

Pease, A (1981) *Body Language*, Sheldon Press, London

Pedler, M (1997) Interpreting action learning, in *Management Learning*, ed J Burgoyne and M Reynolds, Sage, London

Pedler, M, Burgoyne, J, Boydell, T and Welshman, G (eds) (1990) *Self Development in Organisations*, McGraw-Hill, Maidenhead

Perry, W (1970) *Forms of Intellectual and Ethical Development During the College Years: A Scheme*, Holt, Rinehart & Winston, New York

Pfeiffer, J W and Jones, J E (1977) *A Handbook of Structured Experiences for Human Relations Training*, University Associates, San Diego, CA

Piaget, J (1972) *The Child's Conception of the World*, Littlefield, Adams, Totowa, NJ

Polanyi, M (1958) *Personal Knowledge*, University of Chicago Press, Chicago, IL

Polanyi, M (1967) *The Tacit Dimension*, Doubleday, New York

Radley, A (1980) Student learning as social practice, in *Coming to Know*, ed P Salmon, Routledge, London

Randell, R and Southgate J (1980) Cooperation and Community Group Dynamics, Barefoot Books, London

Revans, R (1980) *Action Learning: New Techniques for Action Learning*, Blond and Briggs, London

Revans, R (1982) *The Origins and Growth of Action Learning*, Chartwell-Bratt, Bromley Kent

Revans, R (1983) *The ABC of Action Learning*, Chartwell-Bratt, Bromley, Kent

Reynolds, M (1997a) Learning styles: a critique, *Management Learning 28(2) 115–133*

Reynolds, M (1997b) Towards a critical management pedagogy, in *Management Learning*, Sage, London

Rich, A (1979) *On Lies, Secrets and Silence: Selected Prose – 1966–78*, Norton, New York

Rogers, C (1957) The necessary and sufficient conditions for therapeutic personality change, *Journal of Consultative Psychology*, **21**, pp 95–103

Rogers, C (1983) *Freedom to Learn for the 80s*, Merrill Wright, New York

Rogers, C R (1979) *Carl Rogers on Personal Power*, Constable, London

Rogers, C R (1992) *Client Centred Therapy*, Constable, London

Rosen, S and Tesser, A (1970) On reluctance to communicate undesirable information: the MUM effect, *Sociometry*, **33**, pp 253–63

Ross, S (1991) The termination phase in groupwork: tasks for the group worker, *Groupwork*, 4 (1), pp 57–70

Rowan, J (2001) *Ordinary Ecstasy: The Dialectics of Humanistic Psychology*, 3rd edn, Routledge, Hove, East Sussex

Ruddick, S (1984) New combinations: learning from Virginia Woolf, in *Learning Between Women*, ed C Asher, L DeSalvov and S Ruddick S, pp 137–59, Beacon Press, Boston

Schön, D (1983) *The Reflective Practitioner, How Professionals Think in Action*, Basic Books, New York

Schön, D (1987) *Educating the Reflective Practitioner*, Jossey-Bass, London

Schutz, W C (1979) *Elements of Encounter*, New Nork: Irvington

Schwaber, E (1983) Construction, reconstruction and the mode of clinical attachment, in *The Future of Psychoanalysis*, ed A Goldberg, pp 273–91, International Universities Press, New York

Shrauger, J S and Schoeneman, T J (1979) Symbolic interactionist view of the self concept: through the glass darkly, *Psychology Bulletin*, **86**, pp 549–73

Silverstone, L (1993) *Art and the Development of the Person*, Autonomy Books, London

Simons, H and McCormack, B (2002) The art of evaluation: artistry, discipline and delivery, Paper presented to Annual Conference of the United Kingdom Evaluation Society, *Arts Based Inquiry – The Challenges for Evaluation*, South Bank Centre, London, December

Skynner, R and Cleese, J (1983) *Families and How to Survive Them*, Methuen, London

Smail, D (2001) *The Nature of Unhappiness*, Constable, London

Stafford-Clark, D (1965) The concept of psychical structure and function, in *What Freud Really said*, ch 6, Penguin, Harmondsworth

Tarule, J M (1996) Voices in dialogue: collaborative ways of knowing, in *Knowledge, Difference and Power*, ed N Goldberger, J Tarule, B Clinchy and M Belenky, Basic Books, New York

Thomas, K W (1976) Conflict and conflict management, in *Handbook of Industrial and Organisational Psychology*, ed M D Dunnette, Rand McNally, Chicago, IL

Townley, B (1994) *Reframing HRM*, Sage, London

Trist, E L and Sofer, C (1959) *Exploration in Group Relations*, Leicester University Press, Leicester

Tuckman, B W (1965) Developmental sequence in small groups, *Psychological Bulletin*, **63**, pp 384–99

Tuckman, B W and Jensen, M A C (1977) Stages of small group development, *Group and Organisational Studies*, **2** (4), pp 419–27

Van Deurzen-Smith, E (1997) *Everyday Mysteries: Existential Dimensions of Psychotherapy*, Routledge, London

Vince, R and Martin, L (1993) Inside action learning: an exploration of the psychology and politics of the action learning model, *Management Education and Development*, **24** (3), pp 205–15

Weil, S W and McGill, I J (eds) (1989) *Making Sense of Experiential Learning*, Open University Press/SRHE, Milton Keynes

Weiss, C H (1998) *Evaluation*, 2nd edn, Prentice-Hall, New Jersey

Winnicott, D W (1965) *The Maturational Processes and the Facilitating Environment*, Hogarth, London

Winnicott, D W (1971) *Playing and Reality*, Penguin, Harmondsworth

Yalom, I (1995) *The Theory and Practice of Group Psychotherapy*, 4th edn, Basic Books, New York

Index